Neal,

appreciate
your kindness
on our Arches/
Canyonlands trip,
Virgil & Marilyn
Hollis

Photographing the
# Southwest

## Second Edition

Volume 1– A guide to the natural landmarks of Southern Utah

Laurent Martrès

This guidebook will take you to the heart of Southern Utah, home to some of the Colorado Plateau's most outstanding highlights. Beyond the five National Parks of the famed "Grand Circle", you'll discover many hidden locations of Red Rock Country as well as Indian rock art and cliff dwellings. The book also makes a quick side trip into Northeastern Utah to explore the remote area around Dinosaur National Monument.

# PHOTOGRAPHING THE SOUTHWEST (SECOND EDITION)
# VOLUME 1 – SOUTHERN UTAH

**Published by PhotoTripUSA™**
An imprint of
**GRAPHIE**
INTERNATIONAL, INC.
8780 19th Street, Suite 199
Alta Loma, CA 91701, USA

All photography by Laurent Martrès, Copyright © 2002-2006, except where noted.
Cover photo: Sunset Point Storm (Bryce Canyon Nat'l Park)
Title page: Toadstool Hoodoo (Grand Staircase-Escalante Nat'l Monument)
Overleaf: Arch on Fire (Canyonlands Nat'l Park)
End of book: Dawn of the Mineral Age (Canyonlands Nat'l Park)

Visit Laurent's web sites: **http://www.martres.com** and **http://www.phototripusa.com**

**Also available in this series:**
*Photographing the Southwest – Volume 2 Arizona*  ISBN 978-0-916189-13-6
*Photographing the Southwest – Volume 3 Colorado & New Mexico*  ISBN 978-0-916189-14-3

Printed in China

**Disclaimer**
Some of the locations described in this book require travel through remote areas, where footpaths and 4-wheel drive trails can be difficult, even dangerous. Travel at your own risk and always check conditions locally before venturing out. The author and publisher decline all responsibility if you get lost, stranded, injured or otherwise suffer any kind of mishap as a result of following the advice and descriptions in this book. Furthermore, the information contained herein may have become outdated by the time you read it; the author and publisher assume no responsibility for outdated information, errors and omissions.

**Publisher's Cataloging-in-Publication**

    Martrès, Laurent.
        Photographing the Southwest / by Laurent Martrès. --
    2nd ed.
        v. cm.
        Includes bibliographical references and index.
        CONTENTS: v. 1. Southern Utah -- v. 2. Arizona -- v.
    3. Colorado & New Mexico.
        ISBN-13: 978-0-916189-12-9 (v. 1)
        ISBN-10: 0-916189-12-0 (v. 1)
        ISBN-13: 978-0-916189-13-6 (v. 2)
        ISBN-10: 0-916189-13-9 (v. 2)
        [etc.]

        1. Southwest, New--Guidebooks.  2. Landscape
    photography--Southwest, New--Guidebooks.  I. Title.

    F787.M37 2005            917.904'34
                        QBI05-200068

# PREFACE
## by Tom Till

I've often said that the Colorado Plateau is a place where two divergent forces, the world's best light and the world's most interesting landscapes, seamlessly combine to create a photographer's paradise. Having been lucky enough to travel worldwide in pursuit of landscape and nature imagery, and also lucky enough to have lived my entire adult life in canyon country, I believe I have the standing to make such a claim, although anyone who has spent much time here knows my words to be utterly true.

As I looked at the places mentioned in the text, I was flooded with a lifetime of memories of the great times I have had exploring, hiking, jeeping, river running and making photographs in the Four Corners area. I was fortunate, beginning in the 1970's, to be one of the first photographers to visit the Subway in Zion National Park, to cruise around the White Rim in Canyonlands without a permit, and to be the only photographer in Antelope Canyon for weeks at a time.

Photographers coming to the area now have a challenge I never faced in those early years: other photographers. Over the decades serious photography has become one of the major activities pursued by visitors to the region. As such, we have an increased responsibility to leave the land as we find it, behave ourselves around other photographers and visitors, and place the integrity of the land above our desire to create images. After you leave this magnificent place, you can also provide a valuable service and help insure its survival as a viable ecosystem by supporting national and local environmental groups who lavish a great deal of needed attention on the preservation of our spectacular deserts. These groups include The Sierra Club, The Grand Canyon Trust, The Southern Utah Wilderness Alliance, The Nature Conservancy, and The Wilderness Society.

I congratulate Laurent on the fine work he has done with these books, on his own wonderful photography, and on his mission to give many other photographers a forum for disseminating their great work. In this regard, he is unique among established western landscape photographers.

*Photographing the Southwest* will be a helpful tool for me when I return to many of my favorite haunts in the future, but I'm also glad that an infinity of canyons, arches, ruins, springs and secret places have been left out of this book. These places are the true heart of the wilderness desert southwest. They are available to all who push a little beyond the established scenic hot spots, and all who are willing to risk equipment, creature comforts, and at times, life and limb. It's all worthwhile in pursuit of the magical light that calls us onward around the next bend of the canyon.

*Tom Till*

# ACKNOWLEDGEMENTS

As with any book of this scope, many individuals have contributed one way or another to a better experience for the reader.

My deepest gratitude goes to Philippe Schuler, whose careful editing of the manuscript and innumerable enhancements to its contents have resulted in a much better book. Philippe—who shares with me an intense passion for the Southwest—brought to these guidebooks a level of precision and excellence that I would not have been able to achieve on my own. He co-wrote several sections and contributed informative textual and pictorial content throughout the various volumes and chapters. He also spent countless hours verifying the relevance and accuracy of the practical information and helped immensely in restructuring the presentation of this Second Edition to make the three books a better read. Human error is always possible, but Philippe did everything he could to ensure that I provided the most accurate information about the locations.

Tony Kuyper has done an outstanding job of editing the Introduction and Photo Advice chapters and I'm very grateful for his help.

Tom Till's wonderful photography has consistently inspired me. Tom kindly wrote the Preface to *Photographing the Southwest* and some of his photography is also featured in this series.

Sioux Bally, of Heartstone Arts, lent her considerable artistry to designing the cover, as well as the anchor pages of each chapter.

The following individuals either contributed information or checked the manuscript for errors: Catherine Barney, Vic & Meg Beer, Julia Betz, Marva Braun, Bruce Chesler, Justin Crofts, Isabel Czermak, David Day, Ron Flickinger, Bruce Fynan, Carol Gil, Leona Hemmerich, Jim Hook, Alex Johnson, Patti Joy, Julia Karet, Michael Kelsey, Patricia Martrès, Gene Mezereny, Bill Mitchem, Harriet & Phillip Priska, Mark Ruehmann, Mike Salamacha, Steffen Synnatschke, Dell Tait, Scott Walton and David Whitman.

My photography & hiking partners Akira Kato, Tony Kuyper, Gene Mezereny, Denis Savouray, Philippe Schuler, Steffen Synnatschke and my wife Patricia accompanied me on many of my adventures in the Southwest and I'm grateful for their company.

Finally, I thank the photographers who have contributed their talent to enrich the pictorial content of this book: Alain Briot, Ron Flickinger, Nolan Thomas Jones, Gene Mezereny, Lynn Radeka, Karsten Rau, Denis Savouray, Philippe Schuler, Steffen Synnatschke, Kerry Thalmann, Tom Till, Scott Walton and Charles Wood.

# ABOUT THIS BOOK

Welcome to the Second Edition of *Photographing the Southwest*.

I like to think of this book as a resource for visitors and photographers to the natural landmarks of the Southwest. The present Volume 1 covers Southern Utah, Volume 2 covers Arizona and Volume 3 covers Colorado & New Mexico.

The object of these books is to document natural landmarks of the American Southwest from a photographic perspective. Some of these landmarks are well known, but many are off the beaten track and seldom featured in more traditional guidebooks. Many are easily accessible and will provide you with unforgettable images and memories.

Some human activity is also covered in the books, but it is essentially limited to pre-Columbian dwellings and rock art of ancestral native Americans. This is due to the fact that cliff dwellings and rock art are tightly integrated into the landscape and can be interpreted as an extension of the natural world. I believe that most landscape photographers would agree with that.

On rare occasions, mention is made of more recent sites due to their proximity to natural landmarks. However, other forms of human activity which greatly contribute to the essence of the Southwest, such as architecture, modern native Americans crafts and rituals, rodeo, etc. are outside the scope of *Photographing the Southwest* and are purposely left out.

If you're not a photographer, you'll find in these books lots of information that more traditional guides leave out. The location of a hidden site, the most beautiful angle, and the best time of the day to view it are equally as valuable for seeing with your own eyes as for photography. These books are for everyone with a passion for the Southwest.

Each volume of *Photographing the Southwest* should be seen as a resource, rather than strictly a guidebook. It supplements other—more traditional—travel guides with specialized photographic information. The information is arranged by geographic areas. Locations whose photographic interest is particularly impressive are listed under these main headings. It also describes how to get there, as well as how and when to get the best shots. It purposely leaves out logistical concerns such as restaurant and hotel accommodations as there are already more than enough excellent travel books on that subject.

In addition to all the new areas covered in this Second Edition of *Photographing the Southwest*, all three volumes include a lot of new commentary and advice concerning previously visited sites.

The chapter on photography has been expanded, despite my initial reluctance to dispense this kind of advice. While I hope you'll benefit from my suggestions if you are a beginning photographer, my primary goal remains to provide you with a comprehensive location resource with which you can unleash your very own photographic talent.

Coverage of pre-Columbian sites has been increased, reflecting the growing interest on the part of the public for exploring the heritage of native Americans and interpreting their rock art. As Val Brinkerhoff, photographer of *Architecture of the Ancient Ones* puts it: "Visit one ancient dwelling site and you're likely to be drawn to experience another, and another, and another."

With these three greatly expanded volumes, my goal is to give readers from all over the world the best practical information to discover and photograph the Southwest. I believe you'll enjoy experiencing the infinite photographic possibilities of the Southwest and make some truly amazing discoveries of your own in the course of your travels.

May this book bring you a slew of new ideas for your creative photography of the Southwest.

—*Laurent Martrès*

*Note:*

**Three companion CD-ROMs containing images of each volume are available:**

*Images of the Southwest - Vol. 1 Southern Utah* ISBN 978-0-916189-15-0
*Images of the Southwest - Vol. 2 Arizona* ISBN 978-0-916189-16-7
*Images of the Southwest - Vol. 3 Colorado/New Mexico* ISBN 978-0-916189-17-4

Each CD-ROM is a companion to its respective book (Vol. 1, Vol. 2 and Vol. 3). You'll get most of the photos from each book—a total of 600+ high-quality Jpegs images in XGA format (1024x768), all in full color, royalty-free for your personal use, arranged by chapters just like in the books. This is an excellent way to "previsualize" the sites—an indispensable part of quality photography. The CDs are Windows and Mac OS compatible.

For more information, visit **www.martres.com** and **www.phototripusa.com**

# TABLE OF CONTENTS

*Looking for the light*

## Chapter 1

# INTRODUCTION

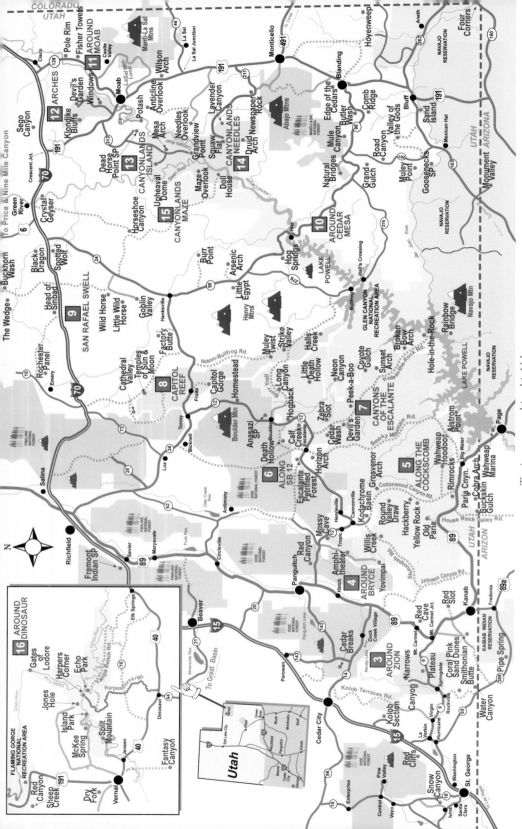

*Territory covered in this Volume*

# LOGISTICS

## Maps

You may be surprised that this book doesn't contain any detailed maps other than the simple one to the left, which describes the general location of the chapters and some of the more prominent sections. The reason for this is that *Photographing the Southwest* has a different purpose than other guidebooks: I like to think of it as an illustrated location resource, providing ideas for discovering or expanding on your previous knowledge of the Southwest. Also, had I chosen to illustrate with numerous maps the locations covered in the three volumes of *Photographing the Southwest,* it would have dramatically increased the size, weight and price of the books, making them impractical to carry on a trip. Any number of small maps I could have included would still not substitute for the real thing. Even with these books, you will need several different kinds of maps to effectively use the information.

Maps play a huge role in several respects. Large scale maps are necessary to get a global perspective of your trip and make initial decisions. Detailed road maps are necessary in order to follow the instructions in the *"Getting there"* sections of the book. You'll find a list of recommended maps in the *Appendix,* along with a short description of each. One particular map—the *AAA Indian Country* map—stands out as an excellent asset in the preparation and enjoyment of your trips. This remarkable map covers about 90% of the territory of *Volume 1* and about half the terrain of *Volumes 2* and *3.*

Additionally, since many of the locations I describe are off the beaten path, 7.5 minute US Geological Survey maps are necessary. Although the information on these maps is sometimes outdated, they are an indispensable tool for locating remote sites and navigating through the backcountry. As it can become expensive and impractical to buy so many different topographic maps, I suggest that you purchase the remarkable *National Geographic Topo! State series* maps for your computer. These Digital Rasterized Graphics files allow you to print your own maps for specific locations. You can print only the portion of map corresponding to your needs, including markers and annotations. While the initial investment in the four *Topo! State series* maps covering the three volumes of *Photographing the Southwest* is sizeable, it will prove economical in the long run if you're going to make extensive use of the books.

The *National Geographic Topo!* maps become a powerful tool when installed on a laptop computer. Used in tandem with a GPS unit, you can track your precise location in real time on your monitor while driving on remote dirt roads. Consider this simple scenario: Driving back from your sunset shoot, you find yourself at a fork and do not remember which branch you came in on earlier. The digitized map and GPS combination makes it extremely easy to find your location and hence the correct turn in order to return home. It's true that you can do this with a mapping GPS alone, but tracking your progress on a computer screen with all the fine detail of a *Topo! State series* map provides a degree of accuracy and comfort that is not possible with the GPS' tiny screen. Entering waypoints from a computer keyboard is also easier and navigating the maps on the computer screen provides a better understanding of the topology—hills to climb, canyons to bypass, etc.—especially if you use relief shading or, better yet, 3-dimensional viewing. If you haven't purchased these maps on CD-ROM, I suggest at least preparing your trips using the excellent *www.topozone.com* web site. Here you can access and print at no charge small-sized excerpts of all topographic maps. There are also commercial web-based topographic services allowing you to print maps with various degrees of information for a fee.

So now that we've entered the realm of digital mapping, let's talk about this other useful tool: the GPS.

## GPS considerations

In the previous edition, I considered it inappropriate to give away GPS points. My philosophy at the time was that readers needed to make their own adventure, performing a minor amount of effort in researching locations. I also considered, and still consider, GPS usage fraught with dangers in the hands of inexperienced users. Knowing GPS coordinates is one thing, but it is no substitute for a topographic map, particularly when it comes to understanding relief.

I have noticed that novice users tend to rely on the "GOTO" function of their GPS, without consideration for the topology. Rarely can one follow the straight line indicated on the GPS. Gullies too deep for crossing and vertical cliffs too high for scaling are common occurrences.

In the early 2000s, a majority of friends and government agency officials shared my concern. The consensus at the time was that giving away GPS coordinates could make things too easy and perhaps dangerous for novice users.

Circumstances have changed substantially since then. Today, GPS coordinates can be found on the Internet for just about any location of interest and the information is freely exchanged between peers with similar pursuits. In this rapidly evolving context, it would be counterproductive to force readers to seek GPS information outside of this book.

Therefore, in this edition, I have chosen to provide GPS coordinates very selectively. I do not want to entice readers to rely totally on their GPS unit. Instead, you'll find coordinates whenever they are truly useful or even indispensable.

I'll reiterate my warning, however. The GPS is no substitute for a topographic map and a compass, and in some cases for plain old instinct and navigational skills. Batteries eventually die, but the compass will continue to indicate your direction. You should always carry spare batteries, a compass and a map… and of course know how to use them.

If you are a novice user, I suggest that you attend a clinic. GPS clinics are available for free at many outdoor equipment stores in cities across the country.

One last bit of advice: do not walk with your eyes riveted to your GPS. Instead, try finding your way around by observing landmarks and following natural paths. Not only will you become a better routefinder, but you'll enjoy your surroundings a lot more. Your GPS is not a toy; use it only when necessary, to make sure that you are on course. Once you've mastered its use and are aware of its potential pitfalls, you may wonder how you got along without it.

The coordinate system used in this book is Degrees, Minutes, Seconds in WGS84 datum. It is the simplest to understand for novice users. It is also the best choice in terms of readability and ease of input: The popular UTM system may have some pluses, but it is not as immediately descriptive when comparing two waypoints. Coordinates expressed in UTM are also easier to mistype. Once typed into your GPS unit, *Topo!* program, or on-line web site, you can simply switch the WGS84 coordinates to your preferred reference system.

## Driving around

The question of the best vehicle to use may naturally arise when you visit an area as vast as the American Southwest. In this *Volume 1* of *Photographing the Southwest*, about 60% of the sites are accessible via paved roads or tracks adequate for passenger cars. An additional 17% of the sites can be accessed via rougher tracks that are still potentially passable by passenger cars if driven with caution in dry weather. The rest necessitate an SUV or some kind of high-clearance vehicle. In a number of cases—not the majority—use of a four-wheel drive (4WD) vehicle and some experience with this kind of driving is required. High-clearance is generally associated with larger tires than on the typical passenger car and is often necessary to negotiate the irregularities of a track, prevent damage to the undercarriage, and avoid becoming high-centered. Complementing high clearance, 4WD, especially in low-range, is useful on sandy or muddy tracks or tracks presenting rock steps and/or particularly steep angles—a small minority of locations in this book.

Road difficulty is examined in detail for each location in the text. Also, in the Ratings section at this end of the book, I rate the difficulty of vehicular access under "normal" conditions, i.e. always in dry weather and long after a rain. In wet conditions or after violent thunderstorms, a track rated accessible by passenger car can become impassable even to a high-clearance 4WD vehicle. The ratings provided should always be confirmed with visitor centers or local authorities, as track condition change frequently based on recent weather and the elapsed time since the last road maintenance. Don't take any unnecessary risks. Towing may cost hundreds or even thousands of dollars should you become stranded in some remote location.

Undoubtedly, using an SUV to explore the locations in this guidebook—even if it isn't 4WD—provides a degree of flexibility and comfort not offered by passenger cars and limits the risk of damage to your vehicle. If you are considering

*A bit of road building…*

car camping on your trip, you may even be able to sleep in your vehicle. Assuming you have a flat surface after folding down the rear seats, a person of average height can usually sleep diagonally. If you own a pick-up, a shell will provide inexpensive and effective protection against the elements.

If you're traveling in your own SUV or pick-up truck, you should always carry a tow strap, a shovel and a small air compressor. The latter will allow you to reinflate your tires after airing down in particularly sandy terrain. If you fly in from another part of the country (or the world) and rent an SUV from a major rental company, be aware that it will rarely offer 4WD. Furthermore, your rental agreement usually prohibits taking the rental vehicle off paved roads, so think twice about where you want to go, as you'll be assuming a major financial risk. One last piece of advice concerning rental vehicles: Always verify the presence of an adequate spare tire and tools to change it. You don't want to be stuck on a remote road just because the crank to operate the jack is missing.

## Hiking

I'm often asked about the level of difficulty of the hikes involved in visiting various locations. The answer depends on a plurality of factors. Many readers are not necessarily avid hikers. While a majority are probably content to carry a lightweight camera, some may be hauling heavy photographic equipment. At the other end of the spectrum, some folks prefer long hikes so they can "get away from the crowds". In *Volume 1*, about 60% of the locations can be visited and photographed with almost no hiking at all or else an easy stroll lasting less than an hour round-trip. An additional 20% of the sites should be accessible to most readers, requiring between one to three hours round-trip with moderate difficulty. About 15% are more demanding, as they require up to six hours round-trip and/or involve some kind of difficulty such as elevation change, orienteering, tougher terrain, obstacles or other risks. A minority require longer, more strenuous hiking or backpacking (mentioned only marginally in this guidebook).

In addition to the descriptions in the text, hiking difficulty is summed up in detail at the end of the book, with ratings on difficulty of access on foot for each location. These ratings are done with the average hiker in mind, i.e. neither a person with mobility problems, nor a marathon runner, in average physical shape (exercising regularly, preferably walking) and having a reasonably good sense of orientation, under normal hiking conditions (in dry weather and average temperatures).

Reading this guidebook, you'll see that visiting the Southwest—even off the beaten track—is not the exclusive domain of hard-core hikers. You'll come to realize that ordinary city folks can find plenty of trips to satisfy their photographic pursuits with only a modest amount of effort. Obviously, you need to set reasonable goals for yourself. Begin your trip with easy hikes, increasing your mileage progressively and alternating hard and easy days. Pay particular attention to the duration of your hikes; some people tend to be overly optimistic, especially if taking lots of pictures.

Always heed the advice of park rangers and professional guides, even if it feels a little too conservative. This is particularly important when hiking in canyon country. Flash floods are a not so rare occurrence in all seasons, although they tend to happen much more frequently during summer. You don't want to find yourself trapped in a slot canyon when that happens.

Hiking equipment should also be considered carefully. It can make a significant difference in terms of security and comfort. Security should not be taken lightly as there is a very real risk of getting lost on backcountry hikes without trails. Although a minority, there are a few such hikes in this guidebook. Start with the Ten Essentials:

❏ A first aid kit
❏ Waterproof matches or a small lighter
❏ A pocket knife
❏ A headlamp (there are very small, lightweight LED models)
❏ Sunglasses (polarized types are nice for photography)
❏ A loud whistle (so you can be located by your party or a rescue team in case of mishap)
❏ High-energy food (trail mix or energy bars)
❏ A topographic map of the area
❏ A compass and if possible a GPS unit (always take a waypoint of your vehicle's location)
❏ Extra clothing in case of a sudden change in weather.

Your digital camera can also be a useful tool when hiking in the backcountry, where there is no trail or no obvious landmark and you'll be returning the same way you came. At each strategic location (such as a spot where you need to go down or ascend a cliff, an intersection of side canyons, or when leaving the course of a wash) turn around and take a snapshot, taking care to place the direction to be followed on returning in the center of the frame. If you have any doubt as to the correct course when you return, just examine the shots you took on your camera's LCD.

A good pair of hiking shoes with good ankle support is essential for hiking in the Southwest. You want good ankle support and soles with good traction on small pebbles and slickrock. Sneakers are definitely inadequate for the trail and should stay in your car. If you're going to wade inside streambeds—this book offers several opportunities to do so—a second pair of shoes, specialized for water activities, will come handy. This type of shoe usually has excellent anti-slip soles. Although not indispensable, they offer an additional level of comfort when hiking in water. Use them with a pair of wool socks or synthetic liners to avoid blisters. For pants, shorts, and shirts, the newer synthetic fibers work very well in the Southwest environment. They breathe well, transferring body moisture away from the skin, and they dry extremely fast (on you or after being washed).

*Flash flood raging*

Don't forget the indispensable fleece jacket and/or windbreaker, which you should always have handy as temperatures can change radically throughout the day. Don't be fooled by the fact that the land looks like a desert; it can get cold very fast, especially at elevation, during the spring and fall months. When hiking in full sun—a common occurrence in the Southwest—consider a solar cap with a "legionnaire" attachment to protect your ears and neck. Also, frequent application of sunscreen to sun-exposed areas is recommended. Sunburn can hurt like hell and has potentially life-threatening health consequences.

There are many good daypacks and photo packs available. Consider one with sufficient capacity to carry not only your photo equipment but also your additional clothing, safety gear and, above all, plenty of water. In summer, dehydration may come easily and without warning. Some of the day-hikes in this book may require a full gallon of water. When hiking in the backcountry, I sometimes encounter photographers carrying "specialized" photo packs for their equipment and only a small hip-bag with just enough space for a couple of energy bars and two pints of water. Not having enough water places you at serious risk in case of unplanned occurrences. Taking the wrong turn or simply extending your visit because every bend of the canyon brings more captivating beauty requires additional resources, especially water. On long day hikes, I usually stash a water bladder behind a tree for the return trip. On extended trips, especially in the Escalante area, I carry and use a water filter.

Trekking poles can be very helpful on hikes that involve lots of ascents and descents. They propel you forward going up and relieve pressure on your knees going down. Your poles can also aid in keeping your balance when wading rocky streams. Note that a trekking pole with a hole on top to screw in your camera is no substitute for a steady tripod!

## A word about lodging

I provide no information or advice concerning accommodations, although I do mention campgrounds on occasion. I have found that my readers have very different traveling styles depending on their individual goals, time constraints, and the level of comfort they require. There are excellent travel guides available that can assist the reader in finding the specific type of accommodations they desire.

Keep in mind, however, that you'll take many of your best photos during the so-called "golden hour", soon after sunrise and just before sunset. As many of the locations discussed in this book are on dirt roads far away from motels, you may have to camp close to the site to be present during the best light. Doing so, you avoid driving at night on backcountry tracks. What would pass as minor impediments during the day can become very dangerous when you discover them at the last second with your headlights. Depending on the situation, you may be able to opt for organized campgrounds, such as the ones found in many national or state parks (where camping is prohibited outside the official campgrounds). Alternatively, there may be primitive camping where you'll just pick your site in the middle of the backcountry if this is authorized, which is the case most on BLM-administered land.

Even if you're following a classic regimen of motels every night, you may want to carry in your car a small tent, a sleeping pad, a sleeping bag, as well as a stash of food and several gallons of water. Should some unforeseen circumstances prevent you from going back to town, you'll be able to improvise a night in the backcountry. You may even become addicted to it once you get a taste of it!

## When to visit

The Colorado Plateau can be visited year-round. Each season possesses its unique charm and presents various advantages and disadvantages.

Summer monsoon storms make for sublime skies, occasional rainbows, soft lighting due to the haze and spectacular sunsets, but there is a high price to pay for that. It's the busiest time of the year on the roads and in the parks. In the last two decades, foreign visitors en masse have also discovered the American West, in organized tour groups or as individuals, crowding the roads and parks, not to mention the motels. In the most popular places, reservations become indispensable and need to be made in advance to guarantee a place for the night. This can create a serious obstacle to the flexibility of your itinerary by imposing a measure of control on your evening's destination.

The intense heat is not generally a problem in the car or on short walks, but it is a factor on long hikes. Summer sees frequent afternoon downpours with all the risks they entail, especially when visiting the numerous canyons described in this guide. Additionally, dirt roads are sometimes closed by water runoff.

Insects can pose a problem in certain areas, particularly at the beginning of

*Summer brings beautiful clouds to the Plateau*

summer when deerflies and biting gnats or "no-see-ums" will attack your skin relentlessly. Unfortunately, it is impossible to predict when and where they will hang out in a particular year.

Finally, the days are at their longest; this allows you to cover a lot of ground and visit many sites. On the other hand, this can considerably limit your photographic opportunities during the day when the sun is high in the sky and your shots will be way too contrasty and with-

out nuance. Bear in mind that the angle of the sun is at its highest in summer. There is no such thing as a "golden hour" at the height of summer, merely fifteen minutes of very good light after sunrise and before sunset. As a photographer, I find summer rather exhausting in Southern Utah and I'd recommend concentrating on Colorado and New Mexico at that time of year (see *Volume 3* of *Photographing the Southwest*).

Autumn is the best time to discover the Southwest. It's still warm, but the heat is less ferocious. In the first part of autumn, days are still long but less grueling. Kids and the majority of grown-ups have returned to work and school after Labor Day. The motels empty out. Prices lower to a reasonable level, the parks are less congested and parking near the panoramic vistas no longer requires you to drive around for ½ hour to find a spot. Hazy days become rare and insects no longer make your life miserable.

Fall colors begin in mid-September in the high country and in early November at lower elevations. October and November are absolutely marvelous in Zion or Capitol Reef as the foliage changes and a new, multi-colored palette of yellow, ocher and red appears with a much softer illumination than in summer. Strong rains are relatively rare, although at high altitude locations such as Cedar Breaks or Bryce, snow is possible. Finally, the sun rises and sets at a lower angle and the "golden hour" lasts quite a bit longer than in summer. This is my favorite season for general travel in the Southwest, as well as for photography.

Winter is the off-season and offers exceptional possibilities to enjoy the surrounding tranquility at incredibly low prices. Also, winter's short daylight hours, as well as the low trajectory of the sun on the horizon, are a blessing to the photographer.

With a bit of care to dress warmly, the dry cold is not disagreeable, though it can make camping less attractive. Winter storms often bring rain or heavy snow to the higher elevations and can last several days. However, a snowfall in Bryce can be an absolutely magical experience when, with these alternate periods of beautiful weather, the air attains an unequaled purity and the sky is an intense blue. By the same token, there are few clouds in the sky and it can be tough to come up with spectacular photography including much sky. Nonetheless, unobstructed views such as those one sees in Canyonlands or the Grand Canyon—to give but two examples—reveal extraordinary distances when there is no pollution, as is rarely the case in summer. Large animals descend from the higher elevations and are frequently and easily observed in the valleys.

The main inconvenience is that certain sites become inaccessible, particularly the North Rim of the Grand Canyon, Cedar Breaks, the Narrows of the Virgin and sometimes the trails of Bryce Canyon (at least without adequate equipment, for these last two). Another negative factor is the lack of color in the vegetation. You'll have to be careful not to include bare vegetation in your images; bare branches and bushes don't make very nice foregrounds.

Spring is a magnificent season, although the weather can be very unpredictable. You are as likely to encounter stormy, wet days as warm and sunny weather. Precipitation is frequent in March and the rivers and waterfalls are at their highest. High peaks are still snowbound, greenery is sprouting, the trees are leafing out and wildflowers abound in wet years. It's a great time to visit the Canyons of the Escalante, among others, when cottonwood trees explode an intense green and temperatures are still tolerable. However, beware of high water levels, which may make it impossible to wade.

The days are getting longer and prices are still not as expensive as during the height of the season. In late spring, insects can also be a great nuisance. No-see-ums, fond of blood and terribly annoying, as well as aggressive deerflies are to be found along watercourses and in washes.

*Arches Nat'l Park in winter*

| Formation / Average layer thickness | Era | Where is it found? |
|---|---|---|
| Claron formation 180 m | Tertiary | Bryce Canyon |
| Mancos Shale 1000 m | Cretaceous | Capitol Reef |
| Dakota sandstone 100 m | Cretaceous | Capitol Reef |
| Morrison formation 120 m | Jurassic | Arches, Capitol Reef |
| Summerville formation 90 m | Jurassic | Goblin Valley, Arches |
| Curtis sandstone 70 m | Jurassic | Goblin Valley |
| Entrada sandstone 250 m | Jurassic | Arches, Goblin Valley, Cathedral Valley |
| Carmel formation 200 m | Jurassic | Capitol Reef, San Rafael Reef |
| Navajo sandstone 300 m | Jurassic | Zion, Escalante, Arches, Rainbow Br., Capitol Reef |
| Kayenta formation 100 m | Jurassic | Arches, Island in the Sky |
| Wingate sandstone 110 m | Triassic | Dead Horse Point, Capitol Reef, Colorado N. M. |
| Chinle formation 200 m | Triassic | Island in the Sky |
| Moenkopi formation 300 m | Triassic | Natural Bridges, Capitol Reef, Fisher Towers |
| Kaibab limestone 90 m | Permian | Grand Canyon, Capitol Reef |
| White Rim sandstone 75 m | Permian | Island in the Sky |
| Cedar Mesa sandstone 360 m | Permian | Natural Bridges, Needles, Maze |
| Cutler formation 420 m | Permian | Monument Valley, Fisher Towers |
| Honaker formation 900 m | Pennsylvanian | Shafer Trail, Needles |

Sedimentary layers of the Colorado Plateau

# A BIT OF GEOLOGY

## Introduction

What makes the Colorado Plateau so special is its amazing geological origins. The sedimentary layers of the Plateau were deposited, one after the other, in horizontal strata and subsequently subjected to erosion by the various elements—wind, rain, and river action—forming fantastic and captivating scenery.

In no other part of the planet does there exist a similar concentration of such singular and varied geologic phenomena. Here the work of erosion manifests itself in such diverse forms as the great depth and enormity of the Grand Canyon, the tight corkscrew shape of Antelope Canyon, the stupendous spans of Arches and Natural Bridges, the incomparable coloration of Bryce Canyon and the fantastic gargoyles in Goblin Valley—all this to our great enjoyment.

The next sections do not pretend to be a course in geology. Although in 30 years of exploring the Southwest I have learned to enjoy recognizing the geologic origin of the sites I visit, I do not have the scholarly background and expertise to discuss this subject in depth, nor is it the main focus of the book. I encourage readers, however, to research this in greater depth for themselves. For a superb, yet very approachable, in-depth exploration of the geology of the Southwest, I invite you to read three books: F.A. Barnes' *Canyon Country Geology*, Thomas Wiewandt's and Maureen Wilkes' *The Southwest Inside Out* and Ralph Lee Hopkins' *Hiking the Southwest's Geology*. Even if you don't have the time nor the inclination to do so, a minimum of geologic knowledge will permit a better understanding of the striking terrain and how it is not merely an inanimate mineral world, but a monumental product of perpetual evolution.

The knowledge of some basic geologic features will enrich your experience of the locations covered in this book:

❐ the various sedimentary layers of the land;

❐ the breaks and swellings that lower and raise the relief of the plateau;

❐ the step-like structure of the Colorado Plateau which falls in successive stages towards the southwest;

❐ the role of the principal waterways in forming the landscape;

❐ the geographic location of the various mountain chains of the plateau;

❐ and finally, the desert ecosystem.

*Capitol Reef has many exposed sedimentary layers*

## Sedimentary Layers

A knowledge, however superficial, of the sedimentary layers that form the Plateau will provide a better opportunity to get the most from your visit to the area. All these layers are uncovered in one place or another. The geology of the Southwest is like an open book and all you have to do is read it with accompanying notes—it couldn't be simpler.

A few formations constitute the majority of those which are most commonly photographed:

❒ the ancient beige Cedar Mesa sandstone of the Permian era, which forms the spectacular spires of the Needles and Maze districts of Canyonlands as well as the bridges and canyons of Natural Bridges NM. It is also seen throughout the Cedar Mesa plateau from Blanding to Hite and down to Mokey Dugway.

❒ the salmon-hued de Chelly Sandstone, which is formed from ancient sand dunes and found in Monument Valley and Canyon de Chelly.

❒ the dark brown and red, strangely-striated Moenkopi, found throughout the Colorado Plateau, but especially well-represented in Capitol Reef.

❒ the outrageously colorful Chinle formation, soft and crumbly, forming numerous badlands throughout the Plateau.

❒ the highly-polished, intense-red Wingate sandstone essentially forming the core of the Island in the Sky and Dead Horse Point. It is also found in the Escalante drainage, at Capitol Reef, Little Wild Horse Canyon and the Colorado Nat'l Monument. It assumes a wild animal quality when striated by desert varnish, reminiscent of a Tiger's fur. It makes a fantastic background for photos of cottonwoods in spring and autumn.

❒ the grayish-red Kayenta sandstone, with its characteristic horizontal layers.

❒ the ever-present Navajo sandstone, encountered everywhere on the plateau. It is often whitish, with occasional hues of red and pink and is best represented by the minarets of Zion, the domes of Capitol Reef and the fantastic slot canyons near Lake Powell and the Escalante River.

❒ the superb Entrada sandstone, star of some of the best photos of the Southwest, finely grained and terra cotta in color; it appears dull under the midday sun but glows a brilliant red during the golden hour. It is found in hard form in Arches, Cathedral Valley, and on the north shore of Glen Canyon, or in a softer, friable form in Goblin Valley, Little Egypt or Behind the Rocks.

❒ the colorful Morrison formation, found throughout the Southwest; it is the material of many badlands photos, a good example being the Painted Desert.

## Other tectonic phenomena

The geologic structure of the plateau is further complicated by innumerable fractures and upheavals caused by volcanic eruption, earthquakes and other tectonic movements of the earth's crust which have shaped the Southwest. Some basic knowledge of the theory of continental drift and plate tectonics will be helpful in understanding these phenomena. Two major tectonic phenomena are worth recognizing and understanding, because you'll be seeing and photographing them often during your travels: faults and folds.

Faults are formed by expansion or compression of the earth's crust, resulting in part of the layers breaking up and sliding. There are relatively few faults in the territory covered by Volume 1: Good examples are the Hurricane fault, which you cross when driving from St. George to Zion, the Uinta Fault, which you can observe in Dinosaur Nat'l Monument and the Moab Fault, best seen from the road to Arches Nat'l Park.

In folds, the layers withstood the pressure by folding instead of breaking. Folds are very common on the Colorado Plateau, especially in the form of monoclines where the layers were bent into a single very steep slope. Good examples of monoclines are the Waterpocket Fold, the Cockscomb and the Comb Ridge. Anticlines and synclines are folds resulting in

*The Mitten fault and monocline from Harper's Corner*

domes and depressions and are rare; good examples of each can be observed in Canyonlands Nat'l Park. When folds actually break, they are called fractures or joints and you'll find plenty of these while exploring the plateau.

## The Grand Staircase

The Grand Staircase starts at the Kaibab Plateau, to the north of the Grand Canyon of the Colorado. The limestone bed of the plateau, 225 million years old, is the first step of the staircase.

The Chocolate Cliffs, a brown color, form the second step. They are found at the south entrance to Zion.

The Vermilion Cliffs, of a deep red hue and between 165 and 200 million years old, form the third step. They are found scattered along an imaginary line from St. George to Page. Without a doubt, the most beautiful examples are found along US 89A where they appear on the horizon, seen from the viewpoint at Horseshoe Bend.

The White Cliffs, which appear white in strong sunlight but are really an ocher color, are between 135 and 165 million years old. They can be seen along the southern part of US 89 in the vicinity of Mt. Carmel.

The Gray Cliffs, 120 to 135 million years old, form the base of Bryce Canyon and are only visible with great difficulty as they are cliffs in name only. Their soft, friable nature causes them to form an almost worn out tread on the Grand Staircase.

Finally the Pink Cliffs, 50 to 60 million years old, that form the top step of the Grand Staircase, of which Bryce Canyon is the most representative example.

During your travels across the plateau, you will cross and re-cross these steps of the Grand Staircase. Yovimpai Point, at the southern tip of Bryce Canyon allows you to view the Staircase almost in its entirety from a single vantage point.

## Mountains

The main mountain ranges of the Colorado Plateau are laccoliths, formed by magma uprisings pushing horizontally and vertically through the thick layers of sandstone. At altitudes of over 9,000 feet and visible for miles around,

*The La Sal Mountains in winter*

they serve as focal points and enrich your journey as you learn to recognize them. It is possible to measure progress as you travel by observing these mountain ranges, adding an extra dimension to just reading the map. For example, as you drive south from Moab on US 191, the La Sals are on your left. A few minutes later, the Abajos appear directly in front of you and a bit to the right. You'll reach them in the area of Monticello and you'll leave them behind near Blanding. In Monticello, Sleeping Ute Mountain is in full view to the east. By the time you reach Natural Bridges National Monument, the Abajos are already well behind and to your right. The characteristic round dome of Navajo Mountain is now in front of you and the Henry Mountains are silhouetted to the left. Traveling the roads of the Colorado Plateau, you will rapidly become familiar with these landmarks, like a seafarer sailing from port to port.

## Rivers

Three principal waterways feed the plateau: the Colorado, the Green and the San Juan rivers. However, many others play an important role in the ecosystem of the Southwest and merit mention for their esthetic qualities:

❒ the Virgin River, which represents for many their first contact with the

Southwest while following its superb gorge between Las Vegas and St. George and which forms the extraordinary Zion canyon;

❐ the beautiful Sevier River, that snakes through the Paunsaugunt Plateau to the west of Bryce Canyon;

❐ the Little Colorado River that feeds into its big brother of the same name and which forms beautiful meanders at the edge of the Grand Canyon;

❐ the Paria River, traversing the Vermilion Cliffs and forming the spectacular deep gorge of Paria Canyon;

❐ the Escalante River, draining innumerable tributaries that would take a lifetime to explore, before emptying into Lake Powell;

❐ the Fremont River, meandering through Capitol Reef and providing awesome autumn scenery on its way to the Dirty Devil;

❐ the Dirty Devil River, which carries waters from the Wasatch Plateau and the San Rafael Reef and joins the Colorado River at Hite, at the northern end of Lake Powell.

Needless to say, there are hundreds if not thousands of smaller water courses, washes and creeks all over the Colorado Plateau. Many become dry in summer but can be awakened into raging walls of water during the monsoon season. Extreme caution must be exercised when wandering along washes at that time.

## FAUNA AND FLORA

The Colorado Plateau is, by definition, an arid area, limited in types of vegetation and animals. The photographer will not find a great variety of animals. Deer, antelope and rabbits are the mammals most frequently encountered by the roadside and they tend to be most strongly concentrated in the heart of the national parks and monuments where they are protected.

There are always mule deer, squirrels and chipmunks begging for a piece of bread on the main park roadways and near the Visitor Centers; an unfortunate habit reinforced by some visitors who want to capture the moment in photographs, despite numerous official warnings not to feed the wildlife. Wherever they're found, coyotes aren't far.

Deer and antelope are found in herds from autumn to spring, and it is not unusual to see them in large groups by the side of the road. Even in summer, your chances of seeing deer are very good. You should

*Cottonwood on Wingate Sandstone*

be extremely cautious when driving at dusk or at night to avoid collisions with animals. Elks are rare on the Plateau but can sometimes be seen.

You will also have the opportunity to observe eagles, falcons, buzzards and the ubiquitous raven, always looking for small mammals and rabbits. At nighttime, it isn't unusual to spot a great-horned owl in your headlights.

Snakes, scorpions, spiders? Yes, they are here, but the visitor would have a hard time finding them, especially in the daytime. If this can reassure you, I have only come close to two venomous snakes in the hundreds of miles I have logged on foot on trails of the Colorado Plateau. Rattlesnakes present little danger as long as you don't alarm them and they'll usually give you advance warning of their presence. Just be cautious of where you step and pay attention to where you place your hands when scrambling around the backcountry. Large stones and holes in the rock serve as a refuge for these cold blooded creatures during hot summer days. I'm sure you've read all this advice before, but you may not have read these two little-known facts: Envenomation is actually infrequent, even if you receive a bite; however, in the unfortunate and statistically small chance that you've become injected with venom, you should be aware that there is a seemingly constant scarcity of antivenin in the Southwest and that a full treatment usually requires 20 vials, at approximately $1,000 a vial. Better carry medical insurance. Scorpions are present in Southern Arizona and New Mexico and are known to inflict an extremely painful sting. Be cautious at night if you're camping out. Black widows are extremely shy creatures and present no danger. If you live anywhere in the southern United States, you learn to live with them. Brown Recluse spiders are also extremely rare, but I do know two persons who have been bitten, including my wife. The bite is nasty, creating necrosis of the local skin tissue and taking months to heal. In case of trouble, call 991 or the Poison Control Center hot line at 1-800-222-1222.

In the arid areas of the Colorado Plateau, juniper, pinyon pine and sagebrush dominate the landscape. In the canyons, cottonwoods line up streams and dry washes. They bloom an intense green in mid to late April and turn yellow and golden in mid-September to late October. Douglas fir and ponderosa pine can be found at higher elevations. Aspens line up mountain tops and rare Bristlecone pines are found in patches above 10,000 feet. All help considerably in making spectacular photography. In recent years, I have witnessed accelerated encroachment by non-native vegetation, in particular Tamarisk. This water-seeking shrub sucks an enormous amount of moisture from the ground and grows thick along rivers and creeks.

*The Tamarisk invasion*

The agencies in charge seem to be lacking the resources to implement its eradication. One unfortunate example of this, among many others, can be found along the banks of the Colorado River near Moab, where huge stretches of the river have become obscured by Tamarisk's galloping growth.

# A BIT OF HISTORY

## Ancient History

In the Southwest, man is very small, while space and time appear immeasurable. Even multiplied by a hundred, what are a few thousand years of known history in relationship to the slow mineral transformation of this Earth, in successive waves, from volcano to mountain, from river to canyon or from ocean to desert? The ruins of the Fremont and Puebloan—or Anasazi—cultures, dispersed over the plateau, are eloquent testimonies to the vulnerability of the human condition when confronted with implacable nature. In contemplating their abandoned pueblos, sheltered under the immense sandstone cliffs, one cannot help but ponder how fragile their protection really was and what a tenuous hold life has here.

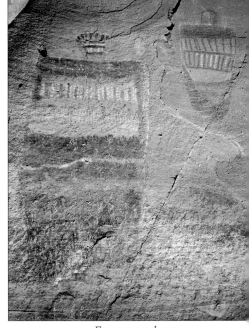

*Fremont rock art*

The Fremont populated a geographic zone situated to the north of an imaginary line that passes through Capitol Reef, extending to the Great Basin in the west and the Rocky Mountains in the east. The Puebloans inhabited the Four Corners region, so-called because it is the junction of the boundaries of the states of Utah, Arizona, Colorado and New Mexico.

The Puebloans are almost always referred to as Anasazi, a term meaning "the Ancient Ones" in the Navajo language. As a matter of fact, the Navajo migrated to this land much later and bear no genetic or linguistic relationship to the Anasazi. The Navajos and Apaches belong to the Athabaskan linguistic group and are closely related to indigenous populations of Alaska and Western Canada. The Hopi, Zuni and other tribes to the south of the Grand Canyon are direct descendants of the Anasazi and Fremont and prefer calling them Ancestral Puebloans—based on the style of their dwellings. These Ancient Ones left the area around 1300 AD under circumstances that are still a subject of debate. It is incorrect to talk about a "disappearance," however, as there is ample proof that the Puebloans migrated to the south and were gradually absorbed by the Hohokam, Sinaguan and Mogollon (pronounced "mug-ee-yon") cultures.

*Traditional Navajo Hogan*
*(take photos only from the road or ask for permission)*

Several theories have been advanced over the years for what we shall call the collapse of their society: The first one presumes that a large meteorite struck the area, blotting out the sun, and rendering the land incapable of growing crops and, therefore, making it uninhabitable. This somewhat messianic theory has now been largely discredited. The second postulates a radical climatic change around the beginning of the 14th century causing decreased harvests. This theory is well supported by scientific evidence garnered from tree-ring dating and showing a first 50-year drought starting around 1130 AD followed by another one, even more drastic, from about 1275 to 1300 AD. A third theory places the responsibility for environmental degradation—mainly the disappearance of topsoil—on the intensive system of agriculture practiced by the Ancestral Puebloans, eventually exceeding the capacity of the system to sustain their needs. Yet another subsidiary theory places the blame on marauding enemies and internal strife. The consensus among contemporary specialists is that all the above factors—with the exception of the meteorite theory for most—combined to make life too hard in the area, causing progressive, rather than sudden, migration to more hospitable land to the south.

Although a sure bet answer still eludes archeologists, what remains is ample testimony to a well-established social order that was able to assure subsistence and artistic production of great merit. Numerous artifacts discovered on the sites attest to this, in particular the baskets, pottery and fabrics. In Southern Utah, a visit to the Anasazi, Edge of the Cedars and Fremont Indian State Parks is strongly recommended for a better understanding of the human history of the Southwest. Similar exhibits can be found in Arizona at the Museum of Northern Arizona near Flagstaff and at Navajo Nat'l Monument. In Colorado, the Anasazi Heritage Center, Chapin Museum in Mesa Verde, as well as the Manitou Cliff Dwellings Museum and the Crow Canyon Archaeological Center are the most prominent centers of Anasazi culture. In New Mexico, the museums at Chaco Canyon Nat'l Historic Park and Aztec Ruins Nat'l Monument are also terrific.

## Recent History

Modern native Americans, early Spanish explorers, Mormon pioneers, ranchers, cowboys, uranium miners, adventurers... the history of the settlement and exploitation of natural resources in the Southwest by native Americans and diverse groups of Europeans is fascinating. Much has been written about it by infinitely better qualified authors and I invite you to discover more about the recent history of the Southwest by reading a short, eclectic—and necessarily biased—selection of works, ranging from factual to fiction, which I describe in the *Other Recommended Reading* section in *Appendix*.

Nevertheless, I'd like to present here a brief compendium of seminal events that shaped the history of this Land:

❏ the Spaniards' explorations: their first foray occurred in 1540—two decades after Cortès' brutal Mexican campaign—when Hernando de Alarcón sailed deep into the Gulf of California and encountered the Colorado River delta. That same year a young Lieutenant in Coronado's army, by the name of García López de Cárdenas, stumbled onto the Grand Canyon with the help of local Zuni scouts. Juan de Oñate, first governor of the region, searched the land extensively—but in vain—for routes to the Pacific Ocean. Expeditions were abandoned for almost two centuries until 1776, when two Franciscan friars, Atanasio Domínguez and Francisco de Escalante went looking for a northern route to link Santa Fe to San Francisco. Their extraordinary five-month long expedition "discovered" many of the Canyon Country sites described in this book.

*The ancestor of the RV*

❏ the first mappings: first by Escalante's cartographer Bernardo de Miera; then by Alexander von Humboldt and later by John Fremont: these successive mappings of the Southwest opened the way for trade and provided the groundwork for the next wave of explorations;

❏ the American explorers: Gunnison, Beale, Seatgreaves, Macomb, Newberry, Wheeler, Hayden and the greatest of all: Major John Wesley Powell all led remarkable expeditions to then uncharted regions of the Southwest, helping to open new routes for the railroad and new settlers;

❏ the Mormon influx: the massive and extraordinarily courageous migration of the Mormons from the Midwest, under extremely inhospitable circumstances, established Utah's Caucasian farming communities and ranches;

❑ the Indian wars: a sad period during which the U.S. government fought, defeated and deported Native American tribes, with people like Kit Carson, Cochise and Geronimo emerging as leaders on both sides of the fence.

## Archeological Sites Etiquette

Rock art and ancient dwellings are a most precious heritage of Native American Indians and humanity at large. They are obviously extremely fragile and when not protected, are often the unfortunate subject of vandalism. When photographing rock art and ruins, the first and foremost rule is: Don't touch. Natural oils from human skin can and will affect glyphs and paintings. Even though a slight touch may only remove a minute amount of pigment or sandstone, when you multiply that by many years and many visitors it will eventually lead to irreparable degradation of the art. Even worse than that is the use of chalk or crayon to enhance or highlight the art for photographs. It compromises the integrity of the art by becoming a permanent part of the design and paves the way for others to add their own mark, thus destroying the precious heritage forever. This is a sad and irresponsible act, which I have observed too many times on otherwise beautiful rock art throughout the Southwest. The Black Dragon (see San Rafael Reef chapter) is a prime example of such misguided alteration. Another reprehensible practice is the wetting of rock art with water to accentuate contrast and texture. Needless to say, you should not cut, chip, or try to remove rock art. The Antiquities Act protects rock art and infractions are subject to very high fines. It is our responsibility as observers and photographers of our era to treat it properly so that it may be preserved as a testimony to those who came before us and for the benefit of future generations.

Please don't blame me as an author for disseminating information about public or lesser-known archaeological sites. Vandals don't read books such as this one, looking for information. In 90% of cases, rock art is defaced by teenagers, mostly males, happening to pass by in groups. One has to conclude that the remaining 10% must be immature adults. The best way to prevent this from happening is through education, in school and at the sites.

Some of the best places to admire and photograph rock art in Utah are Horseshoe Canyon, the Maze, the San Rafael Reef, the San Juan River area, Sego Canyon, Newspaper Rock, Dinosaur Nat'l Monument and surrounding areas. The most outstanding unprotected ruins are located on the Cedar Mesa Plateau. Fortunately, most of the best ancient dwellings are under the protection of some governmental, state or tribal agency.

To visit hard-to-find panels and significantly increase your enjoyment and understanding of rock art, consider joining the Utah Rock Art Research Association, aka URARA (see *Appendix*). ✿

*Cobalt Waterflow*

Chapter 2

SOME PHOTOGRAPHIC ADVICE

*Photographing the Southwest* makes no assumptions about your ability with respect to photography. Whether you are an enthusiastic beginner or a seasoned pro is irrelevant. While this book is essentially a location resource, it also provides specific photographic advice for almost every location to allow you to be better prepared for your visit. The advice is based on my experience in the field, having been at many of these locations several times and under different lighting conditions. In many cases, I have also checked my notes against those of knowledgeable friends or acquaintances.

After examining the indispensable photographic equipment, I'll discuss how to handle a number of generic situations you'll encounter in the field so you can create better images. I ask the more advanced photographers to be understanding if this advice seems trivial; drawing on the feedback from the past edition, many readers seem to appreciate having this quick photographic reference.

# ABOUT EQUIPMENT

## Terminology

The myriad of existing film and digital camera formats creates confusion when discussing lens focal length expressed in the metric system, i.e. millimeters. Since most people understand focal length based on the 35mm camera, I'll be using this as the reference camera throughout the book. Medium and large

*Ancient Patriarch*

format photographers will probably have no problem. Newcomers starting with a digital camera, however, may find it more difficult. The digital camera's sensor size determines the angle of vision for a lens at a given focal length. The focal length inscribed on the lens simply reflects its effective focal distance from the sensor in millimeters. This is the distance the lens must be from the sensor in order to provide sharp focus for an object located at infinity. For each camera system with a different size image capture device, the inscribed focal length will provide a different angle of vision. A focal length that appears to be a very wide angle to a person using a 35mm system may in fact be a normal lens for a person using a digital camera. The difference is due to the size of the sensor in relation to the 24x36mm film size for a 35mm film camera. This size differential is known as the "crop factor". With a 1x crop factor—which exists only for the "full-size sensor" of some high-end digital cameras—the angle of vision is the same as on a 35mm film camera. Cameras with smaller sensors will have crop factors of 1½x, 2x or even larger. Take a 20mm lens for example. On a 35mm camera or a camera with a "full-size sensor" its angle of vision will be very wide angle. For a sensor with a 2x crop factor, the 20mm lens becomes equivalent to a 40mm lens on a 35mm film camera. Therefore, the 20mm lens is considered a "normal" lens on a camera with a 2x crop factor. On a digicam equipped with an even smaller sensor, this 20mm focal length could actually provide a small telephoto effect. Since the final angle of vision is what really matters, I sometimes use additional terminology to describe what the lens does. A 40 to 50mm lens could be described as a normal lens, while 24 to 35mm is standard wide-angle range and anything below 24mm is considered super-wide angle. A 70 to 140mm lens provides a short telephoto effect and from 140 to 300mm is medium telephoto. Larger than 300mm is simply a very long telephoto lens.

## Film vs. Digital

The technology of traditional film and camera equipment is very mature. There is little room for improvement, especially in image quality. Any further improvements in terms of lower grain or better color are likely to be trivial. Traditional film-based photography will eventually become obsolete, although, especially for landscape photography, it will coexist with digital for quite some time. For fine-art photographers, film retains definite advantages. It holds the edge in terms of color subtlety and smoothness, feeling of depth and presence, and the capacity to produce huge, incredibly sharp prints. This advantage is mostly limited to medium and large format cameras. In most regards digital has already equaled or surpassed 35mm in terms of quality and is knocking at the door of medium format.

My advice to newcomers is to go straight to digital. Digital camera technology, although already very usable, will see spectacular development in years to come. Having spent twenty years in the computer industry, I am a firm believer in "Moore's Law", which states that technological capacity doubles every 18 months. There is little doubt that we will see a similar rate of expansion in the digital camera industry, although perhaps not quite as rapid. For the most demanding users, there are still a few stumbling blocks. The shortcomings of sensor size, limited storage capacity, and short battery life will eventually be overcome. Current sensors are already able to produce digital files that are sufficient for most needs, including commercial photography. The last stumbling block to fall will be big enlargements of digitally-captured landscape scenes. However, it's only a matter of time until much larger capture devices are developed to tackle this. Economies of scale will keep driving prices down. After critical mass is achieved we will see miniature cameras capable of producing astonishing results at a very reasonable cost.

As of this writing, there are still a few problems awaiting better solutions. Storage, for example, is still an issue if you shoot lots of high-quality images during a long trip. Standalone devices are already replacing laptops to help you download, archive and review your images on the road. It is becoming increasingly easy to perform a quick review of your images "in-camera" almost in real time. At the end of the day and with the help of a large LCD display a more in-depth review can occur. Anything that isn't a "keeper" can be discarded to make room for more photographs. Battery life also presents somewhat of a challenge in the field. Digital photography requires a lot more energy to power the camera, store the image file, and pre- and post-visualize images on the LCD. This aspect is evolving rapidly and improvements in battery life are likely.

One side benefit of digital photography compared to film—at least with small-sensor cameras—is to allow telephoto lenses to act as if they were even longer. As I explained earlier, the source of this phenomenon is the fact that the footprint of a sensor is in most cases smaller than that of a 35mm film window. A 200mm lens may give you the magnification ratio and angle of view of a 400mm when used with a digital camera with a crop factor of 2x—although it won't provide the same nice blur in out-of-focus areas. While this is a tremendous boon for photographing wildlife, it is not necessarily so for landscape photography where a wide angle and its associated depth-of-field are more useful. In the case of a digital camera with a crop factor of 2x, you'll need to use a 14mm lens to get the actual angle of vision provided by a 28mm lens on a 35mm film camera. To minimize distortion, a digital lens must be built to very high standards, which means additional costs. This explains why a majority a digicams do not have wide-angle lenses and also why quality wide-angle lenses for digital SLR cameras

*Brittlebush & Sandstone*

are so expensive. On the other hand, for an equivalent angle of vision, digicam lenses with a short focal length offer remarkable depth-of-field, which is perfect for landscape photography.

Digital files are also much more practical than film for creative manipulation. Since no scanning is required for digitally-captured images they are more easily made available for computer management. This naturally enhances the photographer's capacity to interpret his work in new ways and to share images with others for fun and to garner feedback.

One final aspect where digital shines is in the area of noise, which is equivalent to grain in film. High-end digital cameras are able to produce clean images with very little noise, up to 400 ISO or more. This allows you to shoot handheld while preserving quality.

Even when noise is present, it can be almost entirely removed without degrading detail using specialized noise reduction algorithms. The images produced by digital cameras can also be more easily enlarged than those that come from film. Because images from digital cameras are inherently clean, they can be more easily "up-rezed," a computer method for increasing the file size, to produce larger prints with excellent results.

## The Middle Way

For a few more years, there is an excellent alternative to all-digital by combining traditional film-based photography with digital scanning. If you own several quality lenses for a film camera—often incompatible with newer digital bodies—you can use them to shoot film, scan the film, and then print your pictures at home using the new generation of photo-quality printers. High-end scanners are capable of extracting every bit of information from a medium or large format transparency or negative to produce stunning prints. This method works extremely well as long as you stay away from low-cost consumer scanners. If you only want to produce a small quantity of large prints, send your film to a professional lab to be scanned on a high-end scanner. Drum scanning by these labs yields the best quality but at a very high cost. Consumer film scanners have improved tremendously and are very usable for enlargements in the 11"x14" to 16"x20" range. They remain difficult to use for negative film, however, and are downright hopeless for B&W film. Mid-range prosumer scanners—although cheap in comparison to drum scanners—are still out of reach for most people. Flatbed scanners with transparency adapters are cheap and convenient, but adequate only to a certain extent. Their advertised resolution and d-max is often a bit optimistic and they do not yield razor-sharp scans despite what the ads would like you to believe. I find them unacceptable for making exhibit-quality work. Based on my own experience, unless you can afford a professional-grade dedicated scanner, you will get better results at a very economical rate by sending your film to a pro lab with a non-drum high-end scanner.

## Prints vs. Slides

This question is now almost obsolete, eclipsed as it is by the film vs. digital debate. Still for film purists and owners of high-end film-based equipment, it is worthy of a brief discussion within the framework of landscape photography. Print film has largely overcome the handicap of poor quality it had compared to positive film, also known as transparency film or slides. The capacity of print film to forgive exposure errors and keep high contrast in check can be useful in certain circumstances. That said, the quality of your prints ultimately depends for the most part on your photo lab unless you scan your own negatives and do your own printing. If you decide to use print film, 400 ISO is the way to go for shooting handheld and getting good depth-of-field. The grain of these fast emulsions is barely noticeable even with big enlargements. However, one has to raise the obvious question: Why shoot film for small prints when you can shoot so cheaply and practically with a digital point-and-shoot camera and have so much more control over the printing process in your digital lab? Print film will certainly be the first to go as digital technology continues to mature exponentially.

Color transparency film, on the other hand, yields high quality results and saturated color but also imposes more constraints than color negative film. First and foremost, correct exposure is absolutely critical. This effectively excludes using point-and-shoot cameras that do not allow for manual exposure compensation. In addition with transparency film you lose at least one stop exposure range compared to negative film. You must constantly concern yourself with keeping the contrast between light and dark areas to a minimum. Finally, although slow color transparency emulsions have almost no grain, it does become an issue at film speeds above 200 ISO. All these factors make it necessary in a number of circumstances to use a tripod if you want to shoot transparency film. It can be a nuisance for many who are on a pleasure trip, but it will go a long way toward high-quality results.

One other advantage of transparency film is that you can see your results easily on a light box. It's easy to determine which images are going to be "keepers". Slide film also scans extremely well, which can't be said of negative film.

In my experience and that of most serious photographers, Fujichrome Velvia is the transparency film of choice to photograph the Southwest. Velvia's high saturation and pleasing colors are particularly well suited to capture the warm light of the Golden Hour on sandstone. Even under very difficult circumstances the results can often be surprisingly good. In fact, there is a well-known saying in landscape photography circles: "Never underestimate the power of Velvia." All this leads me to believe that transparency film will continue to co-exist for quite some time with digital technology in order to satisfy the needs of discriminating users and fine-art photographers.

## Printing your Images

Having processed my own film and prints since I was eleven-years-old, I'm thankful for the memories of my early years in photography, but I'm also glad I no longer have to deal with the "chemical lab". In the mid-seventies I was using the Cibachrome system to process my own color prints. I have been producing inkjet prints for several years now and I have never looked back. The combination of state-of-the-art advancements such as archival inks, fine resin-coated or cotton rag papers, and miniaturized nozzles allow you to create stunning enlargements from digital files at a surprisingly low cost. Print longevity is no longer an issue as state-of-the-art papers rival traditional color prints for permanence. For small prints, a large number of consumer-grade photo printers do an excellent job. For big enlargements, wide-carriage inkjet printers are becoming affordable to acquire and economical to use and maintain. I am personally very satisfied with inkjet prints, but others still prefer laser or LED printers such as the Lightjet and Chromira brands.

There are many option for printing, all of them very good to excellent. The main thing you need to do is to profile your scanner and printer and color-calibrate your monitor. If you are not sure, buy yourself a book or attend a workshop dealing with color management. This is the best investment you can make toward getting high quality results for your prints.

## What to take on your Trip

You will notice that I do not talk much about equipment throughout the book. That is essentially because gear is not a decisive factor in the quality of your photography. Light, the ability to "see", and an eye for composition are much more likely to affect the results than simply pointing an expensive camera at a well-known landmark and shooting.

❐ The camera body is at the center of your photographic equipment, although it is not the most important component in terms of results. Modern camera bodies offer a tremendous number of functions—too many in my opinion. Some of these functions are nonetheless useful, if not indispensable, if you want to go beyond simple snapshots. Single-lens reflex cameras (SLR or dSLR in the case of the digital SLR) have through-the-lens viewing capability which is helpful for precise framing, although many people are just as happy with a rangefinder, optical or electronic viewfinder. Note that the optical viewfinders in digital point-and-shoot cameras usually show only about 70% of the image forcing you to use the LCD for accuracy. This can sometimes result in fuzzy pictures shot with extended arms.

In traditional photography, aperture-priority mode is essential to maximizing depth-of-field. You'll be able to preview the depth-of-field if your camera has depth-of-field preview. Some sophisticated cameras have special modes allowing you to maximize depth-of-field automatically. While this is fine for non-critical shooting, it is no substitute to setting the depth-of-field manually.

Aperture compensation allows you to manually correct exposure under difficult lighting circumstances. Exposure bracketing is very useful to guarantee correct exposure for those critical shots. An all-metal lens mount is also recommended over polycarbonate if you're planning to change lenses often.

One function that has completely vanished on entry-level film cameras is mirror lockup. This is sad because it has been scientifically demonstrated that pictures taken with the mirror up have a higher count of lines per millimeter, which in turn produces sharper enlargements. Fortunately, manufacturers have resurrected this functionality on affordable dSLRs. Rangefinder cameras eliminate the mirror shock problem completely, but they come with their own set of limitations.

❐ Lenses are the most important component of your camera system. High optical quality glass is crucial for producing quality results. Single focal length lenses used to be better than multi-focal length zooms, but high-end zooms are now equally as good and are extremely practical, both in terms of speed, weight and protection of the mirror and internal mechanism from dust and wind. Stay away from low-cost consumer zooms; they yield disappointing results. Digital sensors are even more demanding. High quality lenses are absolutely essential if shooting digitally. A bright zoom covering 28mm to 105 or 135mm works well in the Southwest. If you take a digital or analog point-and-shoot camera, be sure not to settle for 35mm or 38mm at the wide end. It will be not be sufficient in the field. You'll find yourself using the wide angle range most of the time. Needless to say, a super wide-angle (24mm or less) and a long telephoto (200mm and above) will significantly enhance your potential for original shots.

Wide-range zooms (28-200mm and 28-300mm) are deservedly popular as versatile lenses for travel photography, but be aware that they are usually soft at the telephoto end. They are adequate for small prints up to 5"x7", but do not expect high-quality enlargements.

One new development that offers a lot of value to the photographer on the go is the emergence of gyro-stabilized zooms. This technology allows you to gain at least two stops, which may be enough to forego a tripod in non-critical 35mm or digital landscape photography. While this doesn't completely obviate the use of the tripod, especially to maximize depth-of-field, it offers greatly improved sharpness at speeds in the 1/30th and 1/60th range. It allows you to quickly capture those fleeting moments—a furtive ray of light or a rainbow—with increased chances of getting good results.

*Photographing the Southwest can be full of surprises*

As for teleconverters, which generally come with a 1.4x and 2x magnifying factor, only use prime models in conjunction with high-quality lenses in order to get good results. A factor of 1.4 is less radical and less detrimental to overall picture quality.

Whatever lenses you decide to buy, don't be frugal. Too many people buy an expensive body, only to equip it with a mediocre zoom lens. Major manufacturers always have two or even three lines of lenses: a consumer line, a so-called "prosumer" line, and a high-end more expensive line. My advice is to buy a cheap body and the best possible lens you can afford. It will result in sharper, higher contrast pictures, with better color.

❐ I do occasionally recommend the use of filters to enhance and compensate for the shortcomings of film. A UV or Skylight 1B filter will protect your lens without diminishing image quality, but use them with caution on a zoom lens.

Zooms, due to their complex optical construction involving the use of many elements and groups, are particularly prone to flare—the phenomenon of light entering the lens and causing unwanted reflections. I do not personally use these filters, relying instead on my lens shade to protect the lens, but this advice is not for everybody.

A graduated neutral-density filter (or ND Grad) is an essential piece of equipment, especially if you shoot transparencies. It will help keep contrast in check and open up shadow areas. Split neutral-density filters work great when the separation line between lit subject and shadow is very obvious, but these instances are rare in Canyon Country. By all means, use a high-quality filter. Cheap ND grad filters are not neutral and will give a nasty color cast to your skies. In my opinion, you'll be better served by a two-stop filter than one with three stops. Also, a model you can slide up and down in a holder is more flexible than a simple screw-in filter.

A mild warming filter such as an 81a, KR 1.5 or Nikon A2 is also an important filter. It is useful under many circumstances, but most particularly in the shade to remove the blue cast from the sky and when photographing under a strong sun. It adds a slight warmth to your images, without introducing a color cast. These filters work very well in the Southwest.

Most books and articles enthusiastically endorse the use of a polarizing filter, or "polarizer", as a vital piece of equipment to carry in your bag. I am not so enthusiastic and recommend that you use your polarizer with moderation with anything other than print film. This advice also applies to digital cameras. If you have high-quality, high-contrast lenses and shoot on a highly saturated film, such as Fuji Velvia, you won't need one most of the time. Used indiscriminately a polarizer may create skies that are too dark. Also, in combination with a wide-angle lens, the polarizing effect can become too strong, resulting in light falloff in one or more corners of the image. I use my polarizer mostly to eliminate glare on foliage, streams or various textures, but generally keep it in the bag during broad daylight unless the sky is full of fluffy clouds. If you use a rangefinder, carry a pair of polarizing sunglasses and look straight into the lens to see the effect of the filter. Then, based on your experience, apply the proper amount of exposure compensation for your particular filter, usually 1½ to 2 stops. It is also not too hard to use an ND grad with a rangefinder with a little practice.

❏ A lens shade is helpful in preventing flare. Be sure it is designed for your lens to avoid the phenomenon of vignetting, which is light falloff in the corners of your image. This is particularly nasty with blue skies.

❏ Now we come to what I consider the second most important piece of equipment after your lenses: the tripod. A tripod is nearly indispensable for landscape photography, particularly if you shoot transparencies. Good slide film is inherently slow and doesn't lend itself to handheld photography. A tripod also allows you to compose your images more carefully and to keep the horizon straight. Unfortunately there is also price to pay when you need to carry a four-pound tripod on long hikes, especially if some scrambling is involved. Carbon fiber tripods are a good alternative albeit quite expensive. They can shave a couple of pounds from an otherwise heavy piece of equipment. I recommend buying a headless tripod and purchasing your own ballhead. I personally use a combination carbon-fiber tripod and magnesium ballhead. There are now smaller, lighter-weight, and less expensive tripods that do a great job with small digicams and lightweight dSLRs. If you have never used a tripod before when shooting landscapes, you'll be surprised at how much it can improve your photography.

❏ The natural companion of the tripod is fortunately very lightweight: a cable release. It is useful in avoiding camera movement when releasing the shutter, even when the camera is mounted on a tripod. A good quality one costs only a few dollars more than a small flimsy model and is much nicer to use. If you don't want to bother with one, you can also use your camera's built-in timer release. There is one potential pitfall with the timer technique on entry-level cameras: someone may walk right in front of your camera just when it's taking the picture. I can almost guarantee that this will happen in highly visited places, such as Antelope Canyon. Most digital camera manufacturers offer remote control devices, which take care of this problem.

❏ You shouldn't carry your camera and lenses without some form of protection. It is risky to switch lenses in an environment where dust and sand are present, especially with a dSLR. Be sure to protect your camera from the wind when changing lenses and to blow away dust every time you load a new roll or sheet if you shoot film. It's amazing how many frames can be wasted by dust-induced streaks. Consider Antelope Canyon again. There is always a fine dust suspended in the air, although you might not see it. If this lodges in your camera when you change lenses or film, you run the risk of having lines etched across your entire roll. A single speck of dust can ruin all the frames when you rewind. You should also carry a soft airbrush with which to blow away dust from the lens and from the inside of the camera between rolls. Obviously, digital point-and-shoot cameras, also known as digicams, with their permanently attached lenses are almost impervious to this type of misadventure. It's exactly the opposite with a dSLR, which are extremely prone to dust problems. Some dSLRs incorporate vibrating sensors to shake the dust off, apparently with very good results. Dust can also cause malfunctioning of the storage media.

If you carry several lenses, consider a photo backpack. It will also carry your tripod and, with some models, your water bottles. For reasons I explained in Chapter 1, I think it is essential to use a backpack capable of carrying your water. If you are going to venture into wet canyons when the water level is high, you should carry your photo equipment in sealable plastic bags. If your photo adventure involves swimming, a dedicated dry bag is a must to protect your equipment..

❏ If you use expensive, bulky or slow-to-operate equipment, such as medium or large format, I recommend that you take along an auxiliary digicam with a good lens. It will prove invaluable for photographing difficult sections of trails or narrows. A small digicam is also useful for shooting test images before exposing large-format film. Finally, as noted in Chapter 1, a digicam can prove very useful in helping you "remember" your way while hiking in the backcountry.

# IN THE FIELD

In the following sections, I'll discuss how to handle a number of common situations you'll encounter in the course of photographing the Southwest. This advice is based on what has consistently worked for me in the field. It doesn't replace a good book specializing in lighting and composition, and it certainly is no substitute for a workshop with an experienced instructor. If you are a novice user wanting to explore the locations in this guidebook without bothering too much about learning photography, I hope this advice will come handy and will help you bring home better pictures.

## Using Reflected light

I'll start this discussion with what is arguably the quintessential element of photographing the Southwest: reflected light. Let's define reflected light first. Reflection involves two rays of light. One incidental ray strikes a given surface, which in turn sends out a reflected ray. You can immediately guess that the reflective properties of the surface in question impact the quality of the reflected rays. This is where the second ingredient comes into play: sandstone. People often ask me what I consider so special in the Southwest. My answer is that it has the greatest body of sandstone on the planet and that this sandstone comes in a great variety of flavors. The combination of sandstone and reflected light is what sets the Southwest apart. When light strikes sandstone directly, the reflected light has a much warmer color. If the reflected light happens to reach another patch of sandstone that is not illuminated by direct light, it will cause it to glow with warm colors ranging from deep red to soft yellow. Reflected light is the main ingredient of the best photos of the Southwest. It should always be given priority over direct light.

*Golden Wall*

## Photographing Scenics including close Subjects

If your scenic composition includes a close subject, it is often necessary to work with the smallest possible aperture, i.e. the highest settings such as f/22, or even f/64 if you shoot large format, to guarantee maximum depth-of-field. It is very

*Skullrocks & Arch*

disappointing to view a "grand scenic" photograph in which some parts are not razor-sharp. This is even worse if you enlarge the photo.

If you use a sophisticated SLR or dSLR, you may be able to visualize depth-of-field in the viewfinder. For critical landscape work, it is preferable to work with the manual focusing option and to set the distance not as the exact focus when viewed through the lens, but by using the depth-of-field marks of your lens to maximize sharpness within the particular range of distance pertaining to your shot. Unfortunately many modern lenses, particularly zooms, lack depth-of-field marks so it is often necessary to improvise. Another way to guarantee sharpness and to maximize depth-of-field is by using the hyperfocal distance method. As an example, a 35mm lens focused at 10 feet at f/16 yields a sharp image from 5 feet (which is half the hyperfocal distance) to infinity. There are some handy charts you can buy for a few dollars for every camera format. This method is a sure bet to create a sharp-focused image from close range to infinity. In certain cases, you may want to purposely blur the background to isolate your foreground and create an artistic effect using *bokeh* (a Japanese term signifying the out-of-focus area of a photograph).

## Photographing on River Trips

A rafting trip on one of the great rivers of the Southwest can be an exhilarating experience. It's a great way to discover and photograph the inner canyons of the Green, Yampa, San Juan or Colorado Rivers in areas not accessible from the rims. Similarly, a kayaking trip on Lake Powell allows exploring dozens of narrow canyons not accessible on foot or by houseboats. Your primary concern on such trips is to keep your camera equipment dry. This includes not only the body but also your lenses, batteries, film and/or storage devices. It's one thing to have a splash-proof camera, but you'll need to protect your lenses too and take all precautions to avoid immersion. Some cameras are designed to survive a short immersion in clean water, but few will resist dirty water full of tiny particles of sediment. Your film would not like it either.

You'll most likely undertake your rafting trip through an outfitter and many, but not necessarily all of them, provide some sort of waterproof storage for your gear. Before you sign up with an outfitter, ask what kind of storage they use. Nobody will guarantee you that it's 100% waterproof and your contract is likely to say that you carry your equipment at your own risk. Most outfitters use large waterproof aluminum dry boxes. One concern with these is that your gear risks being knocked around badly when your craft is tossed about in the rapids. If you carry expensive equipment, you may ask your outfitter if you can bring your own waterproof container. Many allow it within limits. Some outfitters recommend customized army surplus waterproof containers, also known as ammo cans or rocket boxes, which work well as long as the rubber gasket in the lid is in good condition (they tend to deteriorate over time after being repeatedly drenched and cooked in the sun). There are many other kinds of dry boxes, made of aluminum or plastic, which you can customize to your needs by lining them with foam. You can also choose a simple dry bag if you carry just one camera and lens. If you're kayaking on Lake Powell, you may want to investigate specialty dry bags designed to be stowed along the hull of your kayak. At the high end, the king of waterproof protection is the Pelican box, an expensive solution but worth every penny. In all cases, you should seal your equipment, as well as your film and storage cards, inside zip-lock bags when it's not in use.

Most rafting trips have rather leisurely schedules and tend to stop early in the day so clients can relax in camp. Most locations allow you to hike around and look for photographs. You can scout around and come back later on or shoot in the early morning before breakfast.

## Photographing Running Water

*Raging River*

Waterfalls and running water are great subjects for photography. Many people wonder how to create the so-called "angel hair" effect of soft water. It is actually quite simple: use a long exposure. To achieve the best effect, start by exposing the scene for at least one second. A slow shutter speed of 3 seconds or longer works even better. It's not always possible to achieve such slow shutter speeds under normal circumstances and chances are you'll need a bit of help from some extra equipment. Your first option is to use the lowest ISO possible. If you have a polarizing filter, you can use it to further reduce the aperture by 1½ to 2 stops, thus almost quadrupling the exposure. In most cases, this is still not going to be enough. To get a truly beautiful effect you'll need to resort to a neutral density filter (non-graduated). The most common ND filter adds 6 stops to a scene, so what was a 1/30 second exposure at f/8 suddenly becomes a 2 second exposure—enough for a wonderful image of nicely blurred water. Obviously, you'll need a tripod and some kind of mechanical or electronic shutter release. If you are using an SLR or dSLR, I can't emphasize enough the benefit of mirror lockup.

In some cases, a bluish cast can enhance the beauty of running water. To add a bluish cast, photograph the water in indirect light with the high color temperature of the blue sky providing the illumination. A film such as Fujichrome Velvia, which is optimized for warm color temperature will produce some truly exquisite enhanced blue. Using a digital camera, you may have to experiment a bit with the white balance to achieve the results you're looking for.

## Photographing Water Reflections

There are several key elements to obtaining great reflections on a body of water. First you need side light or backlight—the latter works great as long as it is not directly in your field of vision and you're using a shade. The light should be soft, so as not to overwhelm the scene, eradicating details and creating nasty shadow areas. Next, you need the ambient air to be perfectly still. The slightest trace of wind will agitate the surface and create ripples that will mar your subject's reflection. If the wind shows no sign of abating, try using it to your advantage and concentrate on playing with colors in the reflection. You'll also need some strong foreground element to anchor the composition and add depth, making the viewer feel immersed in the scene.

In most cases, the reflection will be significantly less bright than the actual subject. If it occupies a large portion of the frame, such as in the case of a reflection in a lake, you'll need to use a split or graduated neutral density filter to compensate the exposure and keep some detail in what would otherwise be a shadow area in an uncorrected photograph.

In the following illustration, I used the reflection of the fall colors to create a ribbon of color, while the reflection of the sky allowed me to isolate the rocks. An example of using a neutral density filter to preserve detail in a reflection can be found in my Cottonwood Reflection photograph in the Canyons of the Escalante chapter. In that image I used a graduated filter diagonally to open up the shadows in the lower left part of the image. Arguably the most photographed lake reflection in the Southwest is the famous Maroon Bells scene near Aspen Colorado (see *Photographing the Southwest – Volume 3*).

*Zen Pond*

## Photographing Snow & Ice

If you shoot in winter and spring on the Colorado Plateau, you're bound to encounter snow and ice and you may want to integrate them into your compositions, either as part of a scenic landscape or by themselves.

*Blue Bergs*

Your camera's built-in meter is programmed to render everything a neutral grey, which is of course not what you want with snow and ice. To avoid this, you need to compensate by opening your aperture between 1 and 2 f/stops depending on how bright the scene is. Exposing snow and ice correctly is tricky because you don't want to lose detail in the highlights. In broad daylight, I usually start with a +1½ stop compensation in order to expose the snow so it will be white. If snow is just a background, you'll want to expose your main subject correctly, particularly if it's a person, and let the snow be overexposed.

As with any ordinary scene, shooting snow during the golden hour creates nice shadows, making your photos more interesting. I usually prefer a fair amount of sunlight to make the snow shine, a good example of that can be seen on the Canyonlands photograph anchoring the Introduction chapter, as well as the Fremont River photograph anchoring the Capitol Reef chapter.

A bright sunny sky will create a strong blue cast in the shaded areas, especially when your subject is extremely bright. The Blue Bergs image above was purposely shot without my usual warming filter so that the ice on the frozen lake would turn even bluer. If you don't want the blue cast, use an 81a or 81b filter to provide warmth but making sure that the snow or ice don't look reddish.

A polarizing filter can accentuate the contrast, eliminate glare and restore proper exposure for the sky if the latter is somewhat hazy. If the sky is already very blue, be sure not to overdo the polarizing effect or your sky will be too dark; even more when the sun is at a 90° angle.

An overcast sky during a clearing storm can also work to your advantage by filtering the light, making the snow act as a soft reflector. A good example of that can be seen on the Thor's Hammer photograph anchoring the Bryce Canyon chapter. The soft bright light lit the formation bright red while keeping contrast in check. Digital cameras have an advantage over film as you can fine-tune the white balance by checking for immediate results on your LCD. Print film is also quite forgiving on snow and ice, but transparencies must be perfectly exposed.

## Photographing Slot Canyons

The range of perception of film is greatly limited in comparison with the human eye, and it is impossible to reproduce on film all the nuances that we perceive. Variations of 5 or 8 f/stops are the norm in slot canyons and choosing the best exposure is not easy. Your task consists of perfectly exposing the part that most interests you within the limitations of the film. To do this, carefully select your composition to avoid too many highlights and to minimize large areas in deep shadow. The shadows risk appearing completely black, especially on transparency film, and the highlights can be completely blown out to pure white. Avoid photographing sunlight directly hitting a canyon wall as this is a sure way to exceed the contrast range of the film or sensor. Exposure can be determined by making an intelligent compromise between the various spot measurements obtained on those parts of the wall for which you want to preserve detail. In practice, I find that it is very difficult to overexpose in slot canyons. By increasing the exposure, either purposely or by accident, you will still get good images, albeit with a different gamut of colors. Short exposures yield a lot of yellow as well as deep rust, orange and red, while very long exposures introduce light and deep purple into the palette.

If you do not have a spot meter, either handheld or in your camera, be ready to bracket heavily: Easily said when you shoot 35mm or digital, but almost out of the questions if you carry a view camera. You'll often have to carefully add 1½ to 2 stop overexposure to bring out the detail on the darker surfaces without overexposing the lighter walls. If you add too much, what could be a beautiful yellow light could end up totally white on high-contrast slide film.

Try to find compositions that restrict the EV range to the smallest possible value. Avoid the brightly lit areas, concentrating instead on reflected light. Take plenty of time

*Photographing slot canyons may involve some very messy aspects*

to frame your shots and even more time to take them. Use a very small aperture and long exposure in order to let the beautiful reflected light seep onto your film. If you use an automatic camera, a fast ISO and a steady hand can simulate a spot metering technique. Close in on an interesting detail that is not too brightly lit and lock the exposure by pressing the shutter release halfway. Then move back, recompose, and take your picture. Don't use a flash if you want to preserve the texture of the walls and the nuances of color created by natural light.

Knowing your equipment well is a must. Not only must you be able to operate it without hesitation, but you should also be able to anticipate how your images will look. If there is one thing I have learned from my many visits to slot canyons such as Antelope Canyon, it is that experience can play an important role in increasing the number of high-caliber "keepers" that you'll bring back from your visit.

In some popular slot canyons, be prepared to deal with a steady traffic of visitors who are not necessarily interested in photography and will be in your way. Just be courteous and don't take yourself too seriously and you'll find that people will give you a wide berth. One consequence of such intense foot traffic is small particles of dust pervading the air, a phenomenon exacerbated by some photographers purposely throwing dust in the air to add dimension to the shafts of light hitting the floor around midday. Be sure to protect your equipment as best you can, especially if it's a dSLR, and give it a careful cleaning after your visit.

## Photographing Dunes and Lava Beds

Sand and lava are two subjects that can easily fool your built-in meter and you may get unpleasant results if you use it. Many new automatic cameras have programs that supposedly compensate for specific lighting conditions; however, you will get better results by compensating the exposure manually based on the lighting conditions. For brown and red sand, you should bracket your exposure in small increments of ½ to 1 f/stop based on the effect you want to achieve. For deeply saturated red sand in the evening sun, try ½ stop under and over exposure, as well as whatever your meter says. For extremely white sand in bright daylight 1½ f/stops overexposure works best; in early to mid-morning, late afternoon or when it's overcast, try ½ f/stop overexposure for scenics and 1 f/stop for sand patterns.

*Blue Dune*

Depending on the light, lava usually doesn't need as much correction, as it is more gray rather than pure black. However, if you want to make it darker, underexpose by ¼ or ½ f/stop.

I do not recommend that you shoot sand and lava using print film—or any other bright or dark texture for that matter—unless your goal is to have them scanned professionally or to have custom enlargements made from the negatives.

## Photographing Wildflowers

The two most important factors in photographing wildflowers are the presence of soft, diffused light and the absence of wind. In the case of the light, one thing to avoid is direct illumination by the sun. A cloudy, overcast day always works best. Partly cloudy conditions may provide intermittently suitable conditions.

*Wildflowers in Storm*

If you are really serious about your wildflower photography, you may need a diffuser and/or reflector for the light and a small tent for the wind (and light) if you do macro photography. An acquaintance of mine has built a wonderful little tent/diffuser using a cheap laundry bag, so it is definitely possible to improvise.

Two filters are essential for wildflowers. A warming filter will always come handy to remove the blue cast, particularly at higher elevations and if you shot during the day. An 81a warming filter works best. A polarizing filter is also very useful to remove glare.

I find that high-end digital cameras work well for close-ups of flowers against a blurred background. I prefer film, however, to shoot scenes involving large fields of flowers. A luminous optical viewfinder or a fast lens with wide aperture offers a tremendous advantage. Electronic viewfinders, on the other hand, such as those found in some digicams, make it very difficult to get good results.

When shooting fields of wildflowers, avoid placing your camera too high. You'll get more dynamic results if you shoot at the flower's level. Large format cameras with tilt and shift movements have an enormous advantage. They allow you to concentrate on a close group of flowers while keeping the background in focus to infinity. Digicams with small size sensors can also do the same thing but at a tremendous cost in terms of detail and sense of three-dimensionality.

One common mistake is to be in too big a hurry to take pictures when arriving on the scene. Instead, scan the field for the best flowers, making sure you have an interesting background and paying attention not to include any white or grey sky. Don't be overwhelmed by the color alone; be sure that the flowers you are photographing appear fresh and are wide open. Some older flowers may still look good to you in the viewfinder but may not look their best on a large print.

Arizona and New Mexico are great for shooting wildflowers from mid-March to late April, particularly poppies. Colorado has fantastic fields of wildflowers at higher elevations in late July and early August. You'll find some advice on Arizona shooting locations in *Volume 2* and on Colorado locations in *Volume 3* of *Photographing the Southwest.*

## Photographing Fall Colors

Photographing fall colors in the Southwest is an exhilarating experience. While the Southwest may lack the red foliage of autumn in New England, it adds the incredible yellow and rust colors of cottonwoods and aspens to the grandiose backgrounds of canyons and snowy peaks. Many outstanding fall color locations in Colorado are discussed in greater detail in *Volume 3.*

One filter you absolutely need for fall colors is a warming filter. Once again a Skylight or 81a filter is usually sufficient to get rid of the bluish cast, which is particularly noticeable at higher elevations in Utah and Colorado. A polarizing filter may also be useful when used in moderation.

Film, particularly medium and large format transparency film, will continue to give better results than digital for a number of years, not necessarily in terms of sharpness, but for tonality,

*Autumn colors in Zion*

overall smoothness and three-dimensionality. Fujichrome Velvia 50/100 is the classic film for shooting fall color. Fujichrome Velvia 100F does a better job with the reds and is a little tamer when it comes to controlling contrast. Kodak film usually does a better job with subtle orange hues.

## Photographing Rock Art

Rock art tends to be quite contrasty; therefore it is prone to color casts when photographed with highly saturated films under strong reflected light. Puebloan ruins, often tucked inside deep alcoves, bring the danger of reciprocity failure, particularly for those who shoot large format.

*Finely drawn pictographs on alcove ceiling*

If you shoot under strong reflected light, you are bound to have an exaggerated amount of red on films such as Fujichrome Velvia and Ektachrome VS. If you shoot in dark areas, Velvia will tend to give you an excess of green. In both cases, a slightly lower contrast film such as Fuji Provia will serve you better. The latter offers the finest grain of any slide film as of this writing and it is well suited to accurately reproduce the delicate textures and subdued golden browns of rock art. With large format, an exposure of 30 seconds is common in low light situations. With an additional one stop, you can reduce this to fifteen seconds, thus limiting the color shift.

Large format photographers have the advantage of being able to change plates to match a particular lighting situation. 35mm and medium format photographers must be more careful with the kind of film they load before shooting rock art and small ruins. If you shoot negative film for paper prints, these problems do not really affect you. If you shoot digitally, it might be a good idea to take a custom white balance measurement on the panel, especially if you shoot Jpeg. If you shoot Raw, it doesn't make much difference as you'll be able to adjust the white balance when post-processing your file.

# More on Exposure

If you are working with transparency film and wish to obtain the best results without concerning yourself too much about determining the right exposure, take five different shots at ½ stop intervals—i.e. two on either side of the setting you think is correct. In the case of negative film, this is unnecessary since the density of the highlights and shadows can easily be altered during the printing process. Negative film tolerates up to 2 stops of overexposure fairly well, but does poorly with underexposure. If you are a perfectionist, you can always take a second shot with one stop of overexposure—it is useless to try more. If you are using a digital camera, you have the advantage of seeing the results immediately on your LCD. While this is not very precise, it at least gives you a starting point.

Attention should also be paid to the reciprocity failure characteristics of your film, especially if you are using a tripod and slow transparency film. With exposures of several seconds, certain slide films display a tendency towards incorrect exposure and you risk underexposing the film. There are reciprocity failure tables for the major brands of film on the market. Unless you are taking exposures of four seconds or more, you shouldn't have to worry about this.

# Some Advice on Composition

Composition is fortunately not an exact science or else it would be the domain of engineers. Rather, it is a subtle blend of classic established rules, specific properties of your subject and, perhaps most importantly, your own artistic sensibility. While I can't help you with the last two, this short refresher course might help you remember and use "the rules" during your visit to the Southwest.

❒ Before you think about composition, remember that lighting is everything in landscape photography. An image is rarely attractive without interesting light.

❒ Remember the "rule of thirds" to avoid an unaesthetic horizon line in the middle of your picture or a main subject that is too centered. Visualize your image overlaid by an imaginary grid dividing it into thirds horizontally and vertically. Try placing your key elements at the bottom left or right intersections of the grid, or at the upper left or right intersections if there is an interesting foreground, but avoid the middle of the picture.

❒ Be sure to check that the horizon doesn't appear tilted in your viewfinder. Using a tripod and taking your time is the best way to avoid an unpleasant surprise. If you're having trouble, use a small level in your camera's hot shoe.

❒ Resist the urge to squeeze too much of a grand panorama into a small picture. Results are almost always disappointing due to the lack of a center of interest, unless the sky is particularly exciting. Your image will usually be more interesting if you zoom in on a small portion and include some of that nice sky. Fill most of the frame with your main subject. Too many secondary subjects create clutter and become indistinguishable in a small picture, even though they look good to the naked eye.

❐ Include an interesting foreground and put your main subject slightly off-center when it is distant. This will create depth in your image and reinforce the feeling of presence. Make sure the foreground is not just empty fill-in space, however. If this is the case, it is often better to give the distant subject more prominence rather than having the bottom two-thirds of the frame filled with a boring subject. Always think depth and presence. Some imposing formations may appear smallish in your image if you do not include a reference object, such as trees, a trail or a human silhouette, to provide a sense of scale.

❐ Thoughtfully consider the benefit of telephoto lenses. Long telephotos serve three purposes: extracting details from the landscape, making a subject stand out through creative use of *bokeh* (the unsharp area in a photograph) and compressing the perspective. The compression effect makes your photographs appear rich and dense by allowing several planes to cohabit in one image.

❐ Super wide-angle lenses give excellent results with very tightly-framed close subjects by accentuating—or even esthetically distorting—the graphic, geometric or even abstract properties. Rocks with interesting colors or texture, shapes in sand dunes or badlands, and trees and bushes are examples.

❐ Be mindful of shadows, especially when using slide film, and make use of a graduated neutral density filter if necessary. So called "golden hour" photography is great, but what appears to you as a simple shaded area may look completely black on film.

❐ Above all, be constantly on the lookout for photogenic details around you—rock texture, natural elements with abstract shapes, uncommon colors, reflections, transparent views, interesting vegetation, or tracks and leaves on the ground. Using these elements can create some wonderfully original compositions. Not all of these images will be keepers, but some will yield beautiful compositions that are a welcome departure from the common "grand scenic" images.

## Photographing in National Parks

Most people carry some form of camera and are eager to capture memories of their trip using the recognized icons of the West as a background. National Parks have become incredibly recognizable through movies, advertisements, park literature, and coffee table books, not to mention guidebooks such as this one. No wonder people want to show that they've been there. The glorification of the West creates a desire to accumulate photographs as trophies, and cheap film and easy-to-use digital cameras make this almost effortless. In view of the massive onslaught of people in relatively concentrated areas, we must be mindful of our collective impact on the land.

So far the National Park Service has maintained the view that photographers—whether amateur or professional—should be treated like any other visitors. While there are no specific restrictions imposed on us, we are also expected to obey the rules. Some large-format photographers talk of a stigma attached to

carrying a tripod and bulky equipment in remote places. I carry a tripod at all times and I have never felt singled out in my interactions with park rangers. So should we worry? I personally don't think so. The National Park Service once floated the possibility of requiring permits for professional photographers, but the idea was abandoned. My credo is that we, as privileged visitors to pristine areas, should act as good citizens and be mindful of the environment in order that our impact on the land not force more closures of sensitive areas.

One area where some closures may be unavoidable is backcountry roads. Rumor has it that several roads in Grand Staircase-Escalante National Monument will be closed in the future. There is little doubt that vehicular access off paved roads has the potential to cause substantial damage—not only when vehicles are driven irresponsibly, but also because of sheer numbers. Let's face it, fifteen years ago the term SUV wasn't part of our vocabulary. Today, light trucks and SUVs form the largest segment of the automobile market and they are the vehicles of choice for visiting the Southwest. We must do everything we can to tread lightly, on foot and on the back roads, to avoid damaging the land and to preserve it for generations to come.

## Parting Shots

There is another less palpable, but no less essential ingredient to good landscape photography: an unbridled love for nature and strong emotional connection to the land and your subject. The act of photographing should be an extension of that love, to record the memories and share with others the joy of being there. If your fascination with camera equipment or the physics of photography take precedence over your love of nature in an unbalanced way, it is doubtful that you'll ever achieve great results. Your craft may become technically excellent and you may acquire a nice portfolio to show friends, but you won't be able to communicate emotions if they weren't present when you took the picture. Most people I know who seriously pursue photography of the Southwest have this love of the land within them. Sometimes, however, I meet folks who are more interested in the act of photographing than in enjoying the beauty around them. Over the years I have taken pleasure in asking people whether they would do a particularly strenuous hike to a beautiful spot if they had to leave their camera at home. I have had a few people flatly—and honestly—tell me that they wouldn't. This isn't necessarily a criticism; photography doesn't have to equate to love of nature to be enjoyed as a hobby. I do say, however, that simply being there, quietly enjoying the place and the moment, is far more important than bringing back a few pictures.

Another important axiom of good landscape photography is that it rarely happens by accident. In all probability you'll need to visit a location several times, to see it under different light and in different seasons—perhaps even a few times without a camera—to start pre-visualizing your image. As you observe, think and feel during your time there, you will learn to refine your past experience to

*Opposite page: Furry Feet*

anticipate a change of light or a break in the clouds. Your best images—those which carry the most emotional content—will be the result of careful planning and pre-visualization.

Finally, with your pre-visualized image in mind, you'll rise early—very early—and drag your sleepy body inside a freezing car. You'll drive on the edge of your seat to the now familiar location, peering at the darkness to spot deer on the road through the partially frozen windshield, nervously glancing at the clock and worrying about the changing light on the horizon. Perhaps you'll be chewing on a hard power bar between nervous sips of coffee to warm you up a bit and get your mind in gear. You will walk to your location briskly, plant your tripod firmly, ready-up filters and lenses. You'll wait, floating in a dual state of serene peace and nervous anticipation. And then, the momentous event you came for will happen: sunrise. The land will be bathed in hues of yellow and red and you will understand the reason you must take this journey.

But there is little time for reflection. There is a job to be done—photos to be taken. The adrenaline kicks in and you are totally focused. You shoot like a maniac, oblivious to everything else but your subject, annoyed if someone else suddenly shows up. You shoot and shoot until the incredible light finally becomes a little too bright, a little too crude. When you're done you smile and bask in the deep feeling of joy that overtakes you as you feel one with this place that you love so much. You linger a while to make the feeling last, letting the sun warm you up, your body still weary from lack of sleep. As you walk back to the trailhead you let your mind wander and play like a puppy. You're proud and ecstatic at having experienced this cosmic moment. You suddenly become part of the great brotherhood of early-rising nature lovers, and, unbeknownst to you, you've just bonded with the fly fisherman in Montana, the ice fisherman in Minnesota and the deer hunter in Idaho!

Months later you sit in your living room looking at the big, majestic enlargement hanging on the wall and you grin happily at the beloved landscape basking in the morning sun. But you also feel something deeper—a special connection. The memories that you bring back from such incredibly poignant and precious moments are treasured as much as the print itself. You may not have the words express it, but that's OK. The picture will speak for you. ✿

*The Organ & the Great White Throne*

Chapter 3

# AROUND ZION

*Tallgrass & Alcove in Zion Canyon*

## ZION NAT'L PARK

Zion is often the first national park visited by travelers making the "Grand Circle" of national parks in Utah and Arizona. It's a spectacular introduction to the discovery of the Colorado plateau.

For the visitor with little time, the park consists of essentially two parts: the canyon and the plateau.

The canyon is deeply cut (between 2,000 and 2,500 feet), which doesn't make for easy photography because of the great contrast between the sunlit summits and the valley plunged in deep shadow. In 2000, the NPS has instituted a mandatory shuttle service to reduce the congestion and pollution in the canyon's interior, thus putting an end to everyone's misery trying to find a parking spot at the popular locations. The service is running smoothly and will deliver you and your camera gear to the location of your choice in the canyon in a much healthier frame of mind. From early April through the end of October, private vehicles are not allowed on the Scenic Drive. Shuttle schedules vary depending on the season and may be subject to change. In summer 2005, shuttles ran from 5:45 AM (from the Visitor Center) to 11:00 PM (from the Temple of Sinawava) and left every 6 minutes during peak hours (9 AM to 8 PM); they left every 15 to 30 minutes outside of peak hours (the interval gets shorter the closer you are from peak hours).

The shuttle trip to the end of the canyon takes 45 minutes. Note that the Visitor Center's parking area is usually full by mid-morning; in that case, you must first take another shuttle from Springdale to the Visitor Center. While in Springdale, you should make it a point to visit Michael Fatali's gallery for a look at his beautiful and inspiring images.

If you are visiting by car outside the mandatory shuttle season, you can travel with the sun as it crosses the valley and harvest a great crop of photos. If you travel by motorhome, note that there are parking restrictions in the canyon and you will need an escort to go through the tunnel on Scenic Byway 9.

If possible, the most interesting way to arrive in Zion is by way of the plateau from the east entrance, since the views are particularly spectacular coming from Mt. Carmel. In addition, illumination is best in the morning at the principle viewpoints of the plateau.

If you follow this advice, you have two possibilities: Visit Zion at the end of your "Grand Circle" or make a detour through Kanab. In practice, spending the night at Kanab is very feasible if you leave from Los Angeles in the morning. If you leave from Las Vegas, you are only three hours from Zion and you'll be hard pressed to resist the attraction of starting from the canyon.

I will begin our visit at the plateau, but the choice is up to you. In any case, the universe of Zion will not disappoint you.

## The Zion Plateau

All of the southeast area of the park, between the east entrance and the tunnel, is absolutely spectacular and offers numerous photographic possibilities. It is without doubt one of the most fantastic landscapes you'll encounter. The rock walls, some white, some pink, some red, possess extraordinary rounded forms, whereas the summits are ornamented like minarets. A sculptural sensuality emanates from this topography that defies the imagination. The ground switches from polished to checkered within a very short space. Stone tumuli scorched raw by the wind, burst forth here and there from a ground alternately smooth and lined. It's an incongruous landscape, kneaded, molded and painted as if by some crazy

*Winter twilight on Zion Plateau*

*Sandstone tumulus typical of the Zion Plateau*

pastry-chef. Coming from the east entrance, just past Checkerboard Mesa you'll see some really interesting eroded hoodoos on the north side of the road, looking like submarine kiosks. It is well worth stopping there to photograph them with a wide-angle to normal lens. About 2 miles from the entrance, you'll come upon a landmark dear to photographers: a little pinion pine growing on top of one of these eroded sandstone shapes. There are a couple of pullout spots on the south side of the road and the tree is about 150 yards to the south.

## Checkerboard Mesa

A short distance from the east entrance station, you'll find the viewpoint of Checkerboard Mesa, one of the most celebrated views in Zion. The prow of the mesa is inclined at a 60° angle and is striated like a baguette fresh out of the oven. The view of Checkerboard Mesa is a classic and it's difficult to take an original shot even by changing the viewing angle. It is mostly the unusual cross bedding of the Mesa, more than its own beauty, which makes for the interest in this photo. From the parking between the east entrance station and the mesa, Checkerboard Mesa can be photographed at just about any time of the day, although it looks best from mid-morning until mid-afternoon, with the sun on the left. A medium wide-angle to standard lens will work best; from the pullout right at the base of the mesa, you'll need a 20mm to 24mm. A 20mm will allow you to shoot upward while framing pine tree needles. Walking in the direction of the Canyon, you'll find a small hill to your right. This makes an excellent vantage point at Sunset to shoot the East Temple silhouetted against the evening sky. A medium zoom will be helpful in fine-tuning your composition.

## Canyon Overlook Panorama

About 5 miles from the east entrance station, you reach this viewpoint from a parking area located just before the entrance to the tunnel. The pretty trail is about a mile long round-trip, with interesting views of the beginning twists and turns of Pine Canyon, a favorite slot for canyoneers. The viewpoint overhangs the Great Arch—which is in fact an alcove—that you can see and photograph while descending the switchbacks leading into the valley. From this often windy viewpoint, you'll gain a bird's eye view of the entrance to Zion Canyon. The view is sometimes hazy, but very pretty on a clear day. Pine Creek and the switchbacks of the main road are visible below, but they only become sunlit in mid-morning during the summer and the middle of the day in winter. Very early in the morning, you can isolate the West Temple and the Towers of the Virgin with a short, 85 to 100 mm, telephoto by concentrating on the golden rock face and eliminating the problematic shadow areas. By the end of the morning, the walls are basking in direct sunlight and have lost their relief. Of the park's three high observation points (Angel's Landing and Observation Point are the other two) this one is by far the most accessible, but it's also the least grandiose.

## Towers of the Virgin

At sunrise, this is the most beautiful panorama in Zion. If you love beautiful lights on rock walls, you won't be disappointed. The sun penetrates the valley through the Pine Canyon fault and bathes the summits of the temples in a warm light. Station yourself directly behind the Zion Museum and mount a 35mm lens. This will allow a tight framing of the West Temple, the Sundial, the Temple of the Virgin and the Altar of Sacrifice and keep the shadowy zone at the bottom of the photo to a minimum. I prefer the left side of the railing, which shows less of the rather unsightly trail crossing the empty field. A graduated neutral density filter is mandatory in order to maintain detail in the shadowy zone and to conserve the vibrant red and gold color of the high walls. If you don't have one, but are shooting digital, you can bracket a series of shots and later on digitally assemble the best exposed foreground with a perfectly exposed shot of the golden wall. You can also crop your image into a panoramic format excluding much of the foreground. You'll have about ten minutes before the sun rays irradiate the summits with so much light that the

*Towers of the Virgin at dawn*

shot gets lost. If you are spending the night close by, in Springdale or in Zion, this sunrise vista is a must. Note that even during shuttle season, you are allowed to drive as far as the Museum and park there.

Another good place to photograph the Towers is from the end of the Canyon Overlook Panorama trail, just above the great alcove.

## The Watchman

The Watchman is one of the most photographed icons of Zion Nat'l Park—a trophy shot that almost everyone feels obligated to have in their collection. The Watchman is a sunset location and there are two good locations for shooting it at that time of day. The closest one is to take the moderate 2-mile round-trip Watchman trail from the Visitor Center, leading to a promontory high above the campgrounds from where it is easy to view and photograph it. Unfortunately, your foreground will be limited to a few bushes, trees and protruding rocks. Not a bad shot, but perhaps not as spectacular as the next one.

*The Watchman and fall colors*

The second and most popular location is the bridge near the Canyon Junction shuttle stop. This easy vantage point provides a rather distant view of the glowing mountain face but allows you to include the river and lush vegetation in your vertical framing. I'll grant you that it is a major "cliché" picture, but it's a classic beauty and there is nothing wrong in having a bit of fun shooting it alongside many other photographers. For a touch of originality, this is a good place to experiment with colored graduated filters, if you are so inclined.

*Photo advice:* A mild wide-angle in the vicinity of 28mm to 35mm will allow you to frame the Watchman vertically with some foreground from the promontory at the end of the Watchman trail. A variety of focal lengths can be employed from the bridge.

*Nearby location:* The Pa'rus Trail is an easy but rewarding 1.7-mile trail between the Canyon Junction shuttle stop and the Visitor Center. The paved trail follows the Virgin River downstream, offering fine views of Bridge Mountain and the Watchman. There is a good photo spot from the river access located behind the South Campground.

## Court of the Patriarchs

Zion Canyon reveals its entire splendor slowly as the sun climbs over the surrounding peaks. After sunrise behind the Museum, your first stop on the scenic drive should be to view the Court of the Patriarchs. You'll get the best results between sunrise and mid-morning. At the end of a short trail, you arrive at a viewpoint where you can photograph the Patriarchs with a wide-angle lens. A 24mm is essential to include all three summits, but you can also get equally good results with a 28 or even a 35 mm, though you won't be able to fit in more than two of the Patriarchs. Finally, a short telephoto lens will let you isolate them individually.

Although the official viewpoint provides an adequate view of the Patriarchs, it has a rather mundane foreground of tree branches, which will turn completely black on your image when the Patriarchs are best lit in the morning. There is a nicer spot across the road, next to the footbridge leading to the Sand Bench Trail. From here, the Patriarchs assume an interesting triangular shape, looking almost like three symmetrical arrowheads when framed with a 21 mm or lower wide angle lens.

## Emerald Pools

The Emerald Pools, especially the lower one, are heavily visited and can be reached by a trail of a little over a mile, round-trip, from the Zion Lodge. Or you can take one of about 2 miles, round-trip, from the Grotto parking area. Add another mile round-trip if you decide to hike to the upper pools. For most visitors, the attraction of this spot rests in the water droplets raining on you from the main wall of the lower pool—a great source of fun for all. In summer, you'll find it quite pleasant to rest under the maple trees and bask in the fine mist of water enveloping you. For the photographer, the main attraction is also the two waterfalls coming out of the Lower Pool but you'll need a decent flow of water to produce a good photograph. I recommend that you come via the middle trail, by turning left past the footbridge near the Zion Lodge. After having negotiated the switchbacks, you'll gain superb open views of the southern part of the canyon from about halfway up the trail. As you reach the pools, you'll also cross an open area with a nicely polished rock surface, affording a really nice view looking down toward the lodge. Walk down toward the lower trail. There are some very good spots at the edge of the trail leading under the waterfalls, although your back will be against the wall and you'll need a 24mm to frame the entire scene. The waterfalls are

*Emerald Pools in springtime*

best photographed in spring and summer or after a rain. They may be reduced to a trickle if it hasn't rained for a while or may even be non-existent.

The upper pool is another mile round-trip and leads to a waterfall with a year-round flow, cascading down a huge red cliff. It is often in the shade and difficult to photograph, but definitely worth the trip to get a close view of the sheer cliffs of Zion. If your time is very limited, however, you'll be better off staying at the Lower Pools and exploring different compositions rather than going to the Upper Pool. To return to the shuttle or your vehicle, continue under the waterfalls on the short Lower Trail. As the walk to Lower Emerald Pools is easy, consider going either before (from the Lodge) or after (from the Grotto) Angel's Landing. The walk to the Upper Pool is a bit harder.

## Angel's Landing

Because of its central location, this is the most beautiful view of Zion Canyon but to access it will require good physical condition and some exertion. Above all, heights must not make you dizzy. The round-trip from the Grotto parking area is about 5 miles. You'll start your ascent following the steep switchbacks of the West Rim Trail before reaching the welcome shade of Refrigerator Canyon. Scaling another series of switchbacks, you arrive at the first viewpoint, Scout Lookout, where you have an exceptional and very steep view of the upper part of the Canyon's meanders as well as of the Temple of Sinawava. The next five

hundred yards require a lot of effort as you painstakingly move forward up a stunning trail, which is more of a rock flank. Chains are anchored in the rock for use as hand holds. Those who are rebuked by the steep climb to the summit should nonetheless consider tackling the first camel hump past Scout Lookout, known as the Neck, to reach the base of the main climb. This part of the hike is only mildly challenging and the view from the base is spectacular, with the almost vertical narrow spine of Angel's Landing close to your lens and a good open view of the canyon.

The vista from the top of Angel's Landing is sensational and well worth the effort. You can see the entrance to Zion Canyon opening up to the right, while in the center you get a breathtaking view of the Great White Throne. To the left, the canyon meanders toward the Temple of Sinawava.

*Photo advice:* Angel's Landing is always dif-

*Angel's Landing from Scout Lookout*

ficult to photograph unless you have a slightly overcast sky or lots of clouds. In the morning, you'll be shooting against the sun and in late afternoon, the western side of the canyon will be in shadow. The best time to shoot is in mid-afternoon. You'll need a very wide angle—20mm or below—in order to encompass the Great White Throne and part of the canyon. Returning from Angel's Landing, you should make it a point to follow the West Rim Trail up for roughly 0.3 mile past Scout Lookout to take advantage of several photogenic viewpoints offering side views of Angel's Landing and an open view of the Great White Throne

*Time required:* 3 hours round-trip. Caution; the end of this trail is not recommended for anyone prone to vertigo. If you have any doubts, skip the end and stay at Scout Lookout, which also offers nice views of the canyon to the north and east. Don't wear sneakers on this hike; you'll need good traction for the end of the trail past Scout Lookout.

## Hidden Canyon

Do not let yourself be intimidated by the spectacular switchbacks leading up from the Weeping Rock parking area. The slope may be steep but the trail—about 1-mile long to the entrance of the canyon—is excellent and the going is fairly easy if you pace yourself. You should know, however, that the upper part of the trail just before reaching Hidden Canyon can be very intimidating to people with fear of heights. Soon after the turnoff to Observation Point, you'll find yourself skirting the edge of the canyon on a somewhat precipitous path; there are chains to hang on to at the most exposed spots. You reach the entrance to the canyon after crossing a very short but pretty little slot canyon with beautiful pools of water.

Once inside the canyon, things get cool and quite in the shadow of a huge wall of sandstone to your right. This is actually the side of the Great White Throne. There are some minor obstructions along the way, that can be easily circumvented. However, shortly after the little arch, the canyon becomes obstructed by larger and larger chokestones and you'll have to go back.

*Photo advice:* The canyon has colorful eroded walls, a nice variety of vegetation and offers plenty to photograph, even in the middle of day; there is an interesting arch ½ mile to your right. Hidden Canyon is also an excellent location for abstracts.

*Time required:* 2 hours round-trip from the parking area.

*Nearby location:* From the same Weeping Rock parking area, a short trail leads behind a curtain of water droplets falling from the rock face—the end result of a two-year voyage through the porous rock. Twenty minutes should be enough for a brief visit. I find Weeping Rock particularly interesting in winter when the seeping water forms a long ribbon of icicles reminiscent of fine lace.

## Observation Point

This is an exhilarating hike to the highest vantage point in the park. The view of the canyon is incredible, although quite a bit more distant and less central than the one from Angel's Landing. Angel's Landing actually appears surprisingly low in front of you. The view to the left is of the top of Cable Mountain and the Great White Throne.

It's a long slug to get there, however, with over 2100 feet of elevation gain, and it feels more like a 10-miler than the actual 8 miles round-trip of the hike. There is a steep 1½-mile section of switchbacks past Mile 2 (near the junction with the East Rim Trail) before you reach the plateau. After yet another ½ mile on level ground, you'll experience a distinct feeling of elation when you reach the end of the trail and take in the awesome view! For those without the time or the interest in going all the way, the section of the trail between Mile 1.2 and 2 is particularly scenic, with sheer vertical walls and fine views of the Echo slot canyon.

*Photo advice:* The panoramic view is awesome but distant; you'll get better images if there are clouds.

*Time required:* About 4 hours round-trip from the Weeping Rock parking area. This hike can be combined with the Hidden Canyon hike, with which it shares the first part of the trail (from the junction add about 1½ hour round-trip).

If you can arrange a car shuttle, hiking the East Rim trail from Zion's East entrance to Weeping Rock can easily include a side trip to Observation Point. Most people do it as a backpack, but a 15-mile dayhike including Observation Point is feasible.

## The Great White Throne

The Great White Throne is without doubt one of the most recognizable symbols of Zion National Park. Unfortunately, it does not allow itself to be photographed as easily as you would like. There are two vantage points: The first one is called Photo Point; it is located just 40 feet down from an unnamed car park, with a spectacular alcove on the other side of the road. A short walk heading northwest along the road from Weeping Rock is required during the manda-

*The Great White Throne (photo by Scott Walton)*

tory shuttle season to reach this car park. The other viewpoint is Big Bend, which is a regular shuttle stop and a prime spot for fall colors.

*Photo advice:* Photo Point offers an unobstructed view of the Great White Throne and the Organ, to the right. Whether you keep to the perfectly satisfactory view from Photo Point, or choose to stroll toward the bank of the Virgin River, the view is always spectacular. The best lighting is in mid-afternoon. Too early in the day, the canyon is shrouded in shadow and later in the evening it is backlit. It took me many visits to Zion to finally get the right light and a picture I was satisfied with. I shot it with a 17mm lens, but a 24mm will work too.

During springtime, tallgrass grows between the viewpoint and the bank of the Virgin, forming a beautiful foreground to shoot the alcove located on the east side of the road, behind the parking spot.

Big Bend Viewpoint is farther up in the direction of the Temple of Sinawava. It allows a rectangular framing of the throne between two walls of the canyon. To the right is the sheer east face of Angel's Landing, where you can occasionally spot climbers doing the two-day ascent. This is a great location during fall colors.

## Temple of Sinawava

This remarkable area, located at the end of Zion Canyon, is one of those special spots that evokes a mystical and spiritual connection with nature. The

happy traveler, intoxicated by the succession and variety of the panoramas of Canyon Overlook, the Towers, the Patriarchs and brief glimpses of the Great White Throne, attains a sort of nirvana when reaching the Temple of Sinawava. The Pulpit rises in the middle of a cove formed by the river. As a result of the twists and turns of the canyon, its lighting is mediocre in the morning and evening. Try timing your arrival for early afternoon, which is the best time to photograph it. Directly from the parking area, you'll have nice reflected light striking the pulpit on the parking side. I find that a normal lens to very short telephoto works best to photograph the Pulpit from here.

Another good location is from the last bend of the road before the parking area. This is a good place to photograph the Pulpit during fall colors or in springtime when the cottonwoods start to bloom. For the ulti-

*The Pulpit at the Temple of Sinawava*

mate shot, be there just after a hard rain when the waterfall is active behind the Pulpit. A short telephoto will let you capture the foliage of the cottonwoods, the reddish pulpit and, in the background, the darker walls of the canyon.

Further on, the 1-mile long surfaced Riverside Walk leads to the Gateway to the Narrows, the entrance to the Virgin River Narrows. The trail, which follows the bank of the Virgin River, offers magnificent views in the spring and early summer, as well as later in autumn when the foliage changes color. At about the halfway point, you'll go past a small cascade worth photographing if it is full.

## The Virgin Narrows

It's an unforgettable memory to go up the Virgin Narrows for 1½ hour or so until you reach the confluence with Orderville Canyon. One of the main draws of the narrows resides in the fact that you are almost constantly immersed in the Virgin River, often up to your knees and sometimes higher. This contributes immensely to the high fun factor of this great hike, although it may be quite strenuous when the water level is high—especially when walking upstream against the current. Outside of summer, the Virgin River can be very cold or its water level too high, so the vast majority of people hike during summer. If you do not want crowds, summer is not the best time; you will also run the risk of flash flooding in July and August. At the entrance to the Narrows, there is a sign-post warning of the potential risks of flash floods and rating the danger for the day. Permits are not required for day-hikers, but the Park Service strictly forbids walking the narrows on days when a storm is threatening. Keep in mind that the risk of thunderstorms is statistically higher after midday than in the morning. Planning your visit to the Narrows in the morning also allows you to avoid much of the crowds and to leave time for other sites later in the day.

If you happen to be there off season, don't let yourself be deterred by air and water temperature: With the proper equipment, you can easily hike the narrows year-round. You can rent a dry suit, as well as Neoprene socks and canyoneering shoes to make the experience safe and enjoyable, although a good pair of hiking boots with good ankle support will also do the job. Under a certain water temperature, this equipment becomes absolutely indispensable; several places rent equipment in Springdale *(check Resources in Appendix.)* Using a dry suit, I have hiked the narrows in late autumn and early spring and have never felt cold, even in water temperatures below 45°F. You should also consider taking a pair of trekking poles to probe the riverbed for treacherous rocks or holes and to keep your balance if the current is strong. A walking stick is fine but doesn't give anywhere near the stability of a couple of trekking poles. If you carry an expensive camera system, you'll find the trekking poles worthwhile. Two poles will also give you much better speed, an asset if you want to go all the way to Big Springs and take a lot of pictures. Otherwise, there is always a stockpile of pretty rough sticks at the end of Riverside Walk, from which you can borrow.

*Opposite page: early morning inside the Virgin Narrows*

At the beginning and the end of the mandatory shuttle season, the timing and logistics of a hike in the Narrows can be a bit more complicated: The water temperature may be cold enough to require a dry suit, however without the presence of your car you cannot change into canyoneering gear at the Temple of Sinawava parking area, nor can you leave your belongings in your car, then switch back when you come out of the Narrows for other hikes inside the canyon. You'll need to leave properly equipped from the Visitor Center and return there with the shuttle in order to recover the equipment that you didn't take with you into the narrows (clothing, food, perhaps bigger and better photographic equipment) before returning into the canyon for other strolls. If your schedule is flexible, you may want to consider hiking the Narrows at the tail end or just prior to the start of the mandatory shuttle season.

The complete descent of the Virgin Narrows from Chamberlain's Ranch requires two full days as well as preparations and logistics beyond the scope of this book.

*Photo advice:* I have to admit that it is cumbersome to carry a tripod into the narrows. It is one more heavy item on top of an already loaded backpack and setting it up and packing it away each time you take a photograph requires serious calisthenics. After a few images, however, you'll get the hang of it: Dump the trekking poles, remove the backpack, deploy the tripod, attach the camera, compose and shoot and then repeat the whole maneuver backwards. It's a chore but that's what you have to do if you want to bring back images with good depth of field, shadow detail and beautiful water action. On the other hand, if

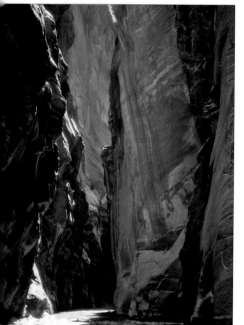

you do not intend to enlarge your pictures too much and don't mind black areas with no detail, you can certainly get away with a fast ISO setting and shoot handheld. For less ambitious photography, this is also a perfect place for a small digital camera. Just remove it from your pocket when an opportunity presents itself and the zoom will let you take excellent pictures of people and scenery. If you are taking an expensive camera, protect it in an airtight plastic bag; should you take an accidental spill, you'll be glad water didn't get into it.

Reflected light in the Narrows is at its best in early to mid-morning during summertime and around mid-day in late autumn and early spring. There is outstanding photography at almost every corner. Remember to look back often, you may be surprised at how light forms a beautiful golden veil over

*Upper Narrows (photo by Gene Mezereny)*

the sandstone from a certain angle. Also, you'll be surprised how the slightest trace of reflected light on a wall will give you excellent results using long exposures.

One of the nice features of the Narrows of the Virgin River is also the opportunity to take photos of people wading in the water, fording the narrows.

*Hiking the Zion Narrows*

*Time required:* If you are short of time, a 1-hour round-trip from the Gateway to the Narrows will suffice to get a glimpse of the place and take some nice shots around Mystery Canyon Falls. A 2½ to 4-hour round-trip is necessary to reach the junction of Orderville Canyon—the final destination for most visitors. If you choose to explore Orderville Canyon, be aware that after an initial easy walk you will encounter many obstructions along the way, requiring you to do quite a bit of scrambling. Instead, I recommend that you continue in the main canyon; its narrowest section begins soon after passing Orderville Canyon and ends roughly ½ mile before Big Springs. Such a trip, from the Gateway to the edge of the Narrows and back, takes about 6 to 8 hours with ample time for photography. If you start at daybreak, this would also put you back at the Temple of Sinawava at an excellent time for good reflected light on the Pulpit.

## Kolob Canyon Viewpoint

The Kolob section of Zion is rather remote from the main canyon and many travelers pressed for time pass it up. That's a shame because the valley that follows the interstate towards Cedar City is very pretty. Also, the road through the park only runs about 6 miles before reaching the Kolob Canyon Viewpoint, making it a very short trip. All along the route, the view of the impressive red rock walls of the Finger Canyons is remarkable. The detour is worthwhile if you decide to go up to Bryce by way of Cedar Breaks. But don't let it cause you to miss the road from Zion to Mt. Carmel, allowing you to cross the plateau. If you have to choose, the plateau should be the first priority.

*Photo advice:* The best time is late afternoon.

*Getting there:* Take Exit 40 from I-15, 32 miles north of St. George and 19 miles south of Cedar City. The Kolob section is frequently closed in winter.

*Time required:* 1 hour round-trip from Interstate 15.

## Taylor Creek

Located in the Kolob section of the park, the Middle Fork of Taylor Creek is a very scenic and highly recommended hike to a fantastic photographic location: a vast grotto-like alcove, topped by two closed arches carved in a 2000 feet cliff. The trail is easy and suitable for families with children. It is only 2.7 miles one-way to Double Arch Alcove on a mostly flat trail. You will cross Taylor Creek

*Double Arch Alcove towers over Taylor Creek*

dozens of times, but none of the crossings presents a challenge.

The canyon walls and vegetation are splendid all along the trail and you'll pass two old cabins on your way. There is a patch of lush green grass and mosses at the back of the lower alcove, which contrasts beautifully with the red rock. This is due to the presence of a spring seep.

Continuing along the stream past the alcove, you promptly reach a small cascade; it is quite spectacular during the wet season, but almost entirely dry during the drier months, when its beautifully polished patina is revealed.

*Photo advice:* A 24mm or 28mm works best to encompass the entire rock wall including some vegetation at the bottom, the alcove and the two arches. It is best photographed around midday under the reflected light from the opposite rock wall, which gives the alcove a fantastic orange and red glow.

In the fall, you'll get the benefit of intense yellows and reds to complement your photos. Some very large pines and spruce trees grow above the first and second alcoves, adding a touch of green to your composition.

*Getting there:* The Middle Fork of Taylor Creek trailhead is about 2 miles from the Kolob Section entrance on I-15 between St. George and Cedar City. This section of the park is frequently closed in winter.

*Time required:* 3 hours round-trip from the parking area.

*Nearby location:* About 1.2 miles past the Middle Fork of the Taylor Creek trailhead, you'll find a large parking area just before a sharp turn. Cross the road and find the unofficial trailhead for the South Fork of Taylor Creek. Heading east into the canyon, the route goes up and down for a while and after one last steep climb, you reach a small hanging valley with nice trees and a lovely meadow. The trail levels off, continuing along the huge, vertical right wall of the canyon until it becomes blocked by chokestones. This is a pleasant hike in a very green, secluded setting, contrasting with the colorful red wall, interestingly eroded in places. There is good reflected light in early afternoon. Count about 2 hours round-trip from the parking area.

## The Kolob Terraces

For those with time and a thirst for more grand vistas of the Zion backcountry, it's possible to cross the west part of Zion from north to south by car. You can start either from Cedar City to the north or from Virgin to the south. The road is known as the Kolob Terrace Road and is classified as a Scenic Backway. The road is paved from Virgin to the Kolob reservoir as well as on the last few miles descending toward UT 14 east of Cedar City. The unpaved section can normally be driven in a passenger car in dry weather; nevertheless, do not leave without confirming road condition with the Visitor Center, as it may be closed due to snow in winter or because of road damage waiting to be fixed.

Although most people choose to drive this road from Virgin, I recommend that you drive it from Cedar City as the views are more spectacular in that direction inside the national park section.

After leaving UT 14 approximately 5 miles east of Cedar City, the road climbs steadily, providing lofty views of the colorful mountains near Cedar City and extending well beyond I-15. It traverses a semi-alpine ecosystem on its way to Kolob Reservoir before crossing the boundary of Zion Nat'l Park. Take the short detour to Lava Point for a distant bird's eye view of Goose Creek and Kolob Creek canyon and the beginning of the West Rim Trail. Soon after that, the road opens up to a series of superlative vistas of the Kolob Terraces, providing a very different view of Zion before descending toward Virgin and UT 9.

*Photo advice:* Between Mile 8 and 15 from Virgin, there are superb views of the Kolob Terraces lit by the afternoon sun, with tallgrass in the foreground. If you are leaving Zion on UT 9 west in mid- to late-afternoon, you won't regret spending an extra hour for a quick jaunt on this highly scenic road.

## The West Rim Trail

Although this 14-mile long trail is often done as a two-day backpack, the entire length of the West Rim Trail can be hiked in one long but surprisingly easy day with a car shuttle—leaving from the trailhead near Lava Point on the Kolob Terrace Road and ending up at the Grotto picnic area in the main canyon. This allows you to limit your weight and take more photographic equipment; just be sure to have plenty of water and snacks. This is a delightful hike, with relative solitude and outstanding scenery all around. The first half of the trail follows Horse Pasture Plateau and is almost entirely flat; it is often in shallow sand and goes through some very lovely forested area. The highlight of the trail is the stretch between Potato Hollow and Cabin Spring. There are two ways to reach Cabin Spring, so be sure to follow the Rim trail to the right almost 1½ mile past Potato Hollow (instead of the Telephone Canyon trail to the left). There are outstanding views into the Right Fork of North Creek, aka Great West Canyon, Greatheart Mesa and Phantom Valley. Past the spring, you'll begin your gradual descent on a good slickrock trail, skirting Mount Majestic and Cathedral Mountain until you reach the vicinity of Scout Lookout, with its outstanding views of the main Zion Canyon, the Great White Throne and Angel's Landing.

## The Subway

This is a fantastic location, but also a long and hard hike, not particularly interesting most of the way if you're coming from the bottom trailhead as photographers have to do. However, the surreal sight that awaits you at the end of the journey makes it all worth it.

*Opposite page: Magical Pools of The Subway*

The Subway is a narrow canyon that has been carved in a tunnel-like fashion by the waters of North Creek. In one meander of the creek, it feels like you are in a tunnel, except for a narrow opening at the top. North Creek gently winds its way on the polished red rock under your feet, flowing over pools of azure and green; small cascades trickle down pour-offs and chokestones further up. The subdued light reinforces the crypt-like feeling of the Subway. It is a very haunting place indeed.

You'll need a permit to visit the Left Fork of North Creek, where the Subway is located; the NPS issues up to 50 of them each day. In summer, you'll be facing fierce competition from groups of young people intent on a day of wading and rappelling. To obtain a permit, you must apply by eMail or fax three months prior to your visit; the permits are issued by a lottery system and results are not immediately known, which makes trip-planning a bit difficult. However, a handful of walk-in permits are also issued bright and early at the opening of the two Visitor Centers *(see details in Appendix)*.

*Back of the Subway (photo by Ron Flickinger)*

*Photo advice:* In summer, you'll want to arrive either in mid-morning or mid-afternoon or you'll find the pools in full sun around midday. In the fall, there is no need for a crack-of-dawn departure as you'll want to arrive around midday. It takes at least 2½ hours to get to the Subway from the bottom trailhead.

At about Mile 4 from the bottom trailhead, you'll come to a series of small cascades over red slickrock that make a very nice picture. Just a bit further, you'll notice a crack in the bedrock on the right side of the canyon floor. The crack channels water from the creek at very high speed, creating the setting for a terrific picture. In the vicinity, you'll also find a large alcove with mosses and other moisture loving vegetation and soon after that, you'll arrive at the bend where the Subway and its pools are located.

Regardless of the format you shoot, you'll need a sturdy tripod in the Subway because light is often very dim and you may find yourself working with very long exposures: 8 to 30 seconds if you shoot slow film and want maximum depth-of-field. This is prime territory for reciprocity failure and you had better know the characteristics of your film and how it reacts to cool dim light. A warming filter would certainly help warm things up a bit, although the very cold blue-green light creates a very ethereal effect.

*Getting there:* This is a long and tiring hike for many people; you must be a good hiker to do it. If you're thinking of taking heavy photographic equipment, you'd better think twice, because you will feel it all the way and back.

You can reach the Subway from two different trailheads. By far the easiest way for a photographer carrying equipment, is to go from "the bottom", a trailhead marked "Left Fork" located about 8 miles north of the Kolob Terraces Scenic Byway turnoff in the town of Virgin. To call this entry "the bottom" is a figure of speech because after only ½ mile of flat walking, you must negotiate a difficult descent down a steep route. A walking stick or pair of trekking poles will make this descent as well as the whole day much easier. Once you reach the bottom, follow the creek up the best you can, crossing and re-crossing many times. This involves a lot of boulder-hopping. A pair of wading shoes works fairly well for this hike. Sometimes there is a visible trail, at other times there is none. It will be a challenge to keep your feet dry all the way but it can be done by detouring over the bigger boulders and crossing with the help of trekking poles. This "easy" way is a compromise which allows you to see only the lower part of the Subway, albeit the most spectacular one.

A few hundred feet past the entrance to the Subway, you'll find the creek blocked by deep pools followed by a cascade and a rocky escarpment which is almost impossible to cross with heavy photo equipment. A rope is sometimes in place along the short wall preceding the deep pools to the right, but don't count on it; Park Rangers routinely remove ropes for obvious liability reasons: A rope exposed to the elements could become time-worn and break while someone is climbing. If you are lucky enough to be there when a group of canyoneers is coming down from the top, you could ask permission to use their rope while it's still in place; chances are they'll be stopping at the Subway for a while and will agree to wait for you. Be careful not to fall, as you'll need to pull yourself hand over hand up the rope, pushing away from the rock with your feet. Once on top, the obstacles are easily bypassed and you can continue up-canyon for a couple of hundred yards inside beautiful narrows, before being blocked by a fall. Along the way, you'll pass by the log immortalized by Michael Fatali in his spectacular *North Pole* photograph.

The other way to visit the Subway is to come from "the top", parking at the Wildcat Canyon trailhead—7 miles past the "Left Fork" car park—and following the Great West Canyon for a while until it meets North Creek. From there, you'll need to wade and swim in chilly waters and rappel your way down several cascades and chokestones until you reach the Subway. You'll then head toward the bottom trailhead and your waiting car shuttle. You'll need a partner or two, as well as some canyoneering experience, to make this trip safe; it is not recommended to take heavy equipment on this one.

*Time required:* 6 to 7 hours round-trip from the bottom trailhead.

*Nearby location:* The lower section of the Right Fork of North Creek can be visited as far as Double Falls in one long 13-mile round-trip dayhike. The falls and the green pool below are very photogenic. Walking inside the lower right fork is somewhat easier than in the Left Fork. The route from Double Falls to Barrier Falls is too challenging for a dayhike and is usually done from Lava Falls as a two or three-day canyoneering adventure.

# AROUND ZION

## The Smithonian Butte

An excellent way to get to Zion is by using the nine mile long Smithonian Butte Scenic Backway. Seen from UT 59 coming from Fredonia, the scenery is magnificent in all seasons with the Canaan Mountains to the east and the tall grass prairie in the foreground. However, it's on the Scenic Backway itself, going toward Rockville, that a surprise awaits you with a spectacular view of the entrance to Zion Canyon. From the mesa, you can clearly see the Watchman to the right of the canyon entrance and the Towers of the Virgin to the left. Just before reaching Rockville, a short detour leads to the old 19th century village of Grafton. Only a couple of structures are still standing today; despite having been renovated in a tasteful manner, Grafton has lost a lot of its old charm.

*Photo advice:* From the highest point on the Smithonian Butte Backway, reached after about 4 miles off UT 59, the angle is just perfect for an early morning or late afternoon shot of Zion. The serrated ridge of the Smithonian Butte comes into view at this spot, looking much like the backbone of a dinosaur.

*Getting there:* The road begins about 14 miles east of Hurricane or 40 miles west of Fredonia on UT 59 and comes out at Rockville, a mere 4 miles from the west entrance to Zion. It is marked by a small Scenic Byway sign. The otherwise excellent road deteriorates rapidly as it plunges toward Rockville and you'll have to exercise caution. Do not take this road after a rain, as it can be extremely slippery. Coming from Rockville, the road is not marked. You'll need to make a turn at a small sign marked Bridge Street from the main road in order to catch it.

*Time required:* A 45-minute detour off the main road.

*Nearby location:* Coal Pits Wash, about 4 miles west of Springdale on UT 9, has one of the densest areas of cottonwoods in bloom during fall and spring, offering outstanding photographic opportunities. A primitive BLM campground, aptly named Mosquito Cove, is at Mile 23½ on the south side of UT 9.

## Water Canyon

In the vicinity of Colorado City, lovely Water Canyon is well worth a visit if you're looking for a secluded place. Nested inside the colorful Vermilion Cliffs, its short narrows offer a refreshing atmosphere with their water-weeping cliffs, scattered greenery and tiny cascades. It also provides access to the vast slickrock benches of Canaan Mountain.

The canyon sees a lot of foot traffic on week-ends and holidays due to its relative proximity to the traditionalist Mormon communities of Colorado City and Hildale. Plan your visit on a weekday if you can; you'll be able to take photographs at your own pace without disturbing the locals, who are not accustomed to see many visitors from outside their community.

From the trailhead, a short 30-minute walk leads to the beginning of the narrows. Along the way, look for an arch on top of the cliff to your right. The first part of the narrows is the most photogenic, but you can go on to an upper level following a slanted ledge to the left. The narrows eventually open up in a slickrock area reminiscent of the Zion Plateau. A steep footpath continues toward Canaan Mountain.

*Photo advice:* Mid-morning or mid-afternoon work best to avoid sharp contrasts. A tripod and long exposure are necessary to capture the flow of water running through the photogenic cracks in the bedrock.

*Getting there:* About 22 miles from Hurricane on UT 59, on the west side of Hildale, look for the Fredonia 33 signpost and turn on Utah Avenue which soon becomes Canyon Street; after 2.9 miles, bear left then make a right on Water Canyon Road, just before the two lanes split to form a loop. Follow the dirt road for 2 miles and park at the end near a reservoir. This road is suitable to passenger cars in dry weather.

*Time required:* About 2 hours round-trip to the end of the narrows.

*Nearby location:* Pipe Spring National Monument, about 19 miles east from the turnoff for Water canyon on UT 59, preserves a collection of buildings erected and used by Mormon pioneers in the last century. Pipe Spring began as a ranch, but was abandoned a few years later after the settlers were killed by Indians. It was subsequently used as a Mormon militia outpost and a fort was built to serve as a refuge for farmers of the surrounding area. The interest is more cultural than photographic, but the site is right along the route and quick to visit. There is a short ½-mile interpretive trail that provides a glimpse into the geology and history of the Arizona Strip. The Monument is located in the middle of the Kaibab Paiute Reservation and the Visitor Center presents many interesting aspects of Paiute Indian culture.

*Water Canyon*

## Red Cliffs

*Red Cliffs pools (photo by Philippe Schuler)*

If you are in the vicinity of St. George and have a couple of hours to spare, consider paying a brief visit to the Red Cliffs Recreational Area; the Red Cliffs are located close to I-15 a few miles northeast of St. George. This small site is heavily patronized by locals on weekends, due in part to its good campground; it is thus preferable to come during the week to take pictures without the crowds. A 15-minute walk on the Nature Trail leads to a lovely narrow canyon with red slickrock walls and to a couple of deep pools. This particularly photogenic spot has good light without too much contrast from mid-afternoon on. You can easily circumvent the main pool by using the moki steps conveniently carved on the right flank of the canyon; the angle isn't too vertical and a rope is also present to assist you anyway. You can then continue inside the pleasant canyon for a few hundred yards before encountering a dryfall that is too difficult to climb.

*Getting there:* 7 miles north of St. George on I-15, take exit 16 to UT 9; after almost 1 mile, take the Old 91 frontage road toward Leeds. After about 4 miles, you'll see the *Red Cliffs R.A.* sign pointing to a narrow tunnel under I-15; from here it's 1½ miles to the park's entrance.

*Time required:* 1½ hour with plenty of time for photography.

## Snow Canyon

Located just a few miles northwest of St. George, Snow Canyon State Park sees few visitors despite its proximity to Zion. And yet, Snow Canyon has plenty of interesting sights along its 5-mile long Scenic Road: Lovely pink sand dunes, colorful sandstone cliffs ranging from white to deep red, spectacular cross-bedding alternating with black lava fields and great views from several easily-reached promontories. All this results in excellent photographic opportunities.

*Photo advice:* The park's diverse colors are best seen from the middle of the afternoon on, but don't go too late or the canyon will be in shadow; early morning should work too. From the south entrance of the park, begin your visit with short and narrow Jenny's Canyon and the Sand Dunes. Next, park just before the campground and hike the picturesque Hidden Pinion Trail to the overlook, which offers a 360° panorama of the canyon. You can shoot grand scenics or isolate nice perspective shots of the canyon north and south. This walk takes approximately 1 hour round-trip. At the Lava Flow Overlook parking area, about 1½ miles farther north, take the trail leading to the lava beds and tubes and ascend the West Canyon Overlook. From this easily-reached vantage point, you gain another great all-around view. There is some highly photogenic red sandstone crossbedding all around this overlook.

After exiting the park through the north entrance, drive north for ½ mile on UT 18 to a trailhead; the 1-mile round-trip trail leads to an interesting white sandstone amphitheater.

As you drive back toward St. George on UT 18, look for a marked dirt road to the right, about a mile past the park's north entrance. This road leads to the Snow Canyon Overlook, which provides a great bird's eye view of the canyon.

***Getting there:*** Leave St. George on UT 18, soon turning west towards Ivins. Follow the signs to the Park to take the Scenic Road heading north.

***Time required:*** At least 3½ hours to drive through the park and do the recommended hikes. There is a very nice campground for those preferring a starry night over one of the numerous St. George motels.

*Snow Canyon crossbedding*

***Nearby locations:*** If you think you've seen enough red rock, you may want to immerse yourself for a while in the radically different atmosphere of Pine Valley. There, you'll find a lovely little Mormon community and a pretty alpine valley surrounded by woods. It is a very pleasant location, visited by few other than residents of St. George and surrounding communities. Coming out from Snow Canyon's north entrance, follow UT 18 north for about 15 miles and turn east for another 10 miles until you find Pine Valley Recreation Area. You can also continue past the pretty Pine Valley Reservoir to the campground and hike on the local pack trails.

While in St. George, you are only 30 minutes away from the heart of the spectacular Virgin River Gorge. The gorge has beautiful narrows in its southern part as I-15 crosses the Beaver Dam Mountains southwest of St George. There is a good rest area and campground about halfway though the gorge, which is the only point where you can take pictures.

# Coral Pink Sand Dunes

This Utah State Park is really worth a detour, at dawn or sundown, if you happen to be in the vicinity. As its name indicates, these are sand dunes of a beautiful strong ocher tint. The extremely fine sand—Navajo sandstone ground and sifted by wind over and over again—becomes an extraordinary coral pink in the setting sun. The dunes are formed by hot air currents coming from the south and accelerating as they pass through Moccasin Gap, seen to the southwest of the viewpoint. These currents lose their speed when coming in contact with cold air masses forming above the Grand Staircase region and deposit sand in this area.

The dunes are spread out over a relatively small area, which makes it easy on the hiker or photographer. From the parking area, you can quickly get to the summit of the two main dunes, which are not more than 40 feet tall. The surroundings are not exactly exceptional, but the White Cliffs to the north and the Vermilion Cliffs to the south allow you to add some depth to these superb dunes. This park should not be missed if you are traveling with children.

*Photo advice:* The interest here is as much along the order of macro-photography than landscapes. Motifs created by the wind and the vegetation stand out from an interesting pink background. Out of season, you can get fantastic panoramic views of the dunes without any trace of footprints on their summits—something you'll be hard pressed to achieve in Death Valley or Colorado's Great Sand Dunes. Contrary to lighter colored sand dunes, like those of White Sands, it is not necessary to compensate by overexposing. A normal exposure will preserve the shadows and relief of the motifs on the sand as well as the beautiful ocher color. Try to be in position on the dunes at Sunset; you'll be treated to an unbelievably pink glow turning into a dramatic red during a brief but miraculous last minute before the sun disappears behind the horizon. In early summer, there are nice big yellow wildflowers near the boardwalks, making good foregrounds for shots of the dunes.

*Sunset on the Coral Pink Sand Dunes*

*Getting there:* The park is located about 15 miles from Mt. Carmel on the Ponderosa/ Coral Pink Sand Dunes Scenic Backway. Coming from Zion or Bryce, leave US 89 about 3½ miles south of Mt. Carmel Junction. If coming from Kanab, exit US 89 about 8 miles north of Kanab. Signs mark the two roads. Watch out for livestock, as they are free to roam along this route.

There is another access from UT 389 southeast of Colorado City via Cane Beds Road; it passes through the Cottonwood Point Wilderness, which has much wildlife. The Arizona section of this road is unpaved but normally passable for passenger cars if driven with caution, except after a rain.

*Time required:* 1½ to 3 hours.

## Red Canyon Slot

Red Canyon consists of two short but beautiful sections of twisted narrows, no longer than 200 feet each, with good photographic potential and no water holes or obstructions of any kind. If conditions are right—i.e. if the extremely deep sand along the way has been packed by recent rains—the canyon can be visited almost effortlessly, as you can drive your vehicle right to its entrance.

*Getting there:* Coming from Mt. Carmel Junction, drive 9.4 miles south and turn east (left) almost 100 yards past the southern route to the Coral Pink Sand Dunes. Coming from Kanab, turn right 2.6 miles past Angel/Kanab Canyon's entrance on US 89. After 0.2 mile on this road, turn left onto marked K2605 and follow it for 1.1 miles, then right on K2672 for 2.2 miles, on an extremely sandy track continuing toward the Red Canyon drainage. An easy 3/4 mile drive inside the drainage brings you to the mouth of the slot (37°10'46" 112°33'32"). A high-clearance 4WD vehicle is a must and you may have to deflate your tires to gain better traction in the sand. Be sure to carry a shovel for added security.

*Red Canyon Slot*

*Time required:* About 2½ hours round-trip.

*Nearby location:* About 5 miles north of Kanab, follow the sign for Kanab Canyon. This good road leads to Angel Canyon, a particularly lovely canyon that can be driven as a short loop. It is the home of Best Friends Animal Sanctuary and Angel's Rest pet cemetery who own the property inside the canyon; however, the road through the canyon is public and you're free to wander about. One of the most interesting feature is Angels Landing, a spectacular dome-shaped cave of red sandstone with a grassy area and amenities in front. This is a wonderful place to stop and relax if you're tired. The canyon also contains rock art and some Indian ruins. The loop ends at US 89 and provides an alternate access to the Red Canyon Slot. You'll find the above-mentioned K2605 track to your right just before reaching US 89.

## Red Cave

Red Cave is a little-known photographer's dream located just a few miles east of Zion Nat'l Park. The texture and color of this slot canyon is reminiscent of Lower Antelope Canyon *(see Volume 2 of Photographing the Southwest),* without equaling the beauty of its Arizona counterpart; on the other hand, it's unlikely that you'll ever find a crowd inside. The canyon consists of two separate sections of spectacular narrows, carved into red sandstone; both are connected by a wide sandy wash at the base of the cliffs. Upper Red Cave has the better photographic opportunities and is easier of access, with only a few minor 3 to 5 feet obstacles to overcome. Lower Red Cave has a technical section requiring a rope just behind its entrance, but it is easily bypassed by continuing on the right hand side above the slot and following a faint path to an easier descent. If it has rained in previous months, you may encounter flooded passages in both slots.

*Red Cave*
*(photo by Steffen Synnatschke)*

*Photo advice:* As with every other slot canyon, Red Cave is best on a sunny day. Plan on being there around noon for the best light. The slot is very dark and a tripod is a must for quality work with good color and depth-of-field.

*Getting there:* Although Red Cave is located on BLM land, it requires crossing private land on a good jeep road built by the owner. You'll need prior permission to do so, either in writing, by telephone or in person *(see Resources in Appendix).* Permission is unlikely to be denied if you can demonstrate to the landowner that you'll act responsibly on his property. The following description assumes that you have obtained prior permission. Coming from Zion NP drive east to Mt. Carmel Junction, turn left onto US 89 and continue 2 miles to Mt. Carmel. Just opposite Tait Lane, turn east on a dirt road, and ford the East Fork of the Virgin River. The road soon enters private land; be sure to close the gate behind you. It climbs to the top of a plateau, winding trough juniper scrub, before reaching a ledge and splitting up. Take the right spur, descending into Sand Wash, and park above the wash 1.6 miles from US 89. Follow the wash eastward for 0.4 mile until you reach the entrance of the Upper Red Cave (37°14'14" 112°38'32"). To get to the lower slot, return to Sand Wash and follow it on foot, westward, for 1.8 miles. Take the smaller Lower Sand Wash to your left, leading directly to Lower Red Cave (37°13'32" 112°38'54").

*Time required:* 2 to 2½ hours round-trip for Upper Red Cave with time for photography; 3½ to 5 hours to visit both slots. ❀

*Thor's Hammer under a fresh dusting of snow*

Chapter 4

# AROUND BRYCE CANYON

*Sunset Point vista (photo by Scott Walton)*

## BRYCE CANYON NAT'L PARK

Bryce Canyon, along with Arches, is the park preferred by the majority of visitors to the Southwest, especially foreign visitors, who come from all corners of the globe to admire and photograph it. The whole world, consequently, has seen images of Bryce and the name immediately invokes a geological phenomenon bordering on the supernatural. A case in point: A software application generating 3-D virtual landscapes is named after this park and its publisher didn't have to explain the choice of name to the public. Happily or unhappily, its proximity to Las Vegas makes access easy. It's unlikely that you'll find solitude or spiritual communion with the environment at Bryce, but you are sure to find a landscape that will hold you in a hypnotic trance the first time you lay eyes on it. It's a landscape filled with weird and incredible formations combined with remarkable nuances of light and saturated with color.

*Time required:* To get the most out of Bryce, it's advisable to stay at one of the lodges or motels in the area so you can visit the park in the early morning hours and until sunset. It's also recommended that you take at least one hike on the canyon trails —an experience that involves a bit of effort.

Allow 2½ hours by car to visit the amphitheater viewpoints and at least 2 hours to hike the canyon. If you don't have much time, go straight to Sunset

Viewpoint. The Rim Trail between Sunrise and Sunset Points and Inspiration Point is an easy walk if you don't want to descend into the canyon proper.

## Sunrise and Sunset Viewpoints

Sunset Point is arguably the best spot to admire and photograph Bryce Canyon. It's also the most popular and you won't be alone. The view on both sides is excellent, looking towards Sunrise Point on the left or Inspiration Point and Bryce Point on the right. The Silent City is set back from the first viewpoint to the right of the parking area. Despite the name of this viewpoint, mornings and late afternoons are both excellent for photography. If your time is limited, Sunset Point is the best place to catch Bryce in all its glory.

Sunrise Point doesn't offer such a spectacular panorama on both sides and the formations are not as densely packed as those are at Sunset Point, but they are just as lovely. It's easier to isolate individual formations from Sunrise Point with a short telephoto lens, however.

*Photo advice:* You can be sure of one thing, all those magnificent photos of Bryce displayed at the Visitor Center or in the gift shops all around the park were taken either early in the morning or late in the afternoon. If you arrive at Bryce during the middle of the day and only stay a few hours, you can't hope to come away with professional quality photos. The canyon's formations must have a warm light skimming their surface, whether from the back or the side, to bring out the relief and color. To bring home high quality photos, you should be at one of the amphitheater viewpoints at dawn and use the rest of the morning to descend into the canyon. Watch out for overexposure, which could wash out the color of the spires.

*Hoodoos in the early morning*

## Inspiration Point and Bryce Point

Inspiration Point offers the best view of the extraordinary conglomeration of spires that make up the Silent City, situated in a recess to the south of Sunset Point. The Rim Trail between Sunset and Inspiration Point displays a constant stream of spectacular views. You can easily stroll it in about twenty minutes.

You'll find the crowds much thinner at both Bryce and Inspiration Points, which could make your photography a lot easier in summer.

## Navajo and Queen's Garden Trails

To really absorb the magic of Bryce, a descent into the canyon is a must. By then you'll understand why old Ebenezer Bryce called this canyon "a hell of a place to lose a cow" as you take in the views, each more spectacular than the last.

*Wall Street section of the Navajo Trail*

Many trails run among the hoodoos and take you right into the middle of these formations. Two of these, Queen's Garden Trail (about 1½ miles) and Navajo Trail (about 2.2 miles) carry most of the foot traffic. This is due not only to their location in the amphitheater and their beauty, but because they are short and easy to reach. All the trails in the amphitheater are connected and you can make a loop using the Navajo and the Queen's Garden Trails, which shortens the entire walk to 3 miles. The Navajo Trail descends from Sunset Point, passing by the famous rock chimney called Thor's Hammer and quickly arrives among the spires of Wall Street, which seem immense when viewed from below. The trek is short and not particularly difficult, except for the ascent on the way back. The Queen's Garden Trail begins at Sunrise Viewpoint; it is rather short and not as steep as the Navajo Trail.

***Time required:*** About 2 hours for the entire loop on the Navajo and Queen's Garden connected trails. Begin at Sunset Point, it's both easier and more spectacular. Each trail will take about one hour to complete separately.

*Note:* These two trails are about 8,000 feet in altitude. It can be extremely hot and dry in summer and it is imperative you carry enough water, a sun hat and sunscreen. You should be able to hike these trails in jogging shoes without problem, but use extreme caution, especially on the steeper parts. These trails are often snow-covered starting in October and continuing until the end of April; at that time, descent can be extremely risky without the right kind of boots. Once inside the canyon, though, snow and ice are less of a problem and the going is not so steep.

*Opposite page: sunrise on the Amphitheater after a winter storm*

## Peek-a-Boo Trail

If you've enjoyed hiking the Navajo and Queen's Garden trails and are craving for more, you'll enjoy the Peek-a-Boo trail. In fact, time permitting, I strongly recommend combining the preceding walks with the Peek-a-Boo Loop; this adds another 4 miles to the walk (including the small connecting trail at the end of the Navajo Trail) for a total of 7 miles and approximately 4 to 5 hours.

*Peeking through a window*

The Peek-a-Boo Loop offers solitude as well as great opportunities for less cliché photography, particularly at the Wall of Wisdom and The Cathedral. In addition to the beauty of the circuit, its variety makes it interesting, with many small switchbacks, passages close to the edge of the ravine and a couple of very short sections dug into the rock. On the other hand, it is a bit of a roller-coaster and often dusty because of the twice-daily commercial horseback rides. It is better hiked clockwise.

If you don't feel like tackling the whole loop on foot, consider a horseback ride. I recommend the A.M. half-day tour, which needs to be reserved at least a day before *(see On the Go Resources.)* Obviously, the odds of getting quality pictures while riding are pretty low, however.

## Fairyland Viewpoint and Trail

You'll find Fairyland Point at the end of a 1-mile spur road to your left, between the Park boundary and the Visitor Center. It's easy to miss this road when entering the park for the first time.

Visitors, who tend to congregate around the more famous viewpoints near the Bryce Amphitheater, frequently neglect this one, as well as the trail of the same name. The Fairyland Loop trail is just as lovely and provides a completely different view of the canyon and its formations. The 8-mile trail meanders through Fairyland and Campbell canyons around Boat Mesa, with a short detour to admire the unusual formation of Tower Bridge. This trail has more open views than the classic Bryce Amphitheater's hikes; another bonus for photographers are the many touches of green and wood sprinkled against the red and orange rock chimneys; on the down side, there is a smaller concentration of spires and hoo-doos. The end of the loop follows the rim for 2.7 miles between Sunrise Point and Fairyland Point but this can be omitted if you've arranged a car shuttle.

If you lack the time to do the entire Fairyland Loop trail or the Navajo/Queen's Garden loop trail, try following the first 1,500 feet of the Fairyland Trail down from Fairyland Point until you reach the promontory visible to the left of the viewpoint. The walk is easy and the views on both sides of the promontory are magnificent.

*Time required:* About 4 hours for the entire Fairyland Loop trail.

## Mossy Cave

Located in the northern section of the park, this extremely pleasant trail, almost flat three quarters of the way and less frequented, was restored in the summer of 2000 after having been closed for a long time, due to partial destruction by a flash flood.

It follows a perennial creek meandering among a spectacular landscape of red spires, before reaching a deep alcove with green veg-etation. A couple hundred yards before the alcove, a spur trail leads to the right to a pretty little cascade. Water level permitting you can cross the stream just above the cascade, where an unofficial but well-trodden footpath leads up to openings in the red spires.

*Getting there:* On the west side of Scenic Byway 12, 4 miles from Tropic or from UT 63 going into Bryce Canyon.

*Time required:* About 1 hour.

*Turret arch near Mossy Cave*

## Yovimpai Point and Rainbow Point

These two viewpoints, at the southernmost tip of the park, appear very differ-ent from the amphitheater. You won't find similar scenery there. This is a superb alpine landscape and an interesting contrast after the amphitheater, if you have the time. From the Visitor Center, the road climbs southward for 17 miles to the heart of a forest where pines and aspens blend. You'll find lots of wildlife here and an almost total absence of cars out of season. From Yovimpai Point, the view takes in all the steps of the Grand Staircase to the south. From Rainbow Point, close to 8,500 feet in elevation, you have a sensational, unobstructed panorama of the Pink Cliffs, the highest tread on the Grand Staircase. The 1-mile round-trip Bristlecone Loop Trail gives you the opportunity to view some ancient bristlecone pines and take spectacular photos of the tortuous forms of these members of the world's oldest living plant species. Some of their cousins in California's White Mountains are 5,000 years old and still growing. On the way back to the main area of the park, you can stop at several viewpoints along the road; however, these are not as spectacular as those from the rim of the amphitheater, arguably with the exception of the Natural Bridge viewpoint.

*Time required:* At least 2 hours round-trip from the Visitor Center. If you're short on time, concentrate on the main amphitheater close to the Visitor Center.

# AROUND BRYCE CANYON

## Red Canyon

Red Canyon, under the jurisdiction of the Dixie National Forest, is an excellent prelude to Bryce if you are coming from Zion. For the majority of visitors, Red Canyon usually means a quick stop along the side of the road to snap a few shots before continuing on to Bryce. That's too bad since Red Canyon has a personality all its own. Its formations are definitely different from those of Bryce and some colors—reds in particular—are even more intense. For off-season visitors, arriving in greater numbers all the time, it's a first-rate alternative to the icy, snowbound trails of Bryce.

*Red Canyon at dusk*

Among the variety of available trails, the easiest and most pleasant is without doubt Pink Ledges, a 1-mile loop of less than 30 minutes, starting from the Visitor Center and passing several extremely esthetic viewpoints. The trail is very easy and a perfect alternative for those who don't want to tackle the Navajo/Queen's Garden loop trail.

Much more difficult is the Photo Trail, located ¾ mile west of the Visitor Center. This short trail climbs steeply to the heights and offers some nice vistas. The contrast between the abrupt halt of the angular formations and the peaceful valley of the Sevier below is interesting to observe.

The Arches trail is an easy 0.7-mile hike, in the western part of the park; it has some good views and red rocks, as well as a photogenic red wall with several windows, hence the trail's name. Along the trail you'll pass a stone structure alleged to have served as a food storage for Butch Cassidy and his gang. To get there, drive about 1½ mile west of the Visitor Center and take Castro Canyon Road, heading north; this dirt road is normally passable by passenger cars. Park at the Losee Canyon trailhead, reached after about 2 miles.

For longer hiking, the Cassidy Trail, about 1 mile east of the Visitor Center, offers the hiker in search of solitude a pleasant stroll far from the crowd in a lovely, steeply banked canyon bordered with trees.

*Photo advice:* In adapting to the angles of the sun, the light is as good in the morning as in the afternoon. If the sun is very strong, be careful not to under-expose the red rock if you use a matrix-type meter. Conversely, take care not to overexpose the rock. A setting of ½ stop on either side should be enough to assure a perfect exposure. The east side of the Pink Ledges Trail is highly recommended for photography.

*Getting there:* Either from Scenic Byway 12 from Bryce or from Scenic Byway 89 connecting Bryce to Panguitch and following the course of the Sevier River.

*Time required:* About ½-hour for a short visit; 1½ to 2 hours if you hike both the Pink Ledges and Arches trails.

## Cedar Breaks National Monument

This National Monument resembles Bryce, though it presents some original formations. Cedar Breaks is laid out in the form of a vast, uninterrupted semi-circular amphitheater, deeper than Bryce is and equally as colorful. Does it merit a detour? Without hesitation, yes, for enthusiasts desiring complete insight into the national parks of the Southwest, but no, for visitors who only have a week to ten days to do the Grand Circle.

Cedar Breaks' location is close to 10,000 feet high and the summit is often subjected to extremely violent winds. Be sure to take a windbreaker on all hikes, even in summer. The Monument closes around mid-October because of heavy snowfalls and remains closed until late May. The plateau is less obstructed than that of Bryce, with some good-size prairies interspersed among the forest pines. Scenic Byway 14 between the valley of the Sevier River and Cedar City is absolutely lovely. In winter, the snowfields of Duck Creek are invaded by snowmobiles, a very tempting sight if you do not mind the noise.

*Photo advice:* Four viewpoints allow you to photograph the amphitheater along the 5-mile long Scenic Drive; each one is a bit different from the other. If you are pressed for time, Point Supreme is probably the best, as well as the most crowded. The Wasatch Ramparts trail is a nice walk with excellent late afternoon and

*Bristlecone Pine at sunset*

evening views and allows you to photograph a rare group of ancient Bristlecone pines at Spectra Point. If you can be there in July, you'll have great wildflowers in the meadows on the east side of the road.

*Getting there:* On UT 148 from Scenic Byway 14 connecting with US 89 to Cedar City or from Scenic Byway 143 connecting Panguitch with I-15. Coming from the north, you'll pass the ski resort at Brian Head.

*Time required:* 1 to 1½ hour to cross the park and take pictures from the viewpoints. Add a couple of hours for a leisurely stroll on the Wasatch Ramparts trail. ✿

*Colorful formation along Cottonwood Canyon Road*

Chapter 5

ALONG THE COCKSCOMB

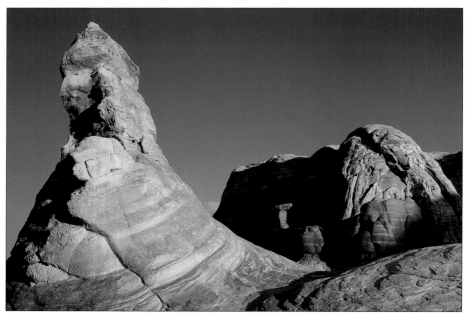

*Rimrock hoodoos catch the morning sun*

# ALONG THE COCKSCOMB

The fantastic Cockscomb is a 50-mile long fault crossing the Grand Staircase and the Vermilion Cliffs National Monuments from north to south, roughly following Cottonwood Canyon Road (BLM 400) and House Rock Valley Road (BLM 700). From the sky, the Cockscomb appears like a giant wound on the earth's crust; it is arguably one of the most remarkable geologic formations of the Colorado Plateau, especially in its section north of US 89 following Cottonwood Canyon Road.

After visiting the principal sites along Cottonwood Canyon Road, we'll explore other spectacular geologic formations located on both sides of US 89 in close proximity to the BLM's Paria Contact Station.

## Cottonwood Canyon Road

Driving the 40 miles of narrow and unpaved Cottonwood Canyon Road is truly enchanting if road conditions are favorable, which is most of the time. There is outstanding scenery all along this popular route: A high plateau to the north including a narrow canyon and an impressive arch, a splendid valley lined with spectacular geologic formations and cottonwood trees in the center, and colorful badlands to the south. In the following sections, I'll describe the various landmarks and side trips along the road in a north to south direction.

Cottonwood Canyon Road is usually passable by passenger cars, with some caution; however, you should always stop to check the weather forecast in Cannonville, Kanab, Escalante, Big Water or the Paria Contact Station before embarking, as rain can make the road impassable. Under no circumstances should this road be driven if rain is threatening. After a heavy thunderstorm, the route can become a muddy morass in just a few minutes and trap any vehicle for hours or even days. Practically every year, some motorists get stranded in the mud for a couple of nights before being pulled out at great cost once the tow truck gets through. The BLM closes the road for extended periods of time when it is deemed too muddy to be passable. If it hasn't rained much during summer, it can also be very sandy in places, especially south of the confluence of Cottonwood Wash and the Paria River.

In the late nineties, the road remained closed for several months after the Paria River destroyed large chunks of embankment. In its current form, the road has one very narrow section that has been bulldozed on a rocky cliff. Exercise caution on Cottonwood Canyon road, as people have a tendency to drive a bit too fast. Also, watch out for Longhorns—seldom seen in Utah—wandering along the southern section of the road.

*Getting there:* Cottonwood Canyon Road officially starts at the end of the asphalted road leading south from Cannonville on Scenic Byway 12 to Kodachrome Basin State Park. If you are coming from US 89, you'll find Cottonwood Canyon Road near milepost 18, about 4 miles past Churchwells when coming from Page and about 2 miles past the Paria Contact Station turnoff when coming from Kanab.

*Time required:* Don't count on using Cottonwood Road as a shortcut, it is a place where you should take your time. Many interesting spots border Cottonwood Canyon Road and you'll want to stop often to explore and photograph, easily stretching the 2 hours it takes to drive it in a hurry into a much longer time. You'll need at least 1½ days to visit all the sites described below with sufficient time for photography. It's possible to camp anywhere along the road since Grand Staircase-Escalante National Monument is jointly administered by the BLM, and their policy concerning camping in the wild is very liberal.

## Round Valley Draw

Located close to Cottonwood Canyon Road, this is an interesting canyon with a good section of meandering narrows that can be hiked in a relatively short time. The wall color is rather pale but there is good texture to the sandstone.

After signing the trail register, hike for about 3/4 mile inside the wash, which is quite open at this point. Some people have driven their 4WD inside the wash right to the beginning of the narrows. Please, don't follow their example; it is illegal to drive off the Monument's existing roadways.

It is easier to enter the narrows right at their onset, a very obvious spot look-ing from above like a corkscrew. The slot immediately starts with a mildly chal-lenging 12 foot drop-off that can be negotiated without help and without any chimneying by most agile persons. A short sling will come handy to drop your bag to the bottom and, later on, to get past the bigger obstacles. Although it's not really deep, the initial part of the slot feels quite narrow and closed up. After a while, the canyon opens up a bit and you reach a first chokestone that is easily circumvented. Soon after that, there is a second chokestone that is much larger and deeper, requiring some careful hand and foot placement to descend to the lower level on the right side. It is best to have a partner for this obstacle.

Once you've cleared the second chokestone, the narrows become very tall, but after another 10 minutes they open up and the canyon becomes much wider. The point where the narrows end is quite photogenic when you look back. From then on, it is less than ½-hour to the junction with Hackberry Canyon, about 2½ miles from the start, where you can retrace your steps.

*Getting there:* About 6.7 miles south of the beginning of Cottonwood Canyon Road at the Kodachrome Basin State Park junction, just after a steep descent, you'll see a marker  on the north side of the road announcing the crossing of Round Valley Draw. A dirt road leaves to the south with a small sign pointing to the Rush Beds; this is your road. Although it is usually in good condition, this road is infrequently maintained and high-clearance is recommended due to deep ruts in places. You may be out of luck after a bad flood and there is a narrow passage over a wash after about 1 mile that can be problematic in some years. I have been there after a flash flood collapsed both sides of the road, leaving only inches on each side of the tires, forcing me to retreat. You'll reach the car park on the right side after about 1.6 miles.

You may also choose to enter Round Valley Draw from the bottom of the narrows, via Hackberry Canyon, by descending a steep trail from the Upper Slickrock Bench Road. You'll find this road 5.8 miles from the beginning of Cottonwood Canyon Road. Be sure to bear left at the Y after you've crossed and closed the fence line behind you and you'll reach the recommended trailhead for people backpacking Hackberry Canyon. The higher car park at the end of the right spur requires a considerably longer descent through very loose scree.

*Time required:* 1½ to 3 hours, depending on how long you wish to stay in the narrows and how far you want to go.

## Grosvenor Arch

About 10 miles from the northern end of Cottonwood Canyon Road, or 2.8 miles past the junction with Round Valley Draw's access road, you'll find the turnoff for Grosvenor Arch. From here, it is only a mile to the spectacular double arch spanning almost 90 feet and towering 152 feet above the ground. The area around the arch is developed, with amenities and an asphalted trail to the bottom of the arch. It is possible to climb to the back of the arch using a steep path on the east side.

*Photo advice:* There is a great angle from the very bottom of the arch, shooting straight up with a very wide-angle lens. The light color of the Dakota Sandstone bestows a warm golden hue to the arch in the late afternoon sun. Early morning works well too, with the roofs of the two spans basked in golden backlight.

*Grosvenor Arch*

## Candyland & The Cottonwood Narrows

About 3½ miles south of the Grosvenor Arch turnoff, you'll come to a saddle dominating some extremely colorful badlands on the east side of the road with another saddle less than 0.3 mile further south; some BLM Rangers like to refer to it as Candyland due its white and red rocks and pinnacles. This is arguably the most spectacular photographic spot on Cottonwood Canyon Road and you can easily spend an hour walking and photographing between the two saddles. This spot has an even better perspective from the south and is best lit in the second part of the afternoon.

On the west side of the road and about halfway between the two saddles you'll find the upper entrance to the Cottonwood Wash Narrows, which run somewhat parallel to the road. Take one of the footpaths going down and go left for the main narrows. These narrows are only moderately spectacular but they present the advantage of being short, with no obstacles, and close to the road.

You can also enter from the south, about 1 mile downstream, from an easily located car park on the west side of the road. From here, follow the footpath crossing the wash and leading to the lower entrance. About 0.2 mile from this lower trailhead, to the left, is an interesting sandstone wall with many intricate patterns.

*Eroded shapes on Cottonwood Canyon Road*

## Heart of the Cockscomb

Right at the heart of the Cockscomb, there is an excellent undeveloped camp-site about 5 miles south of the lower entrance to the Cottonwood Narrows (it is less than 10 miles south of the Grosvenor Arch turnoff). This makes a good base for exploring the sights along Cottonwood Canyon Road and have good light after sunrise and before sunset.

Continuing south on Cottonwood Canyon Road about 0.8 mile from the campsite, you'll notice near the west side of the road a group of white limestone bluffs sticking out at an impossible angle with shades of purple-colored clay on their backside. This fascinating hogback is a great spot for photography. You can reach a good vantage point (37°18'58" 111°53'07") painlessly by walking in a broad circle from the south without having to traverse any gullies. This spot is best photographed just before sunset.

About 1¼ miles south of the campsite, you will cross a low pass over some badlands with an incredible view of the serrated ridges of the Cockscomb mono-cline. Park at the pullout for a great mid-telephoto shot compressing the perspec-tive of the monocline. This is best photographed in the morning.

*Serrated ridge of the Cockscomb fault*

As you near the towering shape of Castle Rock, domi-nating the ridge to your right, the road now levels off inside the fault. One major prob-lem you'll soon notice as you search for photo opportuni-ties, is the almost constant presence of electrical lines marring the landscape.

About 15 miles south from the Grosvenor Arch turnoff, you can drive up the Brigham Plains Road (BLM 430) to the top of the Cockscomb. From here, you'll have a fantastic bird's eye view of the fault. It makes a great photograph looking north, preferably in late afternoon. Looking west across the fault, you'll see the unusual cross-bedding of Yellow Rock and, in the distance, you will catch a glimpse of Mollie's Nipple and No Man's Mesa. The beginning of Brigham Plains Road is extremely steep and a bit intimidating, but it is not difficult to drive as far as the crest, which is less than a mile away from Cottonwood Canyon Road. Go back the same way and don't expect to make a loop continuing on the Brigham Plains Road as it becomes really bad further up and most people turn back when things get nasty.

# Lower Hackberry Narrows

If you feel you've been in your car too long and are in need of a good hike to stretch your legs. Lower Hackberry Canyon is just the place for you: an easy, refreshing jaunt inside a spectacular setting. There is, however, one minor caveat: Hackberry Canyon has a perennial stream and requires frequent wading in ankle-deep water, so you must be willing to get your feet wet; I must add that there is some quicksand—nothing dangerous but your legs can sink to your knees into the soft watery sand. Take a pair of wading shoes or some boots you're not afraid to waste; there is no scrambling involved, so an old pair of running shoes would do just fine.

After parking, cross Cottonwood Wash and enter the deep, vertical walls of Hackberry Canyon. The narrows are immediately very deep but large enough at the top to be well lit. The sandstone walls, already beautiful from the get-go, turn a very dark red after 1 mile. A tall sandstone needle called Finger Rock appears on your right. Around Mile 1.7, the canyon becomes suddenly wider for about 2 miles and looses part of its appeal so this can be a good place to backtrack. If you continue on, look for some cairns and a faint footpath to your left at about Mile 4.3. A short walk leads to the well-preserved remains of the Frank Watson cabin.

*Getting there:* Drive back north ¼ mile on Cottonwood Canyon Road from the Brigham Plains Road junction, about 15 miles south of the Grosvenor Arch turnoff, and find the car park on the east side of the road.

*Time required:* About 2 hours to see the best part of the narrows; at least 4 hours to see the Watson Cabin.

# Yellow Rock

Near the junction of Cottonwood Canyon Road and Brigham Plains Road, you can also climb to little visited Yellow Rock, a vast expanse of colorful slick-rock with a large amount of yellow–as the name implies–but also many patches of beautiful reddish and pastel sandstone as well as some spectacular cross-bedding somewhat reminiscent of the Coyote Buttes. The 360° view from the top of Yellow Rock is simply awesome. This is an outstanding photographic destination and one of my favorite spots in the Paria area. I have visited it numerous times and each trip has led to new discoveries and interesting photography. I have no doubt that you'll feel the same way. Be forewarned, however: The beginning of the trail is a very steep hill with a 45° incline and very loose rocks; be extremely cautious if you decide to attempt it. Although it is not physically hard per se and there is no danger of falling a long way, the potential is there to hurt yourself or twist an ankle, especially during the descent. It is preferable to do this hike with a partner.

The hill takes less than 20 minutes to climb until you reach a saddle. From there, you can see into the mouth of Hackberry Canyon to the north. The trail then turns into a well-trod path, cairned at regular intervals. It climbs steadily for a short while until the enormous humpback of Yellow Rock comes into full view. It is an impressive mass of colorful, cross-bedded sandstone. Although appearing very distant at first glance, due to the lack of perspective, you'll be surprised later on at how quickly you reach the first slab of sandstones.

Look behind you and take your bearings, noting the tall sandstone outcrop looking like horns not far from the point where you emerged from the hill. When you later come down the top of Yellow Rock across the slickrock, remember to aim just to the left of this outcrop.

There are now several ways to reach Yellow Rock itself and it's up to you to decide. You cannot see everything under the best light in a single outing, so pick one direction and go; you can't go wrong anyway.

You can leave the main footpath and go north; you'll then come to a patch of serrated dark rocks eroded into Gothic shapes. Continuing in the same direction while descending toward the sea of slickrock, you'll notice some remarkable rocks resembling petrified wood. A bit further yet, you'll find yourself looking once again into Hackberry Canyon. At this point you can start hiking west, making a gradual ascent on some truly amazing slickrock slabs.

If you continue on the main footpath from the spot where I suggested that you look back at the horned outcrop earlier on, you'll soon reach the base of the sea of slickrock. You can chose to climb directly to the top of Yellow Rock, where you'll find the largest patches of yellow and orange, or you can follow some distantly spaced cairns on the slickrock, circumnavigating the base of Yellow Rock to the left, which is the south side. Once again, you'll be treated to some lovely, multicolored slabs of slickrock. A small outcrop in the form of a Thibetan stupa will come into view on the south side of Yellow Rock. This is a good place to aim for, as you'll be following long slabs of slickrock looking like scales of giant snakes along the way.

Climbing to the top of Yellow Rock from its eastern side is much easier than it seems and provides a breathtaking 360° panoramic view. To the north, you see Castle Rock; to the west, the Paria drainage with No Man's Mesa and Mollie's Nipple in the background; to the southwest the badlands of Old Paria and in the distance the reflection of cars on US 89; to the south you see Yellow Rock Valley and the Box, a deep canyon cutting through the Cockscomb fault,

*The Camel*

linking the Paria to Cottonwood Wash; to the northeast, you get an awesome view of Cottonwood Canyon Road and the stego-saurus-like fins of the monocline stretching in the distance at the center of the fault.

Time permitting or on another outing, you can rejoin the trail circling Yellow Rock to the south and hike to a rock garden in a valley to the west. Better yet, you can aim toward the impossibly colorful area which you can see to the south and explore it to your heart's content. With a car shuttle and a partner, an outstanding cross-country tra-verse can also be undertaken in the direction of the Box.

*Getting there:* Park at the junction of Cottonwood Canyon Road and Brigham Plains Road (BLM 430). If you're coming directly to Yellow Rock from the south, this car park is located about 14 miles from US 89. To find the Yellow Rock Trail, aim southwest toward an opening in the

*Stupa on the south side of Yellow Rock*

Cockscomb in the first drainage about 300 yards south of the mouth of Hackberry Canyon. You don't have to look for a footpath; it is easy to cross anywhere the couple hundred yards of brush separating the road from the bed of Cottonwood Wash, where you may have to wade a bit if the creek isn't dry.

*Photo advice:* The best light is in late afternoon and until sunset. Most of the sea of slickrock in front of Yellow Rock is in the shade ½ hour before sunset. Watching sunset from the top of Yellow Rock is an exhilarating experience, so it's best to do your photogra-phy on the sea of slickrock prior to that. All kinds of focal lengths can be used on Yellow Rock, from a super-wide angle to accentu-ate the unreal look of this site to a telephoto compressing the cross-bedding's perspective. You may want to consider a slight amount of underexposure to further accentuate the colors.

*Time required:* Plan on a minimum of 2½ hours; however, this area can be explored for hours on end.

*Near the top (photo by Philippe Schuler)*

*Nearby location:* The Box of the Paria is a short but pretty 1-mile canyon cutting through a portion of the Cockscomb fault and linking Cottonwood Wash to the Paria River near the Old Paria town site. You'll find an access road to your right about 2.3 miles south of the junction of Cottonwood Canyon Road and Brigham Plains Road. In the dry season, it is possible to drive the entire length of the canyon in a 4WD vehicle, fording the rocky bed of the Paria River several times in shallow waters. This is a quick and fun mini-adventure leading to some large eroded windows and sheer walls with good reddish color, Of course, it can also be done in the reverse direction. There is no "road" per se in the canyon, just some tracks following the wash, fording the Paria at the best possible places. It is a little sandy at the north end but otherwise suitable for any SUV. If you are driving a passenger car or when the Paria is high, you'll have to do this hike on foot.

## The Wahweap Hoodoos

The Wahweap Hoodoos are some of the most beautiful white pedestal rocks in the area and are being more and more photographed by visitors from all over the world.

As of this writing, there are still two ways to get to the Wahweap Hoodoos but this could change at any time. It is a very fragile area and an impact study could one day conclude that the existing infrastructure does not support unrestricted access. One or more access road could become closed, so be sure to obtain the latest information from the BLM Visitor Center in Big Water before going.

The easiest way to access the Wahweap Hoodoos is from the southern end of Cottonwood Canyon Road. From US 89, about 4½ miles west of Churchwells, take Cottonwood Canyon Road for about 1½ mile, turn right onto BLM road 431 and follow it for about 4 miles until the junction with Brigham Plains Road (BLM 430). This is a fairly good road, except for the crossing of Coyote Creek near the last junction, which can be rough in some years. At the junction, take the right fork and follow BLM 431 straight ahead, bearing east and following the most heavily used tracks. ½ mile after passing Coyote Creek, you'll reach a stock pond with a dam. The road is infrequently maintained after the pond and may deteriorate, forcing you to detour to avoid washouts. Be sure to drive very slowly and carefully from this point on. At about Mile 8 from Cottonwood Canyon Road, you'll pass the White Sands Jeep Road to your right (I'll come back to this road in the White Rocks section below); stay on the main track, going east. After about a mile, BLM 431 descends into a vast depression, at the bottom of which it continues eastward for another mile or so toward Wahweap Wash. As of this writing, a sign posted just before the right turn into the wash warns that driving in the wash is prohibited. Park your vehicle here and continue south on foot for about 20 minutes; the first group of hoodoos is located 1 mile downstream and to the right (37°09'45" 111°42'45"). This is the most spectacular group, which I also refer to as the "Towers of Silence". A second group, larger but less impressive, is located in the next bend of the wash. I like to call this one

"Hoodoo Central". A third group, less interesting despite the presence of a very tall hoodoo, is located a couple of hundred yards further downstream.

The second, and longer, access to the Wahweap Hoodoos starts from the little community of Big Water. Leave US 89 at Big Water, drive through town and at the Y with Smoky Mountain Road, bear left on Nipple Creek Road (BLM 327) heading northwest. Follow it along the ponds of the Fish Hatchery for 3.8 miles until you reach the Wahweap Creek crossing. Park there along the right side of the road or, if the stream is not high and you've got a high-clearance vehicle (and no sign prohibits it at the time of your going), bear left and drive into the wash heading north for about ½ mile until you reach a large fence across the

wash. You are now at the confluence of Coyote Creek, Nipple Creek and Wahweap Creek. Wahweap Creek is the main wash heading north to the right of Coyote Creek; the latter, heading west, being narrower and having redder cliffs. Walk in Wahweap Creek for almost 4 miles until you find the first hoodoos—including a very tall one—at the foot of the left cliffs. The walking is easy and it will take about 1-¼ hour to get there at a normal pace. As described earlier, there are three groups of hoodoos along the cliff, so the first group you are now approaching on the left was the last group on the right when coming via BLM 431. Each group is separated from the others by a couple hundred yards. Do not linger too long at the first group; your time will be much better spent at the second group—Hoodoo Central— and better yet at the last group—the

*Towers of Silence in Wahweap Wash*

Towers of Silence—which is the most interesting photographically.

*Photo advice:* All the Wahweap Wash hoodoos are best photographed from sunrise to early morning regardless of season. During the winter months, however, there is no direct light on the Towers of Silence but a very nice soft light instead. In summer, the Towers are directly illuminated from sunrise on while the tall siltstone cliff in the background remains in shadow. This allows for nice contrasty shots making the Towers stand out, although the background will tend to have a slight bluish cast.

Under direct light conditions, be sure to apply at least +½ stop to +1 full stop of exposure compensation to your shots or they'll turn slightly greyish. A mild warming filter can yield pleasant results, although the whites will not be as pure as without filtration. Digital shooters can experiment with different white balance settings to get several variations in tonality.

The Wahweap Wash hoodoos area is all silt-stone and offers many possibilities to turn small details into fascinating abstracts.

Be sure to tread lightly and not to bump any formations with your feet or tripod. Leave this amazing and delicate area as pristine as possible, so those who come after you can enjoy it just as much.

*Time required:* If coming from BLM 431, count on about 2 hours round-trip from your car to explore and photograph the two most interesting groups of hoodoos. Half a day from the longer Big Water access.

## The White Rocks

The White Rocks are located in a seldom-visited area north of Churchwells and west of the Upper Wahweap Creek drainage. It consists of outstanding badlands, white hoodoos and red capped towers. The soft white shale, remnant of an ancient seabed, is often twisted into remarkable shapes by erosion forces. It is a fascinating area to explore and photograph.

*Photo advice:* There are many different groups of hoodoos with a different orientation inside this wide area and it is impossible to recommend a perfect time of day, except to say that early morning and late afternoon are both good times for the White Rocks hoodoos, whether in the lower or higher sites. If you want them in full sunshine, mid-morning or mid-afternoon is definitely the better time. They can also be successfully photographed in the shade, but they do acquire a blue cast that can be easily removed with a warming filter or in a digital darkroom. However, do not use an aggressive warming filter or you will lose the pure white color of most of the hoodoos.

*Cocky Hoodoo in the White Rocks*

*Getting there:* There are two main sites in the White Rocks area, one at the bottom of the plateau and the other one on top. Access to the lower site is from the little town of Churchwells. Coming from Page on US 89, turn right at a red dirt road located ½ mile before Churchwells. It is BLM road 435 and is easy to miss. Follow it north for about 3 miles until you come to a cow fence, with a gauntlet and a reservoir to your right. The prominent landmark to the north is called Chimney

Rock. From there, easy to spot tracks lead straight-ahead. Follow the less obvious tracks to the right, cross the fence at the rightmost gate and continue due north for almost 1½ mile to reach the end of the canyon, an area which is great fun to explore and photograph, preferably in mid- to late-afternoon.

Accessing the higher White Rocks site from the top of the plateau and exploring it above Chimney Rock involves a longer and more adventurous road trip. From US 89, take Cottonwood Canyon Road and follow the directions given in the Getting there section of the Wahweap Hoodoos. When you are on BLM 431 just north of Chimney Rock, about 4 miles past the junction with the Brigham Plains Road, you'll see a spur road to your right; this is the beginning of the White Sands Jeep Trail. Follow it southeast for about 1.3 miles. This one is a very rough road and a 4WD vehicle is necessary. Park on the small promontory soon after a fence. Just to your right, look for an easy entry into a small and rather flat canyon; there are some surprisingly beautiful reds and pinks with many other subtle

*The Great White Ghost*

nuances on the slickrock and the going is easy. Continuing to the right just under the rim, you'll soon discover some impressive and very colorful hoodoos. Be sure not to step onto the fragile cryptobiotic soil in this area.

Next, come back to your car and walk in an easterly direction following the nearby fence. After only a few hundred yards, you'll reach the edge of a large canyon full of hoodoos, in which you can descend via a sand dune and explore to your heart's content. Very few people come to this spot, a good thing because the area is very fragile. It can also be somewhat hazardous to visit this canyon on your own; I recommend going with a partner.

Driving back on the White Sands Jeep Trail toward BLM 431, stop about halfway right where the road is at its lowest point; from this point, walk westward to the edge of the cliff. Just below you is a huge hoodoo; it is surrounded by many smaller ones peppered along the cliffs of a large white amphitheater with striking touches of purple in places. It is possible to descend cautiously into this amphitheater and explore some of the hoodoos. Some are really spectacular and can be photographed with Chimney Rock in the background.

*Time required:* For the lower site, about 1½ hour round-trip from Churchwells, with time for photography. Half a day for the higher site, accessible via the White Sands Jeep Trail, when combined with the visit of the nearby Wahweap Hoodoos.

## The Rimrocks Hoodoos

The Rimrocks is an outstanding area of badlands and hoodoos, located just north of US 89 between the southern end of Cottonwood Canyon Road and the Cockscomb fault. It contains a large number of fascinating hoodoos, mushroom rocks and rock towers. The most prominent and accessible landmark of the Rimrocks is Toadstool Hoodoo, a spectacular sandstone spire, shaped a bit like the Seattle Needle with a larger rotunda at the top. The area around Toadstool Hoodoo offers endless photographic opportunities, at different times of the day. About 30 feet from Toadstool Hoodoo is another prominent hoodoo, shorter and rounder. They are close enough to each other to make an oft-photographed duo. About 200 feet behind Toadstool Hoodoo, near the cliff, is a series of striking rock-capped sandstone towers, perfect for a late afternoon shot. Once you're done photographing Toadstool Hoodoo, follow the cairns on the rim to the west for about 300 yards until you come to a somewhat hidden recessed area to your right. It contains several large white towers, capped with brown slabs of hard rock. This area is in deep shadow until late morning, which will give a strong bluish cast, so it is best photographed in late afternoon.

Back on US 89, about a mile further to the west of the car park, lies another recessed canyon full of spectacular white towers coiffed with cap rocks. You can see this area with the naked eye from the Paria Contact Station across the road, but it is best observed with binoculars.

*Photo advice:* Early morning and late afternoon both work well, with a preference for the afternoon; there are plenty of formations so you're guaranteed to find some that will be correctly exposed. Toadstool Hoodoo itself can be photographed successfully from different angles, with a variety of focal lengths and under various light conditions.

*Getting there:* On US 89 near milepost 20, about a mile east of the turnoff for the Paria Contact Station, there is a small pullout space and a cow fence on the

*Hoodoos come in all shapes and sizes*

*Rimrock hoodoos in late afternoon sun*

north side of the road. The access is unmarked so you'll have to pay close attention, but there is an electric line running perpendicular to the road at that point. Cross the opening in the fence, sign the register a bit further on and follow the wash to the north for about 15 to 20 minutes. There is also a footpath running along the wash; cairns are laid out in the second half to indicate the best way. Climb the low badlands at the end and the hoodoos will come into view. Despite the fact that the area north of the Paria Contact Station is fenced, it is all public land and can be explored on foot, at your own risk. This area is very fragile, so tread lightly.

It takes quite a bit of effort and route finding to climb to the other ledge, where the white hoodoos visible from the Paria Contact Station are located. Few people visit this area, so it's best to go with a companion. Cross the fence north of US 89 opposite the Paria Contact Station's road and walk northeast to the mouth of the canyon. You'll notice that the canyon ends in three arms, follow the right arm though a slot canyon, then scramble up carefully to the ledge, where the hoodoos will come into view.

*Time required:* At least 1½ hour round-trip from US 89 for the Toadstool Hoodoo area alone.

## Old Paria

Old Paria (also known as Old Pahreah) is an easy side trip off US 89 between Kanab and Page, accessible to all passenger cars except during or after a rain. It is an area where history meets breathtaking Chinle formation badlands

*Old Paria (photo by Philippe Schuler)*

for a highly rewarding photographic journey. The good dirt road starts innocuously enough but soon becomes roller-coaster like as it straddles a narrow ridge dominating colorful badlands on the right side. As the road dives down into the Paria valley it can become washboard-like, requiring some caution. You'll soon arrive at the Paria movie set, now consisting of two newly reconstructed Old West buildings, originally erected in 1963 for the filming of Western movies. In 1999, the four original buildings were badly damaged during a flash flood. With some local assistance, the BLM removed them and rebuilt two new structures higher up, hopefully making them impervious to flash floods; it also added some amenities. The old set used to integrate well into the landscape and made for nice pictures; it will take a while for the new set to absorb the patina of time and look authentic.

A few hundred yards down the road, you'll find the Old Pahreah cemetery, the only remaining testimonial to human presence in the area. Take a walk through the cemetery; it is a very moving reminder of the hard life of the early settlers who tried to eke out a living in this desolate area. About ½ mile further, you end up on the banks of the Paria. Across the river is the actual location of Old Pahreah, but nothing remains standing. Following the river to your right, you'll soon enter a pretty 1-mile long canyon known as the Box of the Paria; it leads through part of the Cockscomb fault to Cottonwood Wash *(see "Nearby location" under the Yellow Rock section).*

*Photo advice:* In the vicinity of the movie set or the cemetery, take some time to explore and photograph the amazing badlands—some of the most colorful you'll ever see in the Southwest—especially in the warm late afternoon light. If you are lucky enough to have a dark stormy sky, with streaks of light falling on the badlands, you'll be rewarded with amazing contrast and beautiful hues. If rain seems imminent, be sure not to linger in this area; on your way back, even with a 4WD vehicle, you may not be able to climb the steep ramp just past the movie set. Instead, take your pictures from the pull-out on the flat ridge, immediately after the ramp. It has a splendid view looking down into the badlands.

*Getting there:* At the Historical Marker, about 40 miles northwest of Page or 10 miles northwest of the Paria Contact Station turnoff on US 89, take the good BLM 585 dirt road heading north and follow it for 5 miles to the movie set.

*Time required:* About 1 hour round-trip from US 89.

## Paria Canyon

Paria Canyon is arguably the most famous classic backpacking trip of the Southwest. Most people take 3 to 5 days to hike the 38 miles from the White House trailhead near US 89 to Lee's Ferry on the Colorado River. If you do not have that much time or are not inclined to backpack, you can also get a very good idea of what Paria Canyon looks like by day-hiking down from the White House trailhead. You can walk to the confluence of the Paria and Buckskin Gulch and back in a moderately difficult 15-mile round-trip taking the better part of a day. The first few miles are usually dry most of the year, but you should expect numerous water crossing, muddy areas or water holes further down and even some knee-deep wading before the confluence. There are some outstanding features to see in Paria Canyon, even on a day hike. At Mile 2, you'll reach the Windows, an area of deep holes—small and large—carved by water and wind and spread in three groups separated by several hundred yards on both sides of the canyon. The narrows really begin at Mile 4, becoming progressively narrower and more spectacular. At Mile 6.7, powerful Sliderock Arch makes a great picture. The confluence with Buckskin Gulch, at Mile 7.3, is truly majestic. Time permitting, you can follow Busckskin Gulch for at least a mile and explore narrows even darker and narrower than those of Paria Canyon.

*The Windows in Paria Canyon*

*Photo advice:* As usual in narrows, it's best to be there in mid- to late-morning to take advantage of reflected light. The area around the confluence of the Paria and the Buckskin offers truly spectacular shots.

*Sandstone and Mud*

*Getting there:* Take US 89 from Page (30 miles) or Kanab (43 miles) and turn off at the sign indicating the "Ranger Station" (aka Paria Contact Station) near milepost 21. There, get the latest weather and trail information (also posted on the registration board when the station is closed), and, if chances of rain are slim, proceed to self-register and pay your day-use fee. Unlike the nearby Coyote Buttes, there is no quota limiting the number of day hikers into Paria Canyon and nearby Buckskin Gulch. There is a limit of 20 permits a day for backpackers, regardless of which trailhead is used. The Paria Contact Station sells an excellent map called *the Hikers Guide to Paria Canyon,* which is very helpful for backpackers.

The White House trailhead and campground are at the end of a 2.2-mile dirt road going south. It is suitable for passenger cars.

*Time required:* At least 7 hours including a short foray into Buckskin Gulch. Before embarking on such a long day-hike, however, you should consider the much easier and shorter trip into Buckskin Gulch from Wire Pass, described in the following section.

## Wire Pass — Buckskin Gulch

This foray inside Wire Pass and a short stretch of Buckskin Gulch will give a quick, but spectacular insight into the narrows of the Paria River area. Many people consider Buckskin Gulch as having the most interesting narrows on the Colorado Plateau.

Do not venture into Wire Pass and Buckskin Gulch if bad weather is threatening. Once in the canyon, you won't be able to get out in case of flash floods. The enormous tree trunks lodged in the walls several feet above you testify to the force and height of the flash floods that can hit any time of the year, but particularly in summer.

The marked trail begins at the Wire Pass parking area and follows the dry bed of the wash for about 1 mile before reaching the entrance to the first narrows. These narrows, a few dozen yards long, will give you a little preview of what

*Opposite page: Sliderock Arch dwarfs a hiker*

awaits further on. Soon, you enter the true narrows of Wire Pass and move along between very dark walls, over a hundred feet high. Depending on how the last flash flood affected the canyon, you may have to scramble above choke stones as high as 8 feet at the first and/or second narrows; in some years, this may present a mild difficulty to some. You'll eventually reach the junction with Buckskin Gulch at 1.7 miles from the trailhead. Look for some faint petroglyphs at the base of the right wall just at the junction. Follow Buckskin Gulch downstream as long as you like or time permits.

*Inside Wire Pass*

Returning to the junction, go a little way up into Buckskin Gulch instead of returning directly into the Wire Pass narrows. At this spot, Buckskin Gulch frequently contains water and mud-holes, and will give you a good idea of what the narrows look like further down Buckskin Gulch and deep inside Paria Canyon.

*Photo advice:* The narrows are generally around 10 feet wide, with some narrower passages about 3 feet wide. They are also very high and therefore quite dark, except around mid-day. A wide-angle lens will let you maintain the depth-of-field and show the canyon's dimensions despite the wide aperture you'll be forced to rely on. With a firm grip and in good light, it's perfectly possible to photograph with a hand-held camera using a high ISO. Refer to the advice on photographing narrows and slot canyons in the Photo Advice Chapter.

*Getting there:* From the Paria Contact Station turnoff, head west on US 89 toward Kanab for about 4.8 miles (just past Milepost 26). You'll come to a hard-packed dirt road branching off to the left when the highway makes a wide curve to the right, immediately past the Cockscomb. This is House Rock Valley Road (BLM 700). Be careful not to miss it, as it is not clearly visible when coming from Page because of the angle and the fact it is slightly downwards from the highway. Using this well-maintained track, usually passable to passenger cars, pass Buckskin Trailhead at 4.4 miles and continue for another 4.2 miles to the Wire Pass parking area. In summer, House Rock Valley Road can be closed for a while after a particularly strong storm.

*Time required:* 1 hour round-trip to get to the Wire Pass trailhead from US 89; up to 3 hours in the narrows to really enjoy them.

## Cobra Arch

Cobra Arch is a remarkable arch, in the shape of the lithe body of the snake of the same name, complete with checkerboard striations reminiscent of the serpent's scales; its span is about 60 feet long. It is often visited by backpackers coming off Buckskin Gulch by the difficult Middle Trail. Photographers will want to take the more conservative approach of coming via Long Canyon Road (BLM 750), but that too isn't an easy affair. After driving on this dirt road, it's a cross-country hike over rough terrain with no trail, requiring a topo map and good navigation skills. It's one location where a GPS will prove really useful. Still the result is worth it, as Cobra Arch is truly unique.

*Getting there:* Take Long Canyon Road (BLM 750), which leaves from the Paria Outpost on the south side of US 89, ½ mile west of the Paria Contact Station turnoff. Be sure to stop at the Paria Outpost and get the latest road information from the friendly owners; this is a great watering hole and eatery for weary hikers returning from the Paria area and the Coyote Buttes. It is worth noting that they provide a 4x4 shuttle service for destinations such as Wire Pass, Buckskin Gulch, the White House trailhead or Lee's Ferry *(see On the Go Resources in Appendix)*. The unmarked dirt road takes you to the Middle Trail trailhead in about 8 miles. The first 4½ miles follow a canyon to the right in a southwesterly direction and are usually well graded. After turning left at a Y, turn left again 0.3 mile further onto the West Clark Bench, heading southeast. The track becomes quite sandy, which may be a challenge in dry years. Inquire on current conditions first and

don't attempt it in a passenger car. Park just past the fence, about 3.2 miles from the last junction (or 8 miles from US 89).

*Cobra Arch*

Ponder the trail marker warning you about the potential hazards of this hike, decide whether you are fit to go, sign the register and follow the fence line south to the ledge overlooking the sandy plain. The view from here is expansive, taking in the Coyote Buttes to the west, the so-called Dive, the Buckskin gorge, and Steamboat Rock to the distant south. To the southeast, you'll notice two promontories: an obvious one less than a mile away and a very large one about 2 miles away. The first one is the one just above the word Dive on your topo map. The larger promontory, in the distance, is the one to concentrate on. Just below it is a straight plateau and another smaller, lower promontory. This is your goal. Check your topo map to reference that point.

Now, walk about a hundred yards east along the ledge until you see the cairn marking the descent (37°02'32" 111°55'10"). Before going down the slickrock ledge, look in front of you and locate the reddish footpath skirting the right side of a small rise, close to the edge of a drop. It's behind this rise that you'll descend to the next step, the sandy plain below the Dive. Descend on the fragile slickrock and follow that footpath, then find the easiest way to descend to the plain. Once you are in the plain, take a minute to get your bearings and take a waypoint if you have a GPS. You'll thus be able to easily locate this spot on the way back and it will make it a lot easier to climb the cliff at the right spot and return to your car. The route to the arch now becomes non-existent and you're on your own. Just make a beeline through the very sandy terrain, crossing a few washes and aiming for the aforementioned promontories. If you follow that straight line, it is only 2½ miles to the arch, taking approximately 1½ hour from the car park. Be sure to look back at regular intervals and get your bearings. When you reach the large promontory, climb through the sand until you reach the slickrock hump, then continue in the same southeasterly direction, dropping down on the other side. You can now see a jumble of rocks in front of you; the arch is hidden behind it. Continue in the same direction and you'll find it (37°01'15" 111°53'44"). Note that the arch is not located at the foot of the main cliff to the left, but a little bit more to the south. I do not recommend this hike in summer, when there is no shade. Trudging back up in the sand would not be pleasant.

*Photo advice:* Cobra Arch is best photographed in mid-afternoon, from its west side, to bring out the snake-like shape and texture. A 24 or 28 mm works well for that shot.

*Time required:* About 5 hours round-trip from the Paria Outpost turnoff on US 89. ✿

*Hoodoo near Boulder Township*

Chapter 6

ALONG SCENIC BYWAY 12

*Kodachrome Basin at dusk*

## ALONG SCENIC BYWAY 12

Scenic Byway 12 easily ranks among the top scenic roads in America, with the section between Escalante and Boulder considered by some to be the most beautiful paved road in Utah. Scenic Byway 12 (or SB 12 for short) passes through some of the most grandiose scenery, winding through spectacular slickrock ridges and canyons, red rock cliffs, pine and aspen forests, alpine scenery and quaint rural towns. This amazing diversity makes it a unique route, and a joy to drive, no matter which way you approach it. Be sure to allocate plenty of time to driving SB 12; not only does this beautiful route have plenty of curves and ups and downs, but it has also numerous pullouts providing great opportunities to appreciate and photograph the awesome scenery.

For the purpose of this book, we will travel SB 12 from west to east. The road begins at US 89, 7 miles south of the town of Panguitch and 8 miles north of the town of Hatch. It ends at the junction with UT 24 in Torrey.

Along most of its length, SB 12 forms the northern border of the vast Grand Staircase-Escalante National Monument. Note that Red Canyon and Bryce Canyon—also located on SB 12—are discussed in Chapter 4; the Escalante Canyons along Hole-in-the-Rock Road (a road connecting with SB 12) are covered in Chapter 7.

## Kodachrome Basin State Park

This small park has some large Entrada sandstone monoliths, but it is the sand pipes—spectacular rock columns forming surreal fingers pointing to the sky—that give esthetic and geologic originality to the place. The columns are cut in a beige colored rock. Lots of easy trails ranging from ½ mile to 3 miles will take you among the formations. Do not miss the short drive to Chimney Rock—the biggest sand pipe anywhere—and to Shakespeare Arch Nature trail, a short ½ mile trail leading to a lovely little arch discovered in 1976.

Campsites and cabins are available, but the park is extremely popular and you must make reservations for summer or holiday camping.

*Photo advice:* Leave the car at the small parking area before the campground and follow the trails. The main paved Nature Trail is marked with several information signs and takes only a quarter of an hour to walk. It's full of interesting views of the finger-like formations mentioned above. For a better view of the park, from the same parking area but on the other side of the road, follow the 1½ mile long Angels Palace trail and its side spur on the plateau, offering good bird's eye views of this area. A few hundred yards south, you can also follow the 1½ mile long Grand Parade trail, which passes by other spectacular monoliths.

The park is magnificent at sunset when the ocher sandstone walls become blood red. It certainly deserves its name. A short 15-minute walk up the Panorama Trail leads to the Ballerina Slipper, which is still lit when darkness already engulfs the rest of the park.

*Getting there:* Leave SB 12 in Cannonville, heading south toward Cottonwood Canyon Road for 7 miles to the park entrance.

*Time required:* 3 hours round-trip from SB 12, including about 2½ hours to tour the park if you're doing all the described hikes.

*Chimney in Kodachrome Basin*

## Skutumpah Road & Willis Creek

Starting south of Cannonville, Skutumpah Road (BLM 500) crosses the western section of the Grand Staircase-Escalante Nat'l Monument following a north-south direction and continues south as Johnson Canyon Road (BLM 501) to meet US 89 about 9 miles east of Kanab. A high-clearance vehicle is recommended. This road rarely experiences closure and is often the best alternative to reach the southern section of the Monument when Cottonwood Canyon Road is closed due to inclement weather. Note that you must cross Yellow Creek—a tributary to the Paria—just after entering Skutumpah Road; this crossing could be difficult after a rain.

Although not as photographically rewarding as Cottonwood Canyon Road overall, it nonetheless provides access to a few interesting narrows, among which Willis Creek and Bull Valley Gorge.

To find Skutumpah Road, drive about 3 miles from SB 12 toward Kodachrome Basin State Park. There is a sign at the beginning of Skutumpah Road indicating Kanab 61 miles. After ascending a steep grade about 1 mile up Skutumpah Road, there is a very nice panoramic view of the valley with Powell Point and the Blues visible in the distance. In late afternoon and with some dramatic clouds, this view lends itself extremely well to a panoramic shot; it shouldn't be missed if you find yourself driving near Cannonville or Kodachrome Basin.

*Willis Creek Narrows*

A few miles further—about 6½ miles from the beginning of Skutumpah Road—you'll find a large and obvious car park to the right with a trail register for Willis Creek. Willis Creek is a lovely little canyon with a year round flow and several short sections of narrows. The creek—accessed on the other side of the road—is extremely easy to explore, having none of the usual chokestones and dropoffs of most narrows in the Grand Staircase and elsewhere.

There are several groups of narrows over the short 1.3-mile stretch leading to the confluence with Averett Canyon. The best group is the very first one, located only 0.2 mile from the trailhead. The canyon walls are less than a hundred feet high and a fair amount of light penetrates inside. The best time of the day is in mid- to late morning and again mid-afternoon to avoid direct light on the walls. Rather than being straight on top, the walls present some very interesting protrusions, making them quite unique and interesting to photograph. The second most interesting group of narrows is the last one, just before the confluence with Averett Canyon.

Although it sounds tempting to return to the road via Averett Canyon, there is a large chokestone close to the confluence of Averett and Willis Creek preventing you from doing so.

Less than 2 miles further south along Skutumpah Road, Bull Valley Gorge has much deeper and darker narrows, as well as a more challenging exploration. It does not offer, however, the same photographic potential as Willis Creek.

## The Blues

Continuing eastward from Cannonville on SB 12, Henrieville offers a very scenic view of fields surrounding a broad sandstone mesa. As you approach the prominent silhouette of Powell Point and nearby Table Cliffs Plateau, SB 12 climbs up through an area of grey shale badlands called "The Blues". The road winds up to the top on a steep 12% grade and the area is notorious for accidents. A large overlook is located on the left side of the road, offering a panoramic view of the blueish badlands below the pink cliffs of 10,000-foot-high Powell Point. You are looking directly at 3,000 feet of vertical relief from the badlands to the top. The badlands can look dismally greyish in broad daylight. The only way to restore some interesting color is to photograph them early in the morning or late in the afternoon.

## Escalante Petrified Forest

As the name indicates, this Utah State Park was once an ancient forest engulfed millions of years ago by an inland sea. You'll find many multicolored pieces of petrified tree trunks as the trail reaches the plateau. Because of its close proximity to the town of Escalante, a quick visit is easy to include in your plans and should not be missed if you've never been to Petrified Nat'l Park in Arizona—although the latter is on a much larger scale.

The moderately difficult Wide Hollow trail winds about a mile through juniper and pinion pines before reaching the petrified trees and a viewpoint overlooking Escalante. The Sleeping Rainbow Trail spur adds about 3/4 mile to your visit. It's a bit of an up and down climb and footing can be tricky in places, but it's a worthwhile detour to take for close-ups of the most beautiful and colorful petrified trunks.

*Photo advice:* To get good color, it's best to photograph the petrified wood away from direct sunlight. If the sun shines brightly, look for pieces of wood shaded by junipers or improvise some kind of reflector. In addition to the large quantity of petrified trees, you'll find a forest of pygmy junipers and ancient dwarf pines that make for interesting photos.

*Getting there:* Located next to the lovely Wide Hollow Reservoir, on a side road about 1 mile west of Escalante.

*Time required:* You'll need 1½ hour for a comfortable visit. There is not much to see near the parking area, except for some sample trunks for display, so if you don't have time or don't care to walk, don't bother with this detour.

*Nearby location:* A short distance from this State Park, you can see a lovely little pictograph with a unique design representing people holding hands in a circle. Unfortunately, this isolated petroglyph has been vandalized and its location, which is unmarked, is a bit hard to find. About 4½ miles west of the town of Escalante, take the graded Main Canyon Road leaving SB 12 northwest. Reset your odometer and drive exactly 1.6 miles from the junction with SB 12. Look for a faint path on the right side of the road, just before a tiny hill covered with boulders; the path gently climbs to the right for about a hundred yards toward a tall rock with the pictograph on its south face (37°45'56" 111°42'42"). It is best photographed in early to mid-morning or on an overcast day.

## Smoky Mountain Road

The Kaiparowits Plateau is crossed north to south by Smoky Mountain Road (BLM300), a 77-mile dirt road connecting Escalante to Big Water on US 89.

The Kaiparowits Plateau forms the central section of the Grand Staircase-Escalante National Monument. It is a vast, untamed area—one of the most remote in the continental U.S. Below the surface lie immense reserves of coal, which have attracted intense interest from the energy industry. Attempts to mine the coal were initially thwarted by the costly logistics of transporting it from such a remote location and were temporarily put to rest by the creation of the Monument. Unfortunately, the fight is far from over.

Smoky Mountain Road is seldom graded and is sometimes in such poor condition that it is too risky to take. Each year several visitors have to be rescued at great cost, so inquire about conditions at the Escalante or Big Water Visitor Center beforehand. The difficulty rating assigned to this road is for normal conditions, when its surface is dry and graded. Do not consider it a shortcut to Page; it will take you at least 5 hours to get from Escalante to Page, possibly without seeing a single soul. Cottonwood Canyon Road is a shorter and considerably more scenic alternative.

Smoky Mountain Road leaves SB 12 from the west side of the Escalante township. Initially paved, the road becomes graded as it enters Alvey Wash, a broad canyon lined with cottonwood trees. There are several pictograph panels in the wash; the most easily spotted panel is on the west side of the road just before Coal Bed Canyon, about 4½ miles from SB 12. More pictographs can be found on the east side of the road ½ mile south of Coal Bed Canyon. There are also a few granaries tucked here and there under ledges. Arch hunters will want to take Coal Bed Canyon to look for Horizon Arch *(see next section)*. Overall, the rest of the trip on Smoky Mountain Road feels long and at times rather tedious. From a purely esthetic standpoint, the most interesting part of the road is its southern section, from Kelly Grade to Nipple Bench. More can be found on this southern section in *Volume 2* of *Photographing the Southwest - Arizona*.

## Horizon Arch

Horizon Arch is a superb little arch located high on a flat mesa, less than 4 miles from Escalante as the crow flies. It is unfortunately rather difficult to access, as the route is off trail all the way from where you park your vehicle and requires good routefinding skills. The arch's exceptional photographic potential, however, warrants a presence in this book. If you think you'd like to see and photograph it, you should be in good condition, able to climb or descend at a steep angle over slippery talus and/or large boulders. The hike requires rugged shoes with good support, a topo map and preferably a GPS. Do not attempt this hike alone and notify someone of your whereabouts. If something happens to you and you can't walk back, it may be a long time before someone finds you.

After leaving your vehicle in Coal Bed Canyon near the mouth of Mitchell Canyon, walk upstream in the latter wash toward the northwest for about 1.1 miles. Look to your right for a pile of boulders masking the entrance to a smaller wash (37°43'39" 111°39'27"). After scrambling over the boulders, enter the small wash and follow it northeast for 0.4 mile. The wash eventually splits into two arms at a point normally marked by a large cairn (37°44'00" 111°39'33"). Now comes the hard part; although it's only about ½ mile to the arch, it will feel

longer than that. Be sure to take your bearings from this spot, because it will be harder to find the right way coming back from the arch. Instead of continuing in either of the two arms of the small wash, start climbing straight up toward the north, ascending the steep slope on a combination of talus, dirt and slippery red rocks. After reaching the mesa, continue northwest, making sure you're staying close to the east rim.

As you make slow progress through the dense vegetation of the mesa, it comes as a jolt

*Kissing Dragons*

when the silhouette of the distant arch first comes into view. One final effort brings you just below the arch (37°44'24" 111°39'48"). It is befuddling that the forces of erosion have left such an amazing formation standing, although the arch appears quite fragile; it is hoped that it will resist for a long time for the enjoyment of future generations.

*Photo advice:* Horizon Arch is best photographed from the back in late afternoon, but don't linger too much to avoid descending in the dark. There are several good angles all within a 24mm to 35mm range. Photos taken from the bottom front will be more of a documentary nature.

*Getting there:* From Escalante, follow Smoky Mountain Road for 4½ miles through Alvey Wash. Turn northwest into Coal Bed Canyon, paying attention not to miss the track, which is just past the wash bed and makes a sharp angle. From here on, a high-clearance vehicle—preferably 4WD—is a necessity. Follow the wash, which becomes progressively narrower—alternating between a sandy and rocky bottom—for a little over a mile. Park near the mouth of Mitchell Canyon to your right. Occasionally, there are ponds dug near the entrance to Mitchell Canyon which will stop vehicular travel and add about a mile to your round-trip hike.

*Time required:* About 4 hours round-trip from Escalante.

## Hell's Backbone Road

Scenic Hell's Backbone Road provides access to one of the most outstanding wilderness areas in the Southwest: the Box-Death Hollow Wilderness. The road was built in the Thirties by the Civilian Conservation Corps. It is about 40 miles from Escalante to its junction with SB 12 near Boulder, taking almost three hours to drive, including short stops. Despite a brief hair-raising section around the Hell's Backbone Bridge, this dirt road is easily driven by passenger car in dry weather and before snow sets in.

Starting from the east side of the Escalante township, you'll enjoy an outstanding display of checkerboard sandstone stretching several miles on the east side of the road (this section of the road is also known as Pine Creek Road). Along the way, the Lower Box Trailhead provides access to The Box of Pine Creek, a beautiful canyon tucked in between high sandstone cliffs. About 14 miles from town, take the signed road leading to lovely Posey Lake. Here a short but steep trail leads to a nice overlook with a distant view of The Box. Back at the junction, Hell's Backbone Road continues its ascent, winding through a forested area to reach Hell's Backbone Bridge. The section just before and after the bridge has dramatic views of the Death Hollow Wilderness with its sheer pink Navajo sandstone cliffs contrasting with the green alpine environment (you are at over 9,000 feet elevation). This is an outstanding photo spot one hour before sunset and in the early morning. The road continues on and meets SB 12 about 3 miles southwest of Boulder. If you are based in Boulder and do not want to do the whole loop, the round-trip to the Hell's Backbone Bridge in only 34 miles.

## Death Hollow

So you're tired of crowds and want to have a little canyon paradise all to yourself: Try Mamie Creek, better known as Death Hollow. Contrary to its ominous-sounding name, it is one of the most verdant canyons you'll ever see, thanks to its wide-apart white and pink Navajo sandstone walls and pure mountain water. Wildlife and vegetation are remarkably abundant and people are few.

You may find it strange that I'm touting this area, at the risk of attracting the very crowds that would mar the feeling of solitude of Death Hollow. Not a chance, because Death Hollow is hard to get in and out of, requiring a very long hiking day or a multi-day backpack for many people, as well as almost constant wading. It is one of the least visited narrows in the Colorado plateau and is likely to remain so.

Before planning a trip to Death Hollow via the Escalante River, inquire about the water level at the Ranger Station or you may find yourself wading in frigid water up to your waist. When walking along the banks of Death Hollow, watch for poison ivy; it is advisable to wear long pants.

*Getting there:* Death Hollow is a small tributary of the Escalante, located northeast of the town of Escalante in the Box-Death Hollow Wilderness. It can be hiked from the top by starting from the Hell's Backbone Road as a multi-day canyoneering adventure or it can be reached more leisurely from one of the two trailheads on the Escalante River, by walking to the confluence with Death Hollow. The confluence is located about halfway between the two trailheads with a distance of 14 miles between them. The Escalante Town Trailhead is located just east of town, only ½ mile from the marked turnoff on SB 12. The Escalante River Trailhead is located just past the bridge on the Escalante River, 15 miles east of the town of Escalante.

*Time required:* 2 to 3 days for a relaxing trip. You'll need several hours just to get to the confluence of the Escalante and Mamie Creek. You can then wade your way through the canyon for several miles or until you encounter drop-offs that require technical equipment. In one very long day, strong hikers can do a short one-day incursion from the Escalante Town Trailhead into Death Hollow; with a light daypack you'll need about 2½ hours to reach the confluence, which leaves a few hours to explore Death Hollow before returning the way you came. Avoid doing this lengthy walk on a hot summer day, as the temperature can rise tremendously inside these canyons.

If you are physically very fit, there is yet another way to do a short incursion from the town of Escalante into Death Hollow via a sneak route, requiring that you scramble down, and then up, in excess of 1000 feet of fairly vertical canyon walls. Having done

*Death Hollow Narrows*

this route myself, I don't recommend doing it without the help of a knowledgeable guide. My advice is to take the leisurely route; you'll be able to carry more photographic equipment and come back with better images.

## Escalante to Boulder

This amazing section of SB 12 between Escalante and Boulder is the highlight of this road trip and should not be missed. There are not enough superlatives to describe its spectacular beauty. The road traverses the most outstanding slickrock scenery, rugged and colorful, with delicate hues ranging from white to dark pink.

Coming from Escalante, SB 12 successively passes the Head of Rocks and Boynton Overlook viewpoints before descending toward the beautiful canyon of the Escalante River. There it crosses the Escalante River, providing access to several trailheads *(see the Escalante Natural Bridge, Hundred Handprints and Phipps Arch sections)* before entering the highly photogenic Calf Creek area *(see the Lower Calf Creek Falls section)*.

Past Calf Creek, SB 12 steeply ascends to the unique and spectacular Hogback Ridge. It is so narrow in places that you can see the landscape on both sides of the road, a thousand feet below. This impressive view stretches for miles but is difficult to photograph.

After the descent and just before entering Boulder, look for a big hoodoo high on the hill to your left. You need to cross private property to get to it, so ask for the landowner at the store to obtain permission.

## Escalante Natural Bridge

This is a very pleasant hike along an easy section of the Escalante River. If you have only limited time or are not inclined to walk a long way from you car, this is the hike for you. It will give you some experience of what it is to hike in one of the Escalante canyons and, as an added bonus, you'll see an impressive natural bridge, a nice arch and some Indian granaries. One caveat, though: You'll have to get your feet wet repeatedly, so use a pair of wading shoes if you have one.

From the Escalante River Trailhead, walk a couple hundred feet to the river and cross it. There are usually stones conveniently laid out for crossing or some tree trunk; however things change constantly and it may not be the case when you're there. Some trekking poles or an improvised staff will make it easier to cross. You'll find two trails following the bottom of the canyon. One trail follows the gently moving river close to the sandstone wall to the left, under a canopy of Cottonwood trees. Another, faster trail cuts a more direct line in the middle of the canyon. Both trails force you to cross the river several times. After leaving the shade of the Cottonwoods, you can catch a brief glimpse of the arch (not the bridge) high on the cliff in the distance. In about 45 minutes, a brisk pace on the flat terrain will get you from the trailhead to the Escalante Natural Bridge. You can't see the bridge from a distance as it is somewhat hidden in a side canyon to the left. The best viewpoint is from the river's bank with a few cottonwoods in the foreground; however, it's worth crossing the river one more time and following the short footpath to see the end of the side canyon from under the bridge.

*Escalante Natural Bridge*

Back on the main trail, continue another few minutes upstream and look for a shallow alcove in the cliff to the left; follow the obvious footpath climbing toward it. In the alcove, you can observe and photograph a couple of interesting granaries perched like an eagle's nest; nearby, you can also see a few interesting petroglyphs, unfortunately vandalized. In the fall, this is a great viewpoint to photograph the golden cottonwoods bordering the Escalante.

Return to the river, continue upstream for a few more minutes and the Escalante Arch will come into view on top of the cliff. The arch is small and not spectacular by itself but you may want to photograph the entire cliff, with cottonwoods in the foreground.

*Getting there:* The Escalante River Trailhead is about 15 miles east of the town of Escalante on SB 12. Slow down as you approach the bridge crossing the Escalante River and turn left into the large parking area immediately after the bridge.

*Time required:* About 2½ hours round-trip.

*Nearby location:* If you're interested in a longer hike and can arrange a car shuttle, follow the Escalante River upstream between the Escalante River trailhead and the Escalante Town trailhead. This 14-mile long hike is almost flat with numerous easy river crossings and can also be done the other way around. Most people prefer doing it as a two- or three-day backpack, exploring Death Hollow along the way *(see the Death Hollow section in this chapter)*, but it can also be done in one day. Avoid hot days if possible and do not undertake this hike if there is a risk of flash flooding. In late spring and early summer, you may want to wear long pants and long sleeves to ward off nasty deerfly bites.

Although the canyon has spectacular cliffs in the section close to the Escalante Town trailhead, the sandstone is less colorful and the vegetation less interesting. The above-described section near the Escalante River trailhead is the most esthetically and photographically rewarding.

## The Hundred Handprints

The Hundred Handprints panel, perhaps one of the largest pictograph panels in the Monument, is located just above the Escalante River Trailhead. This unique panel is very close but not necessarily easy to find the first time around. Note that the land behind the cabin is private and fenced; please do not trespass. The following description takes you to the panel outside the private property.

Starting from the parking area, follow the trail heading northwest to the back of the cabin for 100 yards, then leave this trail and take the well-trod footpath to the right for another 50 yards leading to a first rock ledge. Scramble up a few feet to reach the ledge ascending gently to your right and follow it for about 30 yards. Look up to your left and locate a faint path going up steeply. A couple of cairns may be present; if you don't see the cairns, the footpath is located just past a small cactus bush on the ground. Follow this faint path up; it soon angles to the left to reach the plateau. Once there, look at the sandstone outcrop 200 yards in front of you and notice the deep depression in the middle. To the left of this depression, halfway to the top, you'll see a large flat panel with the hundred handprints. You can walk to the bottom of the slickrock below the panel but don't try climbing to the ledge where the panel is located; it is much harder than it looks and it would be very hazardous. From here, you'll need a mid-size telephoto to capture the handprints.

*Hundred Handprints (photo by Philippe Schuler)*

Follow the bottom of the cliff to the left on the slickrock ledge; in a few minutes you'll reach a group of interesting petroglyphs overlooking the Escalante Canyon. If instead you follow the footpath to the right under the cliff, you'll find other petroglyphs that vandals attempted to saw off the wall.

Once you know where the Hundred Handprints panel is, you can easily observe it with a pair of binoculars from the Boynton Overlook on SB 12.

## Phipps Arch

A short trip to Phipps Wash is another good hike from the Escalante River trailhead, although if your time is limited, I'd give the preference to the Escalante Natural Bridge hike. After crossing SB 12 under the bridge, a good trail follows the left bank of the Escalante River, eventually crossing the river about ¾ mile from the trailhead. You then follow the Escalante on the right side, close to the cliff; if the river level is high, there is a bit of shallow wading involved from time to time. Another easy ¾ mile brings you to the mouth of Phipps Wash, to your right and under a dense canopy of cottonwoods. The easy footpath continues up the pretty wash. Maverick Natural Bridge is located in the first side canyon to the west, but fails to impress. Access to Phipps Arch is another few minutes up canyon, but it is high on the cliff and not visible from the bottom. When a broad side canyon appears to the left, look for cairns indicating the beginning of the ascent; although there is a path, it's not always easy to follow. As you get closer to the arch, you'll need to do a bit of Class 4 scrambling for about 12 feet; this may be a bit intimidating for some; just take your time, look for holds and you should be fine. After passing this obstacle, the trail remains steep but presents no other challenge and soon the massive arch (37°45'23" 111°24'37") comes into view.

*Photo advice:* Cross under the arch and go to the other side near the circular sandstone dome. A moderate wide-angle or normal focal lens works best.

*Time required:* About 2½ to 3 hours round-trip.

## Lower Calf Creek Falls

This delightful 5.4 mile round-trip walk follows Calf Creek upstream, inside a wide but beautiful red rock canyon, to where the trail ends at the 126-foot high falls. In my opinion, this is one of the most rewarding short hikes in Utah. The self-guided, interpretive nature trail is sandy, but mostly level and easy to follow, making it a perfect family hike. A leaflet with descriptions for the numbered stakes along the trail is available at the start of the hike. About ½ hour into the hike, stop at number 9 for some interesting rock art. Looking north across the canyon, you can spot in the distance three large painted figures near the bottom of the cliff wall; a side trail crossing the creek brings you there in a few minutes. As you near the falls, the canyon narrows and the trail offers more shade. The desert varnish on the canyon walls becomes more noticeable and offers a pleasing contrast to the tall grasses and cottonwood trees trailside. At the base of the falls is a small pool, which could tempt the summer hiker with a refreshing dip.

*Photo advice:* A lens in the 28mm-35mm range is necessary to capture the entire falls, while a moderate telephoto will capture some interesting details. The morning will find the falls in shade while full or dappled sunlight may be present in early afternoon. The subtle and varied color of the rock and moss behind the falls is best captured without direct sunlight. In the fall, yellow leaves can grace the rock, adding a nice contrast to the scene. Watch out for wind-blown spray from the falls; protect your gear. While the falls are the main subject, don't neglect the grasses, trees, canyon walls and rock art along the way. Beaver dams along Calf Creek can create clear pools reflecting the cliffs and the sky. Avoid weekends, in the high season, when the place is swarming with locals looking for a cool spot.

*Getting there:* About 16 miles east of Escalante and 11 miles west of Boulder on SB 12; turn off at the sign for the Calf Creek Campground. Fee required.

*Time required:* 3 hours for a comfortable pace and time for photography.

## Upper Calf Creek Falls

Although not as tall and spectacular as the Lower Falls, the Upper Calf Creek Falls are easily reached and provide a nice opportunity to relax in the coolness of the water on a hot day. The walk is also quite pretty and not as difficult as it may seem, when looking down from the top. Also, chances are that you'll be alone at the falls, at least outside of the main holidays.

The 2.2 miles round-trip trail is almost entirely on slickrock but is well cairned. Despite a 500 feet loss in elevation, it is an easy descent and the walk back up doesn't feel strenuous if you pace yourself. About a third of the way down, you'll pass through an impressive field of black lava boulders strewn all over the place, in stark contrast with the pale sandstone. These boulders are remnants of volcanic activity from nearby Boulder Mountain. As you approach the falls, the trail splits; take the upper path to the right, leading on top of the falls and some deep pools upstream; retracing your steps, continue on the lower trail to reach the bottom of the falls. The 86-foot falls drop into a large pool under a photogenic shady alcove. The green mosses and fern, the pool and the misty veil of the falls are extremely inviting and you'll want to sit here and relax for a while.

*Getting there:* Access to the trailhead is by a short but rough spur road located on the west side of SB 12, about 5½ miles north of the Calf Creek campground, almost halfway between mileposts 81 and 82.

*Time required:* 1½ hour.

## Around Boulder Mountain

Boulder is one of the last communities of the West to have been linked to civilization with a road. SB 12 opened in 1940 but remained partially unpaved until the mid-eighties and the section crossing the forested area around Boulder Mountain was the last to be paved.

In the hamlet of Boulder, the Anasazi State Park provides an interesting glimpse into the life and culture of the Fremont Basketmakers, who originally settled this region. The museum has many interesting interactive exhibits. Behind the museum, there is a replica of a typical Puebloan-type ancestral dwelling and the excavated ruins of the Coombs site with a partially reconstructed pit-house. Even if you do not visit the Museum, the State Park rangers are an excellent source of information for local hikes and the latest weather forecast. This is helpful if you want to explore the area without driving all the way to the Escalante Visitor Center.

*Opposite page: Lower Calf Creek Falls*

To the north of Boulder, SB 12 turns into a true mountain road while crossing Boulder Mountain—an ancient volcano over 50 million years old. Near the

highest point on the road, you can photograph large groves of aspens. Fall colors are usually at their peak during the second week in October. Of the three viewpoints on the road to Torrey, Homestead (11 miles north of Boulder) is the most spectacular. From here, your eye embraces hundreds of miles around, including the Waterpocket Fold, the Circle Cliffs, and the Burr Trail. SB 12 offers other superb panoramic views of Capitol Reef and the Henry Mountains from the viewpoints at Steep Creek (12 miles north of Boulder) and Larb Hollow (8 miles farther). For photography, the viewpoints on Boulder Mountain are best in the afternoon with a medium to long telephoto. Watch for deer on the road, especially in early morning and evening.

*Pit House at Anasazi State Park*

## The Burr Trail

The Burr Trail (BLM 100) is an old track used by the Mormon pioneers when moving their livestock from the high-altitude pastures of Boulder Mountain to

the warmer grazing areas of the Waterpocket Fold. The trail, asphalted in the 1980's up to the boundary of Capitol Reef NP, crosses beautiful country that is still wild and remote. Just outside Boulder, the Burr Trail passes through a series of beautifully cross-bedded Navajo sandstone petrified dunes; these domes are heavily striated and very photogenic. Then comes Deer Creek and its delightful little campground and soon after that you'll reach the 7-mile long

*Spectacular cross-bedding outside Boulder*

gorge of Long Canyon. There is a pull out on the left side of the road allowing you to contemplate and photograph a superb view of the first ½ mile of the canyon. After that, the road drops down to canyon level and you reach the trailhead to the Lower Gulch Outstanding Natural Area. The road through Long Canyon is pure pleasure, passing through sheer sandstone cliffs with fantastic desert varnish and finely eroded areas. As you exit Long Canyon, a large pullout offers an superb

*Summer Storm brewing over Long Canyon*

panoramic view of the Circle Cliffs, Waterpocket Fold and Henry Mountains, with some highly colorful badlands to your right. 10 miles later, as the Burr Trail becomes a dirt road, the west face of the Waterpocket Fold and Strike Valley come into view very nicely. Soon, you'll be crossing the Fold and reaching the steep switchbacks leading down into Strike Valley. You can drive down the spectacular switchbacks and continue south toward Bullfrog Marina or north toward UT 24 via Notom Road.

*Photo advice:* The road traverses Long Canyon from about Mile 10 through 17 coming from Boulder; its walls are eroded in the form of highly concentrated deep holes dug into the deep-red Wingate sandstone. This phenomenon—known as "Swiss cheese"—makes for great photography, producing highly saturated reds when photographed under reflected light. Scenery along the Burr Trail is best photographed in the early morning and in the afternoon.

*Time required:* At least 1½ hour for a short drive from Boulder to the end of Long Canyon and back. Half a day to drive to the boundary of Capitol Reef and visit Strike Valley Overlook (refer to the Capitol Reef chapter).

## Little Death Hollow

Little Death Hollow is one of the most exciting slot canyons in the Escalante drainage, with just the right amount of technical challenge to spice things up, without being difficult. Although not quite as spectacular as others photographically, this 7 mile long slot canyon can nonetheless yield some great action shots and its beautiful red walls of Wingate sandstone, often pock-marked with spectacular Swiss cheese, are definitely worth shooting.

To visit Little Death Hollow without suffering 8 miles round-trip of nondescript wash-walking from the main trailhead on the Wolverine Loop Road, driving inside Horse Canyon provides an excellent 4WD alternative, weather permitting and assuming the road is in good condition. Horse Canyon Road is usually graded once a year for the benefit of local ranchers and it is suitable for high-clearance vehicle when conditions are right. Horse Canyon is a wide but beautiful Wingate canyon with some absolutely outstanding desert varnish in places—arguably some of the best desert varnish in the Southwest. There are very pleasant primitive camping spots at the end of the road, both near the mouth of Wolverine Canyon and, a few hundred yards further, near the mouth of Little Death Hollow.

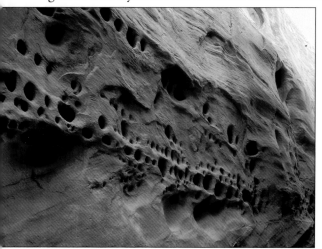

*Fine "Swiss Cheese" in Little Death Hollow*

From the end of Horse Canyon, Little Death Hollow can be followed on foot for approximately 1½ miles before encountering the first truly technical obstacle. All the choke stones before that can be easily scaled or skirted and present no real challenge to a fit person.

At the confluence of Horse Canyon and Little Death Hollow, a 20-minute walk south brings you to the Escalante River where you can rest a while before returning to your vehicle.

As you walk back to your car from the mouth of Little Death Hollow, look for a striking Native American profile formed in the distant sandstone to the left, as the wash opens up.

*Photo advice:* Little Death Hollow is neither very deep nor narrow and becomes very bright around midday. It is best photographed until mid-morning and from mid-afternoon on.

*Getting there:* Take the Burr Trail (BLM 100) for 18 miles from Boulder and make a right on the marked Wolverine Loop Road (BLM 110). After about 5 miles, turn right to enter Horse Canyon Road (BLM 112) and follow this dirt road for about 13 miles until it ends. Before embarking on the Wolverine Loop and Horse Canyon, always check road conditions and weather forecast. There are many patches of clay on the former and some very deep sand 3/4 of the way on the latter. It will be a long walk back if you get caught there during or after a rain.

*Nearby location:* There is an interesting petrified forest area further up on the Wolverine Loop Road, about 5 miles past the junction with Horse Canyon. ❧

*Narrows in the Escalante drainage*

Chapter 7

# CANYONS OF THE ESCALANTE

*Swiss cheese in Red*

## CANYONS OF THE ESCALANTE

The Escalante River drainage is a huge area of colorful sandstone canyons interspersed with plateaus. It includes some of the most remote country in the Southwest. The Escalante, last river in the continental U.S. to be named, meanders slowly in its midst before joining Lake Powell. Its many tributaries form a maze of deep sandstone canyons, containing arches, natural bridges, slot canyons, waterfalls, as well as abundant vegetation and wildlife. These canyons, reminiscent of Glen Canyon before Lake Powell, offer well-prepared visitors some of the finest desert hiking in the world. The few highlights I describe in this book are just a small portion of what lays there, waiting to be explored.

This chapter concentrates on canyons accessible from Hole-in-the-Rock Road and its spur roads. Escalante tributaries whose trailheads are not accessible from Hole-in-the-Rock Road are covered in Chapter 6, Along SB 12.

The Visitor Center in the town of Escalante can help you plan your trip and discover for yourself this incredible backcountry. Escalante is also the site of several motels, B&Bs, and outfitters, making it an excellent base for exploration.

### Hole-in-the-Rock Road

Hole-in-the-Rock Road owes its name to the Mormon pioneer expedition which created it in 1879 to establish a presence in Bluff. In order to cross the Colorado River, they had to cut a primitive route in the cliff *(see the last section in this chapter).* Hole in the Rock road (BLM 200) starts from SB 12 about 5 miles east of Escalante township and heads southwest for about 55 miles until it dead ends at Lake Powell. Except for some short sections and the last few miles of the road, the landscape along Hole-in-the-Rock Road is not especially interesting. The Escalante is far to the east and not visible and the aptly named Straight Cliffs, to the west, are exactly that: straight and barely changing for dozens of miles. However, as you'll find out in the next sections, there is an incredible amount of great scenery to be seen and photographed from its trailheads.

Except during or immediately after a violent storm, the gravel-covered Hole-in-the-Rock Road should not present any difficulties for the ordinary passenger car until you get to Devil's Garden, about 12 miles from the start. Past that point, the road is generally suitable for passenger cars in good weather for about 38 miles. Caution should nonetheless be exercised as the road becomes progressively narrower and more tortuous with potentially delicate passages appearing without warning: Mostly treacherous deep ruts and gullies created by recent rains. The same goes for the side roads leading to the trailheads mentioned in this chapter, taking into consideration the fact that they are even less frequently maintained and generally require a high-clearance vehicle. The last 5 miles of Hole-in-the-Rock Road to Lake Powell are strictly for experienced drivers and rugged 4WD vehicles. In any circumstances, it is advisable to stop at the Visitor Center in Escalante to check on weather and road conditions.

The highlights of this area are described from north to south along Hole-in-the-Rock Road, but this is merely to help locating them. Exploring them cannot be done just following this order due to the great driving and hiking distance. To see them all requires several forays on Hole-in-the-Rock Road over a period of several days.

## Cedar Wash Arch

Anxious to discover the popular highlights of Hole-in-the-Rock Road, few visitors bother taking the time to visit Cedar Wash Arch. It's sad because they'll miss a nicely shaped, soft colored arch that can be seen with almost no walking. Time permitting, try beginning or concluding one of your days on the road by paying it a visit.

From the car park, find the well-trod path straight ahead and follow it for 300 yards until you reach the rim. Turn left and follow the rim—overlooking a lovely valley with almost white sandstone—for another 200 yards until you get a good but distant view of the arch. The arch can be found about halfway from the valley bottom.

*Photo advice:* You can continue as much as you like along the rim of the very pleasant canyon, but the arch actually looks best from a distance with a mid-range telephoto, something like a 135mm. It is best photographed in mid-morning with some sidelight defining edges around its span.

*Getting there:* Almost 3 miles south of the SB 12 and Hole-in-the-Rock road junction, take Cedar Wash Road (BLM 210) heading southwest; although the road isn't marked, there is a sign indicating the wash. Drive about 3.6 miles to the pullout just where the road turns sharply northwest in the direction of the Escalante township. Alternately, you can come directly from Escalante by heading south on Center street and following the dirt road for about 10 miles.

*Time required:* Less than 1 hour round-trip from the Hole-in-the-Rock Road turnoff.

## Zebra & Tunnel Slots

In the Escalante area, these two little slot canyons—especially the short but superb Zebra Slot—are fast becoming the latest craze among the "been there done that" crowd, now that Peek-a-boo and Spooky have become so popular. Still, you're bound to meet few souls on the 2.4-mile one-way trip down Halfway Hollow from the car park to Harris Wash. Arriving at Harris Wash, take your bearings so you can easily locate Halfway Hollow upon your return. Your first goal should be the Zebra Slot so bear left, following the broad wash to the north for about ½ mile until you catch a glimpse of the Zebra drainage to the right. Follow it as it progressively becomes a narrow canyon and then the slot itself (37°39'39" 111°25'02").

The Zebra slot is sandy at the beginning and often filled with deep muddy pools, especially in wet years, but it can also be totally dry. Navigating through the slot is easy at first, but gets tricky toward the end when the slot narrows drastically. You'll have to do a bit of easy chimneying in order to get to the best spot, where you can photograph the beautifully-striated and colorful narrow walls with moqui marbles encrusted in the delicate sandstone. At the end of this spot, you can also scramble up a slightly more difficult dryfall to gain an interesting downward view. Beyond this point, the slot canyon is blocked by a deep pool.

Even with a fast ISO, a tripod is a must. This is a very tight place and you'll need all the depth of field you can get from your lens so the nearest walls are not blurred. The best time to photograph the slot is in mid-morning before the sun strikes the walls directly.

Your next destination is the Tunnel slot. The tunnel, which is about 80 feet long and ends as abruptly as it begins, gets its name from the fact that it is almost closed on top. There is plenty of room to move standing up and no obstructions, except for possible water pools. The Tunnel slot makes for interesting pictures around midday even though its walls are not as colorful or striated as Zebra's. The normal way to get there calls for retracing your steps to the spot where you came in from Halfway Hollow. Continue east for another 0.8 mile inside Harris Wash until you find the wide entrance to the Tunnel drainage to your left (37°39'11" 111°24'26"). From there it is only 0.3 mile to the slot. If you do it this way, you are pretty much guaranteed to find your way to the Tunnel slot, but

*Opposite page: inside the Zebra Slot*

you are looking at almost one hour of walking in Harris Wash with not much to see. An alternate solution is to go cross-country from the Zebra Slot over what I call the "Sea of slickrock" to reach the Tunnel slot directly at its narrow back entrance. Although this is a short cross-country walk, a topo map, a GPS if you have one, and some route-finding skills are essential. For this shortcut, turn left in the first wide opening as you exit the Zebra slot, climbing a gentle slope until you reach a vast expanse of slickrock where you'll find several interesting subjects to photograph. Bear east, leaving a small sandstone hill to your left and skirting a little sand dune. After cresting a low notch, you'll notice a narrow canyon to the east. Aim in that direction, gradually descending on the sandstone until you reach the sandy bottom leading you to the back entrance of Tunnel Slot. Return to Halfway Hollow the normal way in Harris Wash to go back to your car.

*Getting there:* Take Hole-in-the-Rock Road for close to 8 miles until you find a tiny spur road to your right, a couple of hundred yards past a cattle guard. This spur road leads to a corral and has plenty of space to park on the side. Cross Hole-in-the-Rock Road, descend into Halfway Hollow and follow it northeast for about an hour until you reach Harris Wash, where you'll bear left for Zebra or right for Tunnel.

*Time required:* About 5 hours round-trip from the car park for both canyons with time for photography. Trying to combine this hike with a visit to Peek-a-Boo and Spooky slot canyons *(see Dry Fork section)* would be too much; however, you can combine it with a visit to Cedar Wash Arch and the Devil's Garden.

## Devil's Garden

Don't confuse this site with another of the same name located in the northern part of Arches National Park. Escalante Devil's Garden is a small site consisting of petrified sand dunes, weirdly shaped monoliths, small arches and colorful

*Whimsical figures of the Devil's Garden*

hoodoos. Almost by the side of the Hole-in-the-Rock Road, Devil's Garden is a must, due to its proximity to SB 12 and the considerable photographic potential it offers. If you are spending the night in Escalante, it's possible to make a quick visit at sunrise or sunset, even though more time would definitely be warranted. Consider using the nice picnic area for breakfast or dinner after shooting.

There are no marked trails from the parking area and you can immediately wander as you please in the Devil's Garden. However, your natural tendency will be to make a loop around these curiosities following the traces of previous visitors to the top. The spectacular rock formations are among the most beautiful on the Colorado Plateau and are found less than 1,500 feet from the parking area. Some have very strange shapes, reminiscent of Easter Island statues. The elegant Metate Arch is the most recognizable landmark of the Garden, thanks to its remarkable double span.

*Photo advice:* The Golden Hour light is preferred with this type of spectacular formation, but the terrain and the angles vary so it's possible to get some interesting shots even during the day. However, the nicest photos are taken after sunrise when the Straight Cliffs are well lit in the background or just before sunset when the monoliths take on superb golden hues. If you're going to explore other sites along Hole-in-the-Rock Road, my advice is to stop at Devil's Garden first in order to thoroughly check the area and previsualize what you'll want to photograph. This will optimize the short time you'll have later on when you stop to take photographs before sunset on your way back to Escalante. Try some low shots, isolating the formations against the sky to bring out their relief as it's difficult to convey any sense of scale. A 24mm is necessary to frame Metate Arch entirely.

*Getting there:* Take Hole-in-the-Rock Road for almost 12 easy miles from where it branches off SB 12; turn right on BLM 225 for another ½ mile to the parking area.

*Metate Arch (photo by Karsten Rau)*

*Time required:* At least 1 hour on-site if you take photos. If combining this visit with the Dry Fork of Coyote Gulch and its slot canyons—a classic circuit—you'll need at least 6 hours round-trip from Escalante.

# Out of Egypt

The Egypt Bench serves as the entry point to some of the most remote and beautiful tributary canyons to the Escalante River, among which are Fence, Choprock, Neon, Ringtail, the lower part of Twenty Five Mile Wash, and Egypt 3 Slot. Except for the trailhead area which is known for its Carmel formation, the canyons are mostly Navajo and Wingate sandstone, which makes them particularly colorful.

Each canyon can be visited individually in the course of a day-hike, but a backpacking trip of at least 3 days, combining several canyons, will allow you to visit at a relaxed pace with lots of time to photograph during the right light. Note that all the canyons along the banks of the Escalante are located inside Glen Canyon Nat'l Recreation Area and therefore require a backcountry permit if you stay overnight. If you do not want to backpack or if you prefer a little more comfort, several outfitters offer multi-day guided adventures in the area, leading you to the best spots with most of your gear carried by mules or llamas *(see Appendix for reference to some outfitters)*.

If you choose to explore this area on your own, you'll need a good topo map, such as *Trails Illustrated's Canyons of the Escalante*; you'll also benefit from reading additional guidebooks specializing in this area *(see Selected Bibliography in Appendix)*. If you wish to bench-walk between two canyons for fun or to save time, you'll need some route finding skills, a compass and possibly a GPS with spare batteries. You'll also need a hat, sunscreen, insect repellent during deer fly season, and plenty of water. Fresh water can usually be found on the ground in many of the canyons, but it needs to be filtered and treated. Some springs also exist but are not always reliable, especially in summer or during a dry year.

Walking these canyons is generally done mostly on slickrock and sandy ground but count on occasional wading to cross the Escalante River and its tributaries or traverse pools in narrow sections of side canyons. Prior to your trip, inquire about the water level by calling the Escalante Visitor Center; during springtime or a rainy year, you may find yourself wading into frigid water up to your chest. Unless the water is abnormally cold, you'll find this a relaxing experience. Any kind of shoes will work for wading. I recommend using a pair of woolen socks to avoid blisters and ward off hypothermia if the water is cold. A pair of polarized sunglasses will help spot treacherous rocks under water, as well as deep pools.

*Photo advice:* In late spring and throughout summer, cottonwoods explode with green foliage, creating extraordinary contrast with the red canyon walls and wonderful photographic opportunities. There are endless ways to play with reflections in water holes. Outside of Neon Canyon, which is described in the following section, my favorite canyon is Choprock for its numerous photographic possibilities and its many nice narrows waiting to be explored. There is a huge and spectacular alcove located a few hundred yards from the confluence with the Escalante, that makes a great base camp for the leisurely exploration of the entire area.

*Opposite page: Cottonwood Reflection in Choprock Canyon*

*Getting there:* To reach the Egypt Bench trailhead, follow Hole-in-the-Rock Road almost 17 miles from SB 12. Turn left on BLM 240 and follow it for about 9 miles; bear right at the Y and park ½ mile further on a large parking area near the edge of the ridge. A high-clearance vehicle is recommended as the second half of BLM 240 can be too rough on passenger cars, as it crosses several washes and rocky sections.

*Nearby location:* Upper Harris Wash is one of the most easily accessible trailheads. You'll find it about 6 miles down the good BLM 220 beginning about 10 miles from SB 12 on Hole-in-the-Rock Road. It makes an excellent first-time experience for a day hike or even a two-day backpacking trip to the Escalante River. It is about 10 miles each way, with the most beautiful miles—adorned with tall walls and desert varnish—being the last 3 miles before the river.

## Neon Canyon

Neon Canyon and the so-called Golden Cathedral are part of the Escalante drainage and are accessible from the Egypt Bench trailhead; however, they merit their own special mention in view of their great beauty and interest to the photographer.

Located inside the lower section of lovely Neon Canyon, the Golden Cathedral is a tall grotto of Wingate sandstone, with two large collapsed potholes on its roof and a substantial pool of water at the bottom. Wingate is a glorious reddish variety of sandstone often striated with desert varnish, giving it an almost animal fur-like appearance. The superb light-reflecting properties of the Wingate confer a fantastic red glow to the grotto. Around mid-day, beams of light cast whimsical spotlights on the dark-green water at the bottom of the grotto; they also create magical animations on the walls if the wind agitates the water surface or if you skip a stone intentionally. This is without a doubt one of the most spectacular sights of the Southwest.

*Photo advice:* You may want to pare down the amount of photographic equipment you'll take into the canyons if you backpack without an outfitter's assistance. The best time to photograph the Golden Cathedral is between 11 AM and 2 PM depending on the season. You'll want the entire grotto to be in the shade before photographing it. The reflected light from the canyon walls upstream from the grotto is what bestows the glorious golden glow to your images.

In recent years, this spot has become renowned for rappelling and you stand a good chance to bring pictures of canyoneers hanging from their ropes below the potholes. Enthused as you'll be by the Golden Cathedral, don't neglect the wonderful opportunity of photographing cottonwoods alongside Neon Canyon's glorious red walls.

*Getting there:* Follow Hole-in-the-Rock Road almost 17 miles and turn left on BLM 240 toward the Egypt Bench trailhead, as described in the Out of Egypt section. There are a couple of alternatives to reach Neon Canyon from the trail-

*Opposite page: the Golden Cathedral in Neon Canyon*

head: The most scenic, but longer way, is via Fence Canyon or you can make a faster beeline across the plateau. I recommend the latter to photographers only doing a day hike, in order to maximize available time inside Neon Canyon. From the rim near the parking area, locate the ubiquitous mound of sandstone known as Round Dome, about 3 miles to the east-northeast. This landmark is located just behind the entrance to Neon Canyon. Noting the direction of Round Mountain is important—a compass could be useful here—because this natural beacon will often be out of sight as you progress on the plateau below. Descend the sandstone slope following a cairned path, noting the marks of horseshoes on this old horse trail. Once on the sandy plateau, leave the Fence Canyon trail to your left and continue cross-country for about 2 miles toward Round Dome on relatively flat ground, alternating between sand and slickrock. Along the way, look back frequently to memorize the spot whence you started your descent; it can be hard to find when the light has changed on the way back. When you reach the end of the plateau, you'll be overlooking the Escalante River canyon just across from the entrance to Neon Canyon with Round Dome in the background. Follow the rim to the right and locate the sand dune that allows an easy descent to the Escalante River. Find a path through the dense vegetation just across from the sandstone wall to the right of the mouth of Neon Canyon, then cross the river at this relatively shallow spot. Continue inside Neon Canyon for a little under a mile until you reach the fabulous Golden Cathedral. Return to your car the way you came.

Time permitting, you could try exploring the top of Neon Canyon, above and beyond the Golden Cathedral. To do so, backtrack to the confluence with the Escalante. A couple of hundred yards before you reach the confluence, you'll notice to the right a slickrock slope with a forgiving angle. Climb it and you'll find a good trail on top. Follow it to the right until you get past the potholes of the Golden Cathedral. You'll have a magnificent view of the top of the Cathedral and the verdant streambed of upper Neon Canyon.

*Time required:* At least 6 hours round-trip from the parking area; or as part of a multi-day backpack combined with Choprock and nearby canyons. If possible, allow more time to relax on the soft sand at the edge of the Golden Cathedral and to take pictures at different intervals for best results.


## Dry Fork of Coyote Gulch & Slot Canyons

Located about 33 miles outside Escalante township, the Dry Fork of Coyote Gulch is a great opportunity to explore a couple of spectacular slot canyons and have a lot of fun, without major crowds and commercial trappings. The Dry Fork of Coyote Gulch combines several canyons: The narrows of Dry Fork proper and three slots canyons located in side drainages. These are Peek-a-Boo, Spooky and Brimstone.

When you reach the dry riverbed at the bottom of the cairned trail coming from the car park, the narrows of Dry Fork are located immediately to the left. Though not in the same league as the more famous Buckskin Gulch narrows, they are nonetheless quite spectacular. The walls, a lovely ocher color of Navajo sandstone, are about 10 to 15 feet apart and around 70 feet high. A few minutes walking in the narrows gives those who don't want to venture into the slot canyons a chance to shoot some nice pictures.

Peek-a-Boo is an absolute must for slot canyon devotees. It's an extremely narrow and twisted passage about ½ mile long, with beautiful shapes, striations and a unique double bridge. It is blessed with excellent lighting due to the low height of its Navajo sandstone walls. The slot is easy to find, only a couple hundred yards downstream from the narrows of Dry Fork. Follow the dry creek bed of Coyote Gulch eastward until you see the crack in the wall that marks the entrance of Peek-a-boo, to your left (37°28'54" 111°13'00"). You must get into it by climbing up the wall, but toeholds cut in the rock will help and no special equipment is needed. At times, a shallow pool

*Twisted passage*

of water near the entrance to Peek-a-Boo can make things quite slippery. Once you've overcome this part, your progress will be easier. You'll have to wriggle through a narrow hole located about 150 feet from the entrance to be able to explore the upper part of the canyon, where you can only advance one step at a time scraping the bottom of your pants. The most spectacular twists and turns are found barely 600 feet from the entrance of the canyon. Alternately, Peek-a-Boo can also be accessed by climbing a hill to the left of it, and dropping in near its eastern end.

Spooky is the next slot canyon, about ½ mile downstream to your left, north of a big sand dune (37°28'54" 111°12'33"). It's incredibly narrow, with interesting textured walls in places and, as its name indicates, spooky. You can easily enter it from the riverbed of Coyote Gulch and a few steps are enough to give you a good idea of its appearance.

Here is a suggested loop including both Peek-a-Boo and Spooky. It requires some scrambling and route finding, and you should not attempt it if you are alone or claustrophobic! Large people should also make sure they won't get stuck at the end of the loop, which is the narrowest section. This section is near the riverbed entrance of Spooky, so it's easy to check before embarking on the loop. Start with Peek-a-Boo, as it is easier to come back from the top of Spooky.

*Arches inside Peek-a-Boo*

Peek-a-Boo's slot ends up in a shallow wash; locate the cairns going up to your right and follow them and the faint route eastward for about ½ mile until you meet Spooky's sandy wash. Follow it to the right, then proceed cautiously into the slot. This exciting little adventure requires a bit of chimneying or potential crawling on the ground, so large photo backpacks are out of the question.

Brimstone, the third slot canyon, is only for experienced teams of canyoneers and should be avoided by casual photographers. It is located further downstream from Spooky in Coyote Gulch, with a 10-foot drop-off which will be difficult to negotiate on the way back. Once at the mouth of the canyon, you still need to walk another mile in the sand before reaching the narrows. The slot itself is extremely narrow, deep, dark and tortuous. In 1996, a photographer got stuck in Brimstone for eight days, before being miraculously rescued! The story doesn't say whether he got any good images, but it should be enough to discourage anyone who doesn't know exactly what they're doing.

All these slot canyons harbor a dwarf species of rattlesnake. Although it's not known to be aggressive, be careful where you step and put your hands. Given the always present risk of flash flood, be sure to check the weather forecast at the Visitor Center in Escalante before heading for the canyons. May and June may be the best months to visit, as there are less pools of water and mud and the risk of thunderstorms is statistically much lower.

*Photo advice:* Peek-a-Boo is better photographed in mid-morning or afternoon to avoid problems with contrast. Spooky is best lit around mid-day and it is way too dark at other times. A wide angle is indispensable in these narrow slot canyons to capture as much as possible of the rock walls on film, as well as to maximize the depth-of-field and avoid blurring the rock walls in the foreground. A tripod is necessary to work with an opening of f/16 or f/22 if you shoot low ISO. With 50 or 100, you'll find yourself exposing for ½ second to several seconds depending on sunlight. Peek-a-Boo's good overall lighting makes it possible to work hand-held, using ISO 400 or 800, but you may pay the price

*Crawling inside a slot canyon*

in lack of depth-of-field unless you use a digital point-&-shoot. Pay attention not to scrape your lens against the walls and watch for footprints; in the excitement of the moment, it's easy to forget the messy footprints in the foreground.

*Getting there:* To reach the trailhead, follow Hole-in-the-Rock Road about 14 miles past Devil's Garden (this is about 26 miles from the intersection with SB 12) until you see a sign for Dry Fork Coyote Gulch to your left. Follow the very rough, but nevertheless passable, track (BLM 252) for almost 2 miles to the parking area. Be sure to bear left at the spot where the track forks. Leaving the parking area, keep your eyes on the cairns to follow the ½-mile long trail descending from the ridge to the dry riverbed of Coyote Gulch.

*Time required:* About 3 hours round-trip, excluding Brimstone, from the car park. If combining this visit with Devil's Garden, as many people do, you'll need at least 6 hours round-trip from Escalante.

## Coyote Gulch

I have had the good fortune to visit over seventy countries and to trek to the far corners of the world and I rank Coyote Gulch up there with the greatest hikes of all. To me, Coyote Gulch epitomizes the best that Southwest's Canyon Country has to offer: Huge, colorful canyon walls, beautiful desert varnish, remarkable geologic features such as bridges and arches, a perennial stream, hanging gardens of ferns, cottonwoods, great little waterfalls, lots of birds and wildlife, wonderful campsites everywhere. Add to that no bandits, no need for pack animals, no high-altitude sickness, no need to pack gallons of water, shade almost everywhere if necessary, no freezing your bones at night. Above all, it has an unmatched ratio of beauty and enjoyment versus physical exertion and risk. This is a must-see location in one's lifetime, well worth a little advance planning and preparation.

The entire hike is only 12 to 13 miles long on-way, with several possible entry and exit points, thus offering several options.

The best way to visit Coyote Gulch is as a thru-backpack with a car shuttle. I have hiked Coyote Gulch in both directions and my favorite scenario is to start at the Fortymile Ridge trailhead, ending up at Redwell. I have to say that it's a bit more dramatic the other way around because you'll finish with the most outstanding features. In each case, it's a leisurely two-day backpack, but three days will give you more flexibility to kick back and enjoy this amazing canyon and take better photographs. You should consider this option even if you do not have two cars ; it is easy and relatively inexpensive (for a small group) to hire a shuttle in Escalante *(see Resources in Appendix)*. An advantage of this solution is that the 4WD shuttle will deliver you to the Fortymile Ridge trailhead that is a little bit harder to drive to, in some years, because of the deep sand. In contrast, driving to the Redwell trailhead is not particularly challenging.

There is a third entry/exit point into Coyote Gulch at Hurricane Wash, right on Hole-in-the-Rock Road; however, it involves a long, fatiguing trek in soft sand that is a blemish on the rest of the experience. There is a shortcut out of Hurricane Wash with a relatively short cross-country hike to Chimney Rock for a car shuttle, however the road to Chimney Rock is the sandiest of all and there is always the possibility to get bogged down if you don't have a pair of shovels. The Redwell entry/exit is a more preferable option, both scenery-wise and for your legs and your vehicle.

*Coyote Bridge*

In the absence of a car shuttle, all other options require either more time and more effort or less time and less to see. If you want to backpack the entire length of Coyote Gulch without a car shuttle, you'll need to hike a total of about 25 miles in 3 or 4 days. This is of course a great trip if you can afford the time. You can also visit Coyote Gulch over time, splitting your visit into segments. This is a nice incentive to return to this magnificent place.

Note that there is a sneak route in and out of Coyote Gulch at about the halfway point, near Jacob Hamblin Arch. Using this sneak route as an exit is tempting because it allows you to do Coyote Gulch from the Fortymile Ridge trailhead as a day hike with plenty of time inside the canyon. It should not be undertaken by backpackers, unless they have a rope and are experienced climbers. Agile day hikers with good scrambling skills and no fear of heights can negotiate the climb without too much difficulty, but extreme caution is required. You undertake this climb at your own risk, knowing that if you slip or fall you can get badly hurt. Using this route to descend into Coyote Gulch is even more dangerous and I discourage it. Exposure is tremendous and if you panic and freeze while looking down, you'll be in serious trouble.

Finally, if you are very fit and used to long day hikes, it is even possible to hike the entire canyon from end to end in one very long day, using a car shuttle. Once in the canyon, the hike is almost entirely flat, the ground is soft and you don't need to carry any water if you take a filtration device.

Now let's get started and discover this fabulous place together.

I suggest an early start from Fortymile Ridge. It's best if you can sleep at the trailhead. There is no camping but if you are self-contained in your car, you can spend the night there. Start at daybreak and follow the cairns to the northeast, in the direction of the Escalante and Coyote Gulch confluence. This 2-mile long cross-country traverse is mostly on slickrock but is cairned and you should have no difficulty locating the fissure in the top part of the ridge called Crack-in-the-Wall (37°25'09" 110°59'06"). The panorama is spectacular from this point. It is a great pre-dawn shot, but it gets totally lost in bright light shortly after sunrise.

Crack-in-the-Wall does not represent any technical challenge. An initial 10 foot drop to get into the narrow crack is easily negotiated with the assistance of well-placed stones. After that, you'll need to walk sideways and downward for a few dozen feet, pushing your pack ahead of you. It's a bit awkward but everybody manages, although individuals with a substantial girth may think twice before attempting this.

Just below Crack-in-the-Wall, you begin your 600 foot descent in almost 1 mile on a huge sand dune toward Coyote Gulch. It is a well-marked trail. The main rationale for doing this hike in an easterly direction is to avoid hauling yourself up the dune with a heavy load and in full sun at the end of a day, unless you make your last camp near the bottom of the dune and ascend it in the early morning.

Just before arriving in the gulch, you'll see some trail markers; follow a path to the right to hike downstream into the Gulch until you reach the confluence with the Escalante. River level, current and temperature permitting, a short hike in the Escalante reveals nice views of Stevens Arch, high above the canyon.

For a high view of Stevens Arch, hike back into Coyote Gulch and look for a faint path out of the canyon to the right. It is hard to locate from inside the canyon so it pays off to see its precise location during the last stages of your descent on the dune. Coming from the Escalante, it is about 100 feet before the spot where you first crossed the gulch earlier on. After a couple of minutes of hiking up this path, you'll need to scramble up a 10 foot slickrock wall but there are good holds and if you are agile, it shouldn't be a problem. This is the only obstacle on this path. The rest is easy and in about 0.6 mile you'll arrive at the viewpoint after skirting a large mesa on its right side. The view of the massive opening of Stevens Arch is outstanding. Retrace your steps back to the bed of Coyote Gulch and use the same trail you came in to avoid some obstacles in the gulch. In a couple of minutes, you'll be back at the trail markers where you'll go down again into the streambed and begin your journey upstream into Coyote Gulch.

From then on, the hike is pure enchantment. You'll be mostly walking in ankle- to calf-deep water and occasionally climbing out of the streambed to shortcut a meander or circumvent some obstacle. Just take it easy, splashing happily in the shallow waters and stopping often for photography. There is beautiful reflected light and every meander of the river brings a new surprise. The canyon is incredibly riparian and you walk to the constant sound of birds. Lizards and all kinds of insects abound and you may need some protection against gnats in early summer. There are colorful lithe snakes along the banks or in the water and presumably also the odd rattlesnake, but they'll most likely hear you and get out of your way. Springtime and autumn are equally as good. With a mild temperature, this is a dream walk. In summer, be sure to drink a lot, you may forget that your body is thirsty; just scoop and filter water from the riverbed.

You'll pass several beautiful waterfalls during the first quarter of the hike over a 1½-mile or so stretch of the canyon. The first one can be easily negotiated to the left. One presents a bit of an obstacle and you must scramble up 10 feet of slickrock on the right side.

*Hidden Pool (photo by Charles Wood)*

These are the last obstacles. After that, it's miles of easy walking inside the canyon, successively encountering geological features such as Cliff Arch, Coyote Natural Bridge and Jacob Hamblin Arch. If you want to exit the canyon at the Jacob Hamblin Arch, the unmarked sneak route starts near the pit toilets sign, a couple of hundred feet downstream from the arch

Continuing inside Coyote Gulch, the canyon starts widening quite a bit after the confluence with Hurricane wash. At some point, you'll climb on the slickrock and pass a very nice little slot canyon from above before going back into the streambed. There is dense vegetation up to the last mile before Redwell, but the last couple miles offer no shade.

*Photo advice:* Arguably the most outstanding feature of the hike is Coyote Natural Bridge, best photographed from the east side in early to late afternoon. The bridge is then in the shade on that side but receives beautiful reflected light on its well exposed bottom part. Close to the bank, downstream, it's up to you to frame the bridge including some of the riverbed and vegetation if its not basked in direct light. You need to avoid direct lighting at all cost, anything else goes.

I also prefer Jacob Hamblin Arch from the east side, shortly into the afternoon in autumn or spring. There is good reflected light on the arch then and the sun is not low enough to over-irradiate the northern arm of the arch which can be seen through the eastern opening. With a little haze it will shine just right on the cottonwoods below.

All the waterfalls should be photographed in the shade with long exposures to get the best results. A warming filter will bring out the color and a polarizer will attenuate the burn of the highlights. Use a neutral density filter if the light is too strong.

*Getting there:* To reach the Fortymile Ridge trailhead, follow Hole-in-the-Rock Road for about 36 miles and turn left on Fortymile Ridge Road (BLM 270).

Follow this dirt road heading northwest for about 7 miles until its end. The last couple of miles can be very sandy, although I've driven it several times with a 4WD SUV without any difficulty.

The trail leaving from the water tank at Mile 5 of the Fortymile Ridge Road is used by people wanting a quick in and out into Coyote Gulch, using the Jacob Hamblin Arch sneak route both ways. The main benefit of this trailhead, generally accessible by passenger car, is to avoid driving in deep sand to the official trailhead. The time to hike from each trailhead to Jacob Hamblin Arch is about the same, as the shorter distance from the water tank trailhead is offset by the more sandy terrain. A GPS, or at least a compass, is very useful to return to your car from the Jacob Hamblin Arch to either trailhead.

The Hurricane Wash trailhead is located about 33 miles down Hole-in-the-Rock Road, right by the road.

The Redwell trailhead is located at the end of a 1½-mile spur road (BLM 254), normally in good condition. The turnoff is marked at about 30 miles down Hole-in-the-Rock Road.

*Time required:* 8 hours or more for the dayhike loop from Fortymile Ridge trailhead via Crack-in-the-Wall and the Jacob Hamblin Arch exit. A two to three-day backpacking trip allows a longer and more leisurely discovery as far as Redwell or Hurricane Wash and is photographically more rewarding.

*Nearby location:* You can also pay a visit to the tall spire of Chimney Rock, standing out defiantly to the north in the middle of the arid bench–a monkey wrench in the erosion process. As Chimney Rock stands out unobstructed, it is easily photographed during either the morning or evening golden hour. The marked Chimney Rock access road (BLM 255) is located on the east side of Hole-in-the-Rock Road shortly past Mile 32. Inquire about its condition at the Escalante Visitor Center, where you'll most likely be warned that this 3-mile road is the sandiest in the area, with only sporadic maintenance. I have personally experienced no difficulty in reaching Chimney Rock in a high-clearance 4WD SUV with lowered tire pressure, but this is definitely not the place for a passenger car.

## Sunset Arch

Sunset Arch is a beautiful, if somewhat tortured, arch set on a backdrop of slickrock dunes with the whale-like bulk of Navajo Mountain on the horizon. Your initial reaction when seeing the arch is likely to be one of surprise: How can such an arch have formed here, in the middle of these vast sandy bench lands with only a few flat slickrock outcrops and lacking all the usual cliffs, canyons and creeks providing the normal geological context for its siblings? By contrast, Sunset Arch appears to have been deposited here almost artificially, or by some kind of accident of nature, for the sole benefit of photographers and amateur geologists.

In any case, it is easy to explain its success with photographers, thanks to its elegant slender span and compact bulk, sweeping surroundings and ideal orientation for catching the warm golden hour light. Only the long driving time and lack of a graded trail stand between its current isolation and an onslaught of visitors. Let's hope it stays that way, as it would spoil much of the charm of this very special arch.

A short distance to the south of the arch lies another arch, referred to by some as Sunrise Arch. This arch is flatter, more closely wedged into the slickrock bed and less photogenic.

*Photo advice:* As its name implies, Sunset Arch is at its best right before sunset; from October to April, however, you should arrive at least ½ hour before sunset or you'll miss the show, as the sun effectively disappears behind the Straight Cliffs when it's still a little bit high. In contrast to its rather dull appearance during the day, the arch takes on a beautiful brownish-orange color in late afternoon. The late afternoon sidelight also exposes a great deal of detail in the arch and its slickrock base. Set up your tripod in the northeast corner of the sandstone platform and frame Sunset Arch with Navajo Mountain under its span. A 28mm or 24 mm works best for this.

At sunrise, you can also shoot a tightly framed shot of the pink light illuminating the underside of the arch and the Straight Cliffs.

*Sunset Arch*

*Getting there:* Follow Hole-in-the-Rock Road for about 36 miles and turn left on Fortymile Ridge Road (BLM 270). Follow this track for about 4.3 miles and stop at the car park near the water tank. From about Mile 3 on, one can distinguish the faint, isolated silhouette of Sunset Arch, about a mile to the southeast. Look close to the horizon or you will miss it as it is impossible to make out the aperture beneath its span. If you manage to spot the arch, you can park at a pullout exactly 3½ miles from the beginning of the track (37°23'11" 111°03'37") and walk south-southeast.

At the water tank car park, get your bearings before starting the 1-mile cross-country hike traversing the sandy plateau due south. This is the easiest access with the least amount of gullies to cross. Count on ½-hour to reach the arch. Be sure not to drift eastward toward a group of rocks that could pass for the arch, nor to leave the arch behind you if you're not paying close attention. Sunset Arch is located on the upper part of the slickrock area (37°22'33" 111°02'55"). You'll find a compass or GPS very useful to return to your car, especially after sunset.

*Time required:* About 2 hours round-trip from the car park, with time for photography and a brief side trip to the smaller arch close by. Sunset Arch fits well at the end of a full-day outing on Hole-in-the-Rock Road that would also include a visit to Devil's Garden and the Dry Fork slot canyons or Broken Bow Arch.

*Nearby location:* Before proceeding to Sunset Arch, take a quick side trip to Dance Hall Rock by continuing on Hole-in-the-Rock Road for about 3/4 mile past the Fortymile Ridge Road junction and turning east onto the short spur road leading to this historic site. The beautiful natural amphitheater served as an R&R spot for Mormon settlers during their first 1879 expedition to establish a Colorado River crossing. Walking about this impressive outcrop set in the middle of nowhere, one can easily imagine on its walls the long shadows of Mormon pioneers dancing at night around wood fires to the sound of fiddles.

## Broken Bow Arch

The hike down Willow Gulch to Broken Bow Arch passes through some beautiful and varied scenery typical of the wet canyons in the Escalante drainage. This easy but rewarding hike has it all: Lots of slickrock, a perennial stream flowing through a scenic canyon, beautiful vegetation and a chance to see some wildlife. The highlight of the hike, however, is the massive Broken Bow Arch, so named by Escalante schoolteacher Edison Alvey in 1930 when he found a broken Indian bow beneath it.

The 4-mile round-trip hike begins on a well-worn path behind the trail register at Sooner Bench. As you descend, look for a formation shaped like a graduation cap. Upon reaching the wash, head down canyon. The first set of narrows are bypassed by staying high, on the right side of the canyon. The wash quickly broadens but soon constricts into passable narrows. Shortly, a side canyon crosses your path; consider saving its exploration for the return trip if time permits and continue straight ahead in the main wash.

The second canyon encountered is Willow Gulch. As you approach the confluence, you'll notice that the scenery begins to change. Willows and cottonwood appear as the water starts to flow. Take your bearings at this junction for the return trip, bear to the left and follow Willow Gulch down the canyon; it soon

*Broken Bow Arch*

widens into a lovely area for camping or picnicking on the large benches, particularly on the left side of the stream. As you proceed down canyon you may either follow the streambed or the well-worn bypass trails which crisscross it. After a few more twists and turns and a prominent bend in the canyon, Broken Bow Arch comes into view. Caution: there are occasional patches of quicksand along the water's edge about halfway to the arch.

*Photo advice:* Depending on the time of day and on the light, climb the hills to the east or west of the arch to get the right angle. Distant shots yield the best results as tightly framed shots fail to represent the scale of the arch in its environment. While the arch is the main attraction, the willow, cottonwood and beautifully streaked canyon walls along the way also make good subject matter.

*Getting there:* To reach the Willow Gulch trailhead, follow Hole-in-the-Rock road about 42 miles from SB 12. About 1 mile past Sooner Wash, in the flat area of Sooner Bench, BLM 276 goes diagonally to the left, leading to the parking area in 1.4 miles. This dirt road could be difficult for a passenger car.

*Time required:* From the car park, plan on at about 3 hours; more if exploring side canyons and photographing extensively. Including the round-trip to Escalante, you'll need a full day if you want to combine this hike with a visit to Devil's Garden and Sunset Arch.

## Hole-in-the-Rock

Hole-in-the-Rock—which lends its name to the road we've followed in the course of this chapter—was constructed by Mormon pioneers intent on crossing the Colorado River to establish a settlement near Bluff. You have to see this place for yourself to comprehend the incredible engineering feat it was to blast and cut through the rock flanks to reach the Colorado River. Although the place of the crossing is covered by the waters of Lake Powell, most of the trail leading to the ford is still very much like it was.

The descent to the lake shore is not particularly rewarding from a photographic standpoint, but it is a moderate scramble taking about 1 hour round-trip and is well worth doing, considering the historic value and fun factor. As you descend the steep path, you'll wonder how the pioneers managed to lower 80 wagons down and across the Colorado River through this narrow gully. The elevation loss is about 600 to 800 feet depending on the lake's level at the time you read this. The vast majority of people doing this hike are actually boaters coming up from the lake.

The last 5 miles of Hole-in-the-Rock Road are very difficult and definitely beyond the capabilities of low-clearance 4WD SUVs. There is no danger per se, but you may do some damage to your vehicle if you don't have enough ground clearance. Do not rely on older literature describing the end of the road; there has been much damage done to it in recent years and it is mostly maintained by

*Lake Powell from the Hole-in-the-Rock trail*

users. It is now rated 5 with several short but difficult sections and slickrock steps. 4WD SUV drivers should have some prior experience and a partner to spot them.

***Photo advice:*** There are two good spots; my preferred one is on a flat ledge located on the left side of the gully, a couple of minutes down from the top. This ledge is hard to miss; it is wide at first but ends up being just a few feet wide with a sheer drop, so be very careful.

Another good spot is from the rim on the left side of the car park. Just walk up the rim for about 5 to 10 minutes until you find a suitable location.

Of course, if you've never been close to the lake except at a marina, this is your chance to take a swim in the lake and/or snap a few shots. With the lake receding as of this writing, a few trees have started showing up near the shore, making for interesting pictures.

*Time required:* To visit Hole-in-the-Rock is not exactly an easy matter. The one-way trip entails about 55 miles of unpaved road from SB 12 and the last 5 miles are 4WD-only. It takes 2 to 2½ hours to reach the very end of the road, where Hole-in-the-Rock is located, depending on current conditions. Count on 1½ hour here with time for photography and to descend to the lake.

*Nearby location:* Llewellyn Gulch is a spectacular narrow canyon with very good color, leading directly to Lake Powell. It is mainly visited by boaters from Lake Powell but can also be visited from Hole-in-the-Rock Road. In recent years, with the lake level receding drastically, Llewellyn Gulch has seen less traffic due to the increased distance for both hikers wanting to reach the lake and boaters wanting to explore the narrows.

Park ½ mile beyond the cattle guard past Mile 50, just before the road starts deteriorating badly—the first indication that it is 4WD territory from here on. A relatively easy 2-mile cross-country jaunt southeast over rolling domes of red sandstone leads you to the edge of Llewellyn Gulch. ✿

*Wintertime along the Fremont River*

Chapter 8

# CAPITOL REEF

*The Castle at dawn*

## CAPITOL REEF

This extraordinary park is often overlooked by visitors to the Southwest and isn't heavily frequented outside of summer and holidays. This may be due to its geographic location, which makes it less accessible than its better-known neighbors of Bryce and Arches; the fact that there are no well-known icons that would-be visitors can readily identify may also be a factor.

This trend is gradually being reversed due in part to the added presence of Grand Staircase-Escalante Nat'l Monument to the south and a surge of new motels built just outside the park, in Torrey and Hanksville.

Nevertheless, Capitol Reef is one of the jewels of Utah, thanks to its unmatched geological variety, fantastic scenery, surprisingly rich vegetation and lack of crowds. But be forewarned! This park only reveals a small part of itself to the casual visitor. Sure, you can cross it in the course of a few hours, including a short incursion on the famous Scenic Drive, but there is plenty more great scenery awaiting off the beaten track. Plan on at least two days in the park because you need to hike its many trails and explore remote areas with a 4WD vehicle to fully appreciate it.

One of the principal attractions of Capitol Reef is the great geological diversity of its landscape and sedimentary layers. This translates into an extraordinary palette of hues and textures, great for visitor and photographer alike: Cliffs, ridges, domes, canyons, monoliths, badlands come in a huge diversity of colors, which become even more striking during the golden hour. You can better appreciate this exceptional relief with a bit of knowledge of the paleo-environment of

Capitol Reef and the forces of erosion which are constantly at work exposing them. Free brochures are available for travelers at the Visitor Center. Don't miss this opportunity as Capitol Reef, more than any other park, gives you tremendous insight into the geologic history of the Colorado Plateau—the essential ingredient behind these landscapes that we so much admire today.

Torrey, a small town at the west entrance of the park, makes a perfect base for your explorations. Over the course of the last few years, Torrey has seen a great deal of expansion: Where in the 1980's there wasn't a single motel, now there are almost a dozen vying for your business. The beautiful oasis of Fruita, inside the park, is especially nice if you are car camping or want to pitch a tent. During autumn and springtime, it is one of the most pleasant campgrounds anywhere.

## Panorama Point

Coming from Torrey on UT 24, you discover a superlative road, bordered to the north by impressive cliffs that become even more spectacular during the golden hour, mornings and evenings. Among the formations at the base of the cliffs are Chimney Rock and the Castle. Chimney Rock isn't really awesome in itself, but it photographs nicely in the afternoon from the parking area, when the dark red Moenkopi formation capped by the white Shinarump sandstone really stands out. As for the Castle, it offers a remarkable collection of sedimentary layers that can be enjoyed right by the side of the road.

One of the best spots to photograph this area is Panorama Point, located almost 4 miles past the west entrance of the park and 2½ miles before the Visitor Center. From this promontory, you get a splendid panoramic view of the western part of the park with Capitol Dome, the Castle and the Henry Mountains in the distance. A sign claims that this spot is the least polluted in the United States and that, on a clear day, you can see over 130 miles! Even though the validity of this claim is questionable in this day and age, you'll certainly rejoice in the fact that you can see at least 60 miles on most days.

In the morning, Panorama Point affords an excellent view to the west in the direction of Torrey. Toward the east, a 100 to 200mm telephoto lens works great for capturing Capitol Dome and the Henry Mountains in the afternoon.

Continuing almost another mile on the dirt road south of Panorama Point, you can take

*The Henry Mountains from Panorama Point*

the short 1-mile round-trip foot trail to aptly named Sunset Point, which offers a fantastic view in late afternoon. You can use either a normal lens to photograph the various geological strata of the reef or a medium telephoto to capture the shadows of the formations on the red cliffs. From the same parking area, a very short trail leads to the Goosenecks of Sulphur Creek, a promontory above a deep canyon that is unfortunately difficult to photograph because of the shadows, although mornings are better. Nothing particularly awe-inspiring or to compare with the "big guys" (Dead Horse Point, Horseshoe Bend, and Goosenecks State Park), but it's interesting to note that these goosenecks are cut through the same layer of sedimentary rock as that of the White Rim of Island in the Sky fame, a formation rarely seen in that section of the plateau.

## Fruita Oasis

In all seasons, Fruita is an oasis where it's nice to relax between two rocky landscapes. This old Mormon colony is located on the banks of the Fremont River and has abundant vegetation, contrasting heavily with the surrounding desert. Near the Visitor Center, a cabin containing pioneer-era artifacts is visible from the road and warrants a brief stop.

*Fruita Oasis (photo by Philippe Schuler)*

The historic orchards are opened from June through October for public harvesting. Inside the designated orchards, you can eat as much as you want; however, you pay for the fruits you take outside. The vast grassy area adjoining the pleasant picnic grounds with its peaches, wisteria and jacarandas allows you to get some great shots when they're in flower (March and April). The cottonwoods bordering the Fremont around Fruita are magnificent in spring and fall.

Sulphur Creek, which empties into the Fremont River at Fruita, is a lovely walk. Just behind the Visitor Center, a short footpath quickly brings you to a shallow crossing and a series of lovely pools.

The Fremont Gorge Overlook trailhead is located near the Blacksmith Shop. This little-known walk provides a great view of the Castle from atop a high mesa. A mid-range telephoto is perfect to frame the castle and surroundings. After a mile or so, the Castle really opens up and, at about 1½ mile, you'll get an optimum view in mid-morning or mid-afternoon.

*Opposite page: Scenic Drive near Grand Wash*

Just before the campground's main entrance (almost across Gifford House) look for a sign indicating the Cohab Canyon trailhead. After a 0.3-mile ascent on steep switchbacks, you'll come to the entrance of this small hidden canyon with colorful Wingate sandstone walls peppered with photogenic "Swiss cheese". After about ½ mile on flat ground from the canyon's entrance, you'll come to a sign pointing to a spur trail going up to your left; a short walk on this trail leads to two nice overlooks: The North Overlook towers above the Fremont River while the South Overlook offers a photogenic view of Fruita. The round-trip to the overlooks takes about 2 hours from the trailhead. Time permitting, you can continue inside Cohab Canyon, ending up on UT 24 near the Hickman Bridge trailhead. With a car shuttle, you can also take the longer Frying Pan trail, leading south to join the Cassidy Arch trail and ending up in Grand Wash.

## The Scenic Drive

The Scenic Drive, which begins after passing the Fruita campground, offers some spectacular views of geological features such as Grand Wash, Fern's Nipple, the Slickrock Divide and the Egyptian Temple—all this along a 7-mile long paved road. Get yourself one of the mini-guides to the Scenic Drive at the Visitor Center and stop at the various landmarks, following the interesting explanations on the sedimentary origins of the park.

After making sure that no flash flood danger is in the forecast, continue your drive on a good dirt road winding down about 2 miles between the tall cliffs of beautiful Capitol Gorge. This short but spectacular road is passable to any passenger car in good weather. Where the road dead-ends, a 2-mile round-trip foot trail leads toward the end of the canyon, passing by the Pioneer Register and the Waterpocket Tanks (the latter are more interesting when water is present). The 4-mile round-trip hike to the Golden Throne is more strenuous but you'll have good views all along and if you time your arrival at the foot of the Golden Throne toward the end of the afternoon or sunset, you'll really understand how it got its name.

The entire Scenic Road is especially photogenic while driving back from Capitol Gorge in late afternoon. That's when you get the best light on the sensuous, multicolored sandstone walls and layers of Capitol Ridge. Less than a mile past the spur to Grand

*Early morning on the Scenic Drive*

Wash, locate the last little hill before the road starts its descent toward Fruita, park on the right and enjoy one of the most photogenic views in the park. You'll be looking at badlands topped by pillars and cliffs to the right, with the narrow road winding down spectacularly toward the oasis and the Castle in the background. You can use a wide range of lenses to capture either grand scenics or small details of this beautiful landscape.

## Hickman Bridge & the Navajo Knobs

Following UT 24 from the Visitor Center in the direction of Hanksville, the Fremont presents a festival of colors with a number of orchards. The countless tamarisk trees lining the riverbed are particularly photogenic in autumn.

Shortly before reaching the Hickman Bridge trailhead, stop at the Fremont petroglyphs pullout, as well as at the very moving Mormon schoolhouse. The Park Service has constructed a boardwalk that makes it easier to observe and photograph the ancient Fremont glyphs—which are unfortunately badly weather-damaged.

The self-guided nature trail to Hickman Bridge is a short and easy 2½ miles round-trip. The bridge is somewhat ensconced below a ridge and you'll need a 28mm or wider lens to photograph it, framing a part of the canyon below. Press on toward the Rim Overlook Trail, branching from the previous trail after a few hundreds yards from the trailhead, for a series of interesting sights. Soon after the branching sign, the unique shape of Pectol's Pyramid comes into view across the Fremont River. About 0.6 mile from the sign, just past a small reddish butte, look to your left for an outcrop of light-colored sandstone with photogenic black lava boulders. These boulders make an excellent foreground to photograph Pectol's Pyramid from the best perspective. A 28mm or wider lens will yield the best results, but you can also use a short telephoto to concentrate on the Pyramid. The Pyramid can be photographed in the early morning; however, only its left face will be well lit. Mid-to-late afternoon offers better light. A few hundreds yards further up on the trail, you'll be able to catch excellent views of Navajo Dome to the right with a standard lens to short telephoto.

At 2½ miles from the car park, the Rim Overlook provides a nice bird's eye view of Fruita and the Fremont

*Pectol's Pyramid (photo by Philippe Schuler)*

*Navajo Dome*

Valley. Continuing toward the Navajo Knobs for another 2.2 miles until the top of a knob, you'll be rewarded with an awesome 360° vista of the valley and surrounding canyons. Unfortunately, unless you have exceptionally beautiful clouds, this panoramic view is too expansive to yield a compelling picture.

If you've done this strenuous hike in summer, without shade, you may want to stop for a dip in the deep pool located below a small waterfall on the left side of the road, about 4 miles further east on UT 24 past Behunin Cabin. Watch for the strong undertow and, of course, don't venture in the pool in bad weather or during a thunderstorm! A picture of this waterfall was used in the Introduction chapter to illustrate the tremendous power of flash floods in the Southwest.

## Introduction to Cathedral Valley

Cathedral Valley with its huge monoliths and panoramic vistas is, in my view, one of the most remarkable spots on the planet. An incomparable majesty emanates from the place. Its remoteness and the rare presence of other members of our species make you feel deeply privileged to find yourself in such an untrammeled natural sanctuary. This feeling is even more prevalent if you get a chance to camp at the remote campground in Upper Cathedral Valley. From there you can have the whole valley to yourself during the golden hour. Note that dispersed low-impact backcountry camping is permitted on BLM land just outside the park for even more solitude—although I am yet to encounter another visitor at the remote campground in many trips to this valley.

Happily or unhappily, it is not easy to visit and many visitors to the park abstain from venturing there. Few people choose to drive the 57-mile Cathedral Valley Loop crossing many distinctive parts of the valley; the drive requires a minimum of six hours to be thoroughly enjoyed. The Cathedral Valley road is a perfect example of a "feasible" road that's nevertheless risky because of its fragility and isolation. The road is only feasible if you have a high-clearance vehicle. It is not advised to drive the whole road in a regular car—even less so in a camper. Road conditions can vary a lot, depending on whether you are traveling before or after a rain or whether the bulldozer resurfaced the road, usually once a year.

Never set out until you have first inquired of the rangers or one of the local residents as to the condition of the road. The rangers will systematically discourage visitors from adventuring down this and other Cathedral Valley roads in ordinary cars and they do this with good reason: Each year visitors get stuck in the mud or a rut that suddenly appeared from nowhere. As a general rule, a 4x4 tow-truck costs $150 an hour from the time it leaves the garage. The cost of the operation can easily reach more than $1,500 to bail you out.

Always check the weather forecast, as some clay-based parts of the road can be impassable to any vehicle when wet. Fill up your fuel tank; take a lot of water and some food, just in case. Don't forget to buy the cheap, but excellent booklet entitled *Self-guided auto-tour of Cathedral Valley* at the Visitor Center in Fruita. When used in combination with the park map, it is sufficient to do the main loop road. As the mileage of each stop and intersection is precisely recorded, you should encounter no surprises if you stay on the road and check your odometer regularly. However, if you want to drive other roads branching from the main loop road, you'll definitely need to get a topographic map before setting out. This is true of all the roads described below, outside of the main loop road. All these roads include many branching secondary roads that don't show on the large-scale maps and it's easy to set off down the wrong path. Please take this suggestion seriously, as you'll often find yourself consulting the topo map. You can get one of these at the Visitor Center.

Once all these precautions are taken, you can start the loop from the River Ford, located a dozen miles east of the Visitor Center on UT 24. The reason I suggest starting from River Ford is that it's better to cross the ford at the beginning of the loop rather than having to backtrack if, for some reason, you find out that you can't make it or the gate is locked.

If there is no risk of rain later in the day, you could also start before dawn from

*Upper Cathedral Valley monoliths*

Caineville, about 18 miles east of the Visitor Center on UT 24. This allows you to reach Lower Cathedral Valley at sunrise and continue up the valley with the sun behind you. Coming from Torrey, you can stop at the ford first to check it and make sure that you'll be able to cross it later, before beginning the loop counterclockwise at Caineville.

Instead of doing the whole classic loop, it's also possible to reach several parts of the valley from various side roads. Not only will you be able to discover different landscapes, but by combining different approaches, you'll see and photograph the most interesting spots during the golden hour—assuming you can devote a couple of days to the area.

For clarity's sake, the valley's main attractions and their respective access are described separately below.

## The South Desert and the Bentonite Hills

The road overhanging the South Desert and the Bentonite Hills, called the Hartnet Road, begins at River Ford and follows a dry riverbed between the extreme northern end of the Waterpocket Fold and the depression of Cathedral Valley. The Bentonite Hills, about 9 miles from River Ford, are remarkable for their rounded forms and strange checkerboard appearance colored by the Morrison formation. Under the right light, all the colors of the rainbow can be seen. Several exceptional viewpoints are accessible from the road as you follow it to the northwest from River Ford.

*The Bentonite Hills*

At 14 miles from River Ford, a side road leads to the Lower South Desert Overlook. The South Desert is a large valley running parallel to the Waterpocket Fold. The viewpoint yields a splendid view of Jailhouse Rock, with Temple Rock and the Fishlake Mountains in the background.

About 3 miles from the intersection with Lower South Desert Overlook, a 1-mile trail leads eastward cross-country to a saddle with a good view of the great monoliths of Lower Cathedral Valley: Temple of the Sun and Temple of the Moon. If you think this view is beautiful, wait until you're in the valley proper.

About 10 miles further along the road, a short spur road leads to the Upper South Desert Overlook. This overlook is very impressive and gives a good idea of the depth of the South Desert depression if you include a bit of the plateau in the foreground. From the edge of the knoll, those suffering from fear of heights could get weak in the knees.

During the next mile or so, you'll successively encounter spur roads leading to Upper Cathedral Valley Overlook, Hartnet Junction with Polk Creek Road (aka Thousand Lakes Mountain Rd.)—allowing access to UT 72 over Thousand Lakes Mountain—and the Cathedral Valley remote campground. The campground is located just before the switchbacks leading down into Upper Cathedral Valley (all these individual stops are covered in the next section).

*Getting there:* Take the Hartnet road from the so-called River Ford, located 11.7 miles from the Visitor Center on UT 24. The biggest problem will be the Fremont River crossing just ¾ mile past the beginning of the road. You ford the river on a rocky bed, which is usually not too deep, but watch out for potential engine flooding in a low clearance car. The ford is passable most of the time; however, the gate is locked during spring runoff and after rains when even a 4WD can get stuck. Check at the Visitor Center where rangers will let you know if it's passable or not. Beyond River Ford, the track is sometimes passable in a passenger car if you pay close attention and drive slowly depending on whether the bulldozer has been through recently.

*Time required:* 2 to 3 hours to Upper Cathedral Valley.

## Upper Cathedral Valley

Located at the far north end of both the park and the Middle Desert, Upper Cathedral Valley is one of the highlights of Utah. The majesty that emanates from the powerful monoliths and the encircling mountains is reinforced by the isolation and the effort it takes to get here.

If you came from the River Ford via the Hartnet Road, as described in the previous section, you'll catch your first glimpse of Upper Cathedral Valley from the spectacular Upper Cathedral Valley Overlook. The latter is located at the end of a short spur road to the right, past the Upper South Desert Overlook. From the edge of the plateau you can admire the entire Upper Cathedral Valley in all its splendor and capture excellent shots in the second part of the afternoon.

Soon after that, you'll reach the junction with Thousand Lakes Road, coming down from the mountain in front of you. Bear right and ½ mile later you'll come to the primitive Cathedral campground,

*The uppermost giant monolith at Cathedral Valley*

with its six campsites. If you've come equipped, spending the night here will allow you to catch some fabulous evening shots of the extraordinary Entrada sandstone walls as they turn bright red against a background of dark gray sky. Canyon country at its very best!

From here, descend the switchbacks to enter the valley. Less than 2 miles past the campground, you'll come to a sign saying "Viewpoint" on the north side of the road. There, you'll find a narrow footpath leading up to a low plateau with a spectacular close-up view of the two main groups of 500 feet high monoliths and the Walls of Jericho in the background. This easy hike is 2-mile long, round-trip, and offers different angles for photographing the monoliths, which are best lit in the second part of the afternoon.

*Upper Cathedral Valley*

Three miles farther, heading north-east, you'll come to the Cathedral Valley junction. Immediately to your right, you'll see a sign pointing to the Gypsum Sinkhole—a gigantic, sunken artesian well almost 200 feet deep and over 50 feet in diameter. It is well worth the mile-long detour on a good spur road, although it's practically impossible to photograph because of its size.

Next, following Caineville Wash Road on the way to Lower Cathedral Valley *(see below)* you'll be crossing the Middle Desert with its many different geological features.

*Getting there:* There are four possible ways to reach Upper Cathedral Valley. The easiest way for passenger cars and small-size campers to get to this distant spot, in good weather conditions, is from the north, by way of a dirt road leaving from I-70, less than 2 miles east of Exit 91 or west of Exit 86. This wide dirt road, called Baker Ranch Road, is 26 miles long and crosses the forebodingly-named Last Chance Desert. It is usually well maintained for the use of local miners and ranchers, and doesn't present any major difficulties. The main obstacle is crossing Willow Springs Wash, about a dozen miles down the road. After crossing the usually dry ford, the road quickly rolls along and you rapidly reach Cathedral Valley Junction, close to Gypsum Sinkhole. It's also possible to reach Cathedral Valley Junction by following the Caineville Wash Road from UT 24 *(see below)*. The other access point to Upper Cathedral Valley is the previously described Hartnet Road from River Ford near UT 24. Perhaps the most scenic access is by way of Thousand Lakes Mountain Road (aka Polk Creek Road) coming west from UT 72. About 12 miles north of Loa on UT 72, take the dirt road to the right for almost 5 miles in the general direction of Elkhorn Campground. This road is usually in excellent condition until you reach a high altitude pass (at about 10,000 feet) in the Fishlake National Forest. At the fork in the road, do not take the Elkhorn Campground spur to the right; instead, continue straight ahead for about 7 miles, following the signpost indicating Cathedral Valley. Here the descent becomes quite tricky and it is out of the question to take an ordinary passenger car over this portion of the road. Only a high-clearance vehicle can make it, preferably 4WD during winter or spring runoff. This route is especially remarkable as it makes a spectacular transition between two radically different ecosystems, one a high-altitude alpine environment and the other the exceptional desert of Cathedral Valley. There are exceptional photographic opportunities, especially in autumn, when you'll pass through strands of yellow aspen mingling with green conifers before reaching the ocher color of the desert. These mountains are the habitat of a great variety of wild animals—in the course of one trip, I counted almost a hundred mule deer coming down the side of the mountain in great leaps and bounds.

*Time required:* You can reach Cathedral Valley Junction in approximately 1 hour from the I-70 off-ramp, provided you don't stray off the path. A topo map will help you sort out the many side roads. You should also be able to reach Hartnet Junction from UT 72 in about 1 hour. Count on 2 to 3 hours for the other routes. Getting there is one thing, but it's a shame if you can't devote at least a couple of hours to exploring this exceptional spot.

## Lower Cathedral Valley

Lower Cathedral Valley is better known by the name of the two fantastic monoliths that it harbors. The Temple of the Sun and the Temple of the Moon illustrate many coffee-table books and well-deserve their names. Reaching up 400 feet from the desert ground as if trying to grasp the heavens, these two solitary temples cut an imposing profile against a rich blue sky of unmatched purity. At sunrise, these "high priests" of the mineral universe don their incandescent garments for a brief, fleeting moment, to celebrate the miracle of nature.

Both monoliths can be photographed individually at close range or you can shoot them together from nearby Glass Mountain, using a short telephoto to collapse the perspective of the two Temples and the

*Temple of the Sun & Moon*

cliff behind them. The hoodoos at the foot of the cliff are also quite nice. Glass Mountain itself—a small mound consisting of selenite crystals—is an interesting geological curiosity, but doesn't make for an interesting photograph.

*Getting there:* To get to Lower Cathedral Valley and the famous Temples of the Sun and the Moon, it's best to come from the Caineville Wash road described below. It is the easiest and fastest way to get there for sunrise and, under good conditions, you can make it in a passenger car, although it's going to be a bit bumpy. Coming from I-70 via Cathedral Valley Junction, you'll pass numerous washes between the two valleys about a dozen miles apart and the state of the road can be extremely variable.

The Temples are located about 16 miles from the Caineville entrance on UT 24. A spur road about a mile long leads from the main loop road to the foot of the Temples and to Glass Mountain.

*Time required:* 3 hours round trip from Caineville; 2 hours one-way from either I-70 or UT 72.

## The Caineville Badlands

The Caineville Badlands are a vast isolated expanse of dark gray hills of Mancos shale striped with interesting colors. Traveling through the heart of these badlands on the Caineville Wash road, you'll encounter from time to time round blocks of basalt tossed out by the explosion of Boulder Mountain about 50 million years ago and then later deposited here by glacial action. These badlands are actually very deep, forming a bed of sedimentary rock between 2,000 to almost 3,000 feet thick. While contemplating this extreme desert universe, it's easy to imagine the Inland Sea that once covered this part of the valley.

You can also observe badlands directly from UT 24. There are a couple of spots on the north side of UT 24 near Caineville where you can actually drive on BLM land and get close to the badlands for further exploration. The badlands along UT 24 and Caineville Wash road are best photographed in late afternoon. East of Caineville, you'll notice the imposing presence of Factory Butte rising on the horizon like a tall ship to the northeast *(see San Rafael chapter).*

*Getting there:* You'll find the Caineville Wash road about 18 miles east of the Visitor Center on UT 24. A sign by the side of the road indicates the distance to Lower and Upper Cathedral Valley. This road will take you right into a fantastic universe of badlands in just 2 or 3 miles, passing the northern edge of the Bentonite Hills. If you want to continue on to Lower Cathedral Valley, this road can usually be negotiated with a passenger car by driving carefully, if the weather conditions are right, but it's a long drive (about 32 miles round-trip) and you'll be bounced and jolted the whole way.

*Time required:* Less than an hour for a quick excursion into the heart of the badlands; 3 hours round-trip for the drive alone if you continue on until Lower Cathedral Valley.

## The Waterpocket Fold

Located in the southern part of the park, this strange and spectacular geologic formation is unfortunately less spectacular when seen from the ground than in the superb aerial photograph that decorates the NPS brochure. But it still warrants a detour if you can afford the pretty full day that it will take to drive the 125-mile loop described below. Note that this tour—one third of it on dirt roads—encompasses the superb Burr Trail, described in the Along Scenic Byway 12 chapter.

*Badlands along the Notom-Bullfrog Road*

You can get to the Waterpocket Fold by way of the Notom-Bullfrog Road which starts off UT 24, 9 miles east of the Visitor Center. This road is paved along the first 6 miles and well maintained thereafter, so it's suitable to passenger cars in dry weather. However, there is a wash before Sandy Ranch that can present problems after a rain or if it's icy in winter; check with the Rangers.

You get a very good view of the Henry Mountains to the east and the strange nipples of Capitol Dome to the west from the top of the hill, just after you reach the unpaved part of the road. The Waterpocket Fold doesn't really become visible until after you pass the spur leading to the Cedar Mesa campground, about 22 miles from the junction with UT 24. Even there, this extraordinary geological phenomenon remains a bit disappointing when seen from the Notom-Bullfrog road, especially in comparison to aerial photos.

Instead you may want to concentrate on details in the landscape. This area contains amazingly colorful stripes of tuffa, lining up the badlands on the east side of the road. They are best photographed in early morning, when still in the shade, or in late afternoon. However, to really bring out the color, nothing beats an overcast or rainy day; just remember to eliminate the sky from your image.

*Waterpocket Fold badlands*

Less than a dozen miles further, you'll come to the well-marked junction leading west to the Burr Trail. As you reach the base of the fold, the dirt road climbs toward the Circle Cliffs in a series of steep and spectacular twists and turns carved in the flank of the hill. Unless the road has been weather-damaged, these switchbacks are usually passable in a passenger car in dry weather.

Shortly after the switchbacks, you'll encounter on your right the 4WD road leading to Strike Valley Overlook and Upper Muley Twist. These are the only points from which you can capture the true expanse of the Waterpocket fold. After another few miles, the Burr Trail becomes paved and leads to Boulder, where it joins UT 12. You can then drive north on UT 12 and west on UT 24 to complete the loop.

Instead of turning on the Burr Trail, you could continue on the Notom-Bullfrog Road all the way to the Bullfrog Marina, where you can cross Lake Powell by ferry to Hall's Crossing and either descend towards Monument Valley or climb back up towards Moab *(see Around Cedar Mesa chapter)*.

## Strike Valley Overlook & Upper Muley Twist

Strike Valley Overlook is a remarkable vista point, accessible via a short hike, from where you can photograph the wide expanse of the Waterpocket Fold. It is a must if you are entering or exiting Capitol Reef from the Burr Trail.

From the same trailhead, Upper Muley Twist offers a very rewarding, albeit strenuous, hike and yields more panoramic views of the Waterpocket Fold. The views are a little more open than at Strike Valley Overlook, especially to the north, but are also harder to photograph successfully.

*Getting there:* Via the Burr Trail from Boulder, or via the Notom Bullfrog Road (from UT 24 or from Bullfrog). The junction with the dirt road to Upper Muley Twist Canyon is about 1 mile west from the top of the Burr Trail switchbacks. You can drive the 3 miles to the trailhead only if you have a 4WD or high-clearance vehicle. After the first ½ mile, the road becomes very rough, but it is quite scenic and not dangerous. It's actually a good place to hone your boulder straddling skills if you are not an experienced four-wheeler. Do not attempt this road with a low clearance vehicle. You would become high-centered or would damage your undercarriage. Following the road on foot makes for a very pleasant hike, although you would not want to do this hike in summer.

Strike Valley Overlook is about ½ mile east from the trailhead parking and offers a fantastic panoramic view of the Waterpocket Fold. At the edge of the rim, follow it to your right to the very end of the cairns for the best photographic location; you'll find a rock outcrop that makes a good foreground to add depth to this otherwise huge panorama. Use your wide angle in moderation, otherwise you'll end up with an image that doesn't carry enough visual impact. A 35mm will work well, allowing you to include enough of the valley while emphasizing the gentle curve made by the Waterpocket Fold to the south.

If you prefer to explore Upper Muley Twist, just follow the wash at the trailhead until you reach Saddle Arch on your left, at a little under two miles. This arch is not easy to spot at first, but it is almost opposite the small sign to the right of the wash indicating the Rim Trail. It is a very rough climb up the Rim Trail; you'll reach the top in less than 30 minutes and the rim of the plateau in another 10 minutes on flat ground. From there, the trail follows the rim north for another two

*The Waterpocket Fold from Strike Valley Overlook*

miles, offering spectacular views of the Waterpocket Fold.

You can either retrace your steps or do the full loop coming back through the Upper Muley Twist Narrows, which are not particularly spectacular. Upper Muley Twist gets awfully hot in summer; take plenty of water if you want to do the full loop. You'll need minor route finding skills, following widely spaced cairns; some easy scrambling over slickrock is also required.

*Time required:* For Strike Valley Overlook, about 2 hours from the junction with the Burr Trail if you reach the trailhead by car; a half day if you reach it by foot; a full day for the Upper Muley Twist loop.

## Halls Creek

Halls Creek Overlook is one of the least visited viewpoints in Capitol Reef as it is a very long way from the Visitor Center and town amenities, requiring a high-clearance vehicle. It does, however, offer an outstanding view of the lower west side of the Waterpocket Fold as well as the back of the Circle Cliffs and it is well worth the detour if you are traveling on the Notom-Bullfrog Road.

From Halls Creek Overlook, the view of the Waterpocket Fold to the north is very expansive and well lit from early to mid-morning. Looking straight across the valley, you can distinguish the outline of Brimhall Bridge, with its double span tucked inside an imposing canyon carved out deep inside the cliff.

The overlook serves as a trailhead for Brimhall Bridge, as well as for a hike to Hamburger Rocks to the north and for the long trek to the Halls Creek Narrows far to the south. For these three hikes, you'll first need to descend 800 feet on a steep trail leading in 1.2 miles to the bottom of Halls Creek. Going up during the return trip can be strenuous on a hot summer day.

*Hall's Creek from the Overlook*

Once in the valley, you'll find the entrance to Brimhall Canyon about 0.2 mile south across the stream. Don't be fooled by the easy hike inside the initial part of the canyon. Although Brimhall Bridge is less than a mile from this point, it is quite an adventure which should not be undertaken alone. Soon after climbing the slippery slope of a dryfall, you reach a 100 feet long narrow passage, usually filled with dark water, which you must wade deep or even swim. Exiting at the end of this pool requires a hard scramble on large boulders—difficult to do when you're wet. You must then climb a steep slope on loose rocks to reach a ridge, where you gain your first close view of Brimhall Bridge. For the best angle, follow the ridge to the south and, with caution, find your way down to the creek. I don't recommend Brimhall Bridge as a photographic location, unless you are specifically prepared or sure that the narrows are dry; otherwise, you may not even be able to carry your camera across and out of the deep pool and it may not be worth the effort.

From the bottom of Halls Creek, you can also choose to hike north in the main wash to the photogenic Hamburger Rocks, a small group of dark red dwarf hoodoos with oval shapes, set on a bed of light-colored sandstone. You can sight them west of Halls Creek after about 2 miles. Continue walking until you're below them and climb up a short distance to reach them. The hoodoos are just south of the Muley Tanks on your topo map.

Continuing 7½ miles south along the wash from the foot of the switchbacks below Halls Creek Overlook is the only way to reach the serpentine 3-mile long Halls Creek Narrows, with their tall colored walls and perennial water flow. This 22-mile round-trip cross-country trek is usually done as a 3-day backpack.

*Getting there:* From the partly paved/partly graded Notom-Bullfrog Road, about 44 miles south of UT 24 or 23 miles northwest of the Bullfrog Marina, take the signed track heading southwest to Halls Creek Overlook. Follow it for about 3 miles until the spur to the overlook. This track is very rocky in places and requires high clearance; although not technical, it is not suitable for passenger cars due to sharp rocks that could easily puncture a tire. ❧

*Goblin Generals*

Chapter 9

THE SAN RAFAEL SWELL

*The beautiful Buckhorn Wash pictographs*

# THE SAN RAFAEL SWELL

The San Rafael Swell is one of the last great wilderness areas of the Southwest without National Park or Monument status. Although this area has been under consideration for more robust federal protection at various times in the past, it is unlikely that the current status quo will change. If this were to happen, it would undoubtedly attract a much larger number of visitors. For now, few people are aware of its expansive panoramas, monoclines, buttes, deep canyons, and rock art and even fewer are venturing on its confusing network of dirt roads. And indeed many people representing a wide spectrum of interests and political sensibilities would rather keep it this way.

The most prominent feature of the Swell is the San Rafael Reef, an imposing circular plateau located west of the Green River on either side of Interstate 70. The Reef takes its name from its shape, that of a serrated reef dominating this wild desert region. This reef consists of several sedimentary layers pushed almost vertically into position by the shifting of tectonic plates. It is truly a majestic sight, although it only reveals its true magnitude from the cockpit of a small aircraft.

In the course of this chapter, we will discover a number of remarkable natural landmarks and rock art sites, starting out from the town of Hanksville and heading north to explore the area around I-70 between Green River, Fremont Junction and Price.

# Factory Butte

I have to admit that I am particularly fond of Factory Butte, despite the fact that it generally elicits a big yawn from other photographers. I don't exactly know why I'm so fond of it, but I suppose it's simply because of its awesome shape and sheer volume—a cross between a gigantic nuclear power plant and the Titanic. Every time I drive along the Fremont River, on my way in or out of Capitol Reef, I feel a pinch of excitement when the majestic butte comes into view. It took me several tries to capture a satisfactory photograph of Factory Butte, however. Once, for lack of adequate scouting and preparation, I missed the sunrise by a few minutes despite getting up at the crack of dawn. Finally, I decided on a more systematic approach. I scouted various locations in the evening, alongside Muddy Creek road, photographing until nighttime before returning to Hanksville. The next morning, I made sure I arrived at the chosen location with a few minutes to spare; I firmly planted my tripod, waited and was finally rewarded with a fantastic sunrise shot—the warm light illuminating the Martian foreground and bringing up extraordinary shadows on the lovely badlands at the base of the butte.

*Photo advice:* Excellent views of the butte start opening up on the eastern side at about 4 miles from UT 24 on Muddy Creek Road. Factory Butte is best photographed at sunrise from a spot less than 7 miles on Muddy Creek Road, just before the dirt track going toward the butte. There are also lovely badlands on the southern end of the butte that can also be photographed in late afternoon.

*Red Planet*

*Getting there:* Drive about 11 miles from Hanksville toward Capitol Reef on UT 24 and turn right on a dirt road leading toward the butte; an information panel located soon after the beginning of the dirt road will reassure you that you are on the right track. A word of warning: Do not try to cross Muddy creek as a shortcut to Goblin Valley, unless you have talked to a BLM ranger in Hanksville and confirmed the creek is passable. The creek often has quicksand and it is very easy to get stuck there. A tow from Hanksville will cost you at least $800 and your engine may become silted beyond repair.

## Goblin Valley State Park

In Goblin Valley, erosion has carved an extremely pliable variety of Entrada sandstone into extravagant shapes offering your astonished eyes a spectacle of goblins, ghosts and other fantastic creatures seemingly awaiting a magic wand to awaken them and start them walking as if in an animated motion picture. If you are on a family vacation, it's almost guaranteed that your imagination will be as stimulated as that of your children.

A formation called the Three Judges greets you on the left as you enter the park; it is worthy of a photo in late afternoon. But it's at the covered viewpoint at road's end that the most compelling sight awaits you—a vast army of goblins, camped in the depression below the parking area, mineral creatures looking like something out of a Tolkien story.

Start your visit by enjoying and photographing this panorama right from the observation point, as it is truly superb. In summer, you risk catching in your viewfinder lots of Lilliputian-sized humans photographing these ferocious goblins. This formerly little-known park now receives about 85,000 visitors a year. Out of season, you'll have it all to yourself.

Goblin Valley has two official foot trails: The mile-long Carmel Canyon loop with its landmark Three Judges formation and the 3-mile long Curtis Bench trail, offering a superb view of the Henry Mountains from its highest point.

However, the most rewarding walks, from a photographic standpoint, consist of descending into the depression from the covered viewpoint and walking among the goblins where you can let your imagination run wild.

*Goblin Valley from the main viewpoint*

*Photo advice:* Avoid visiting Goblin Valley when the sun is high in the sky as your pictures will have too much contrast and will look flat under a uniform sky. Ideally, early morning or evening is best, as the main view of the depression is oriented to the south. You can take excellent shots from the covered vista point using a variety of lenses. A telephoto will work well to compress the perspective and make the goblins very dense on your picture. Walking among the goblins, the formations located on the left side of the basin generally offer the best photographic opportunities. There is a particularly remarkable spot that you should photograph: Crossing the basin at 1 o'clock in the direction of the cliffs, look for a large copper green dome. It may look quite far from the observation point, but it's really only a short 10-minute walk. Climbing up, you'll find a passage leading behind a group of very high formations. You'll come out into a veritable fantasyland of spires and chimneys.

*A strange mushroom rock*

*Getting there:* The turnoff from UT 24 is located 24 miles south of I-70 and about 20 miles north of Hanksville, at milepost 137. Drive west for 5 miles then turn left toward the south and drive 6 miles to reach the entrance of the park. Herds of antelope are sometimes visible along the road.

*Time required:* At least 1½ hour if you want to photograph extensively and wander around among the goblins. A night walk can be a magical experience during the full moon.

*Nearby Location:* Mollys Castle is a fortress-like rise located 1½ miles east on a spur road leaving from the Park entrance. More remarkable are the lovely "detached mansions" located on both sides of UT 24, about 5 miles south of the turnoff. These beautiful groups of goblins and mushroom rocks are extremely photogenic in the morning or evening sun when coming from Hanksville.

## Little Wild Horse Slot Canyon

This highly rewarding hike, both very visual and tactile, lets you penetrate right into the heart of the San Rafael Reef. You're guaranteed to bring back some nice memories and shots from a trip inside Little Wild Horse Canyon. Access is easy and the walk through the slot canyon is not difficult. This explains why Little Wild Horse Canyon has become a classic hike and one of the most visited locations in San Rafael Reef, especially in season and during legal holidays.

*Exploring Little Wild Horse Canyon*

After parking your car, take the trail leading to the dry wash bed and follow it for a few hundred yards. As the riverbed narrows, about 10 minutes after leaving the trailhead, you'll come to a sort of dry waterfall about 8 feet high. The best way to get around this obstacle is to ascend the inclined plane on the left side, just a few yards before, and return to the wash just after the dry fall.

Continue about 200 yards past the dry fall and turn right at the easily missed fork into Little Wild Horse Canyon. The other fork leads to Bell Canyon.

A popular loop hike, not explored in this guide, is to follow Little Wild Horse Canyon for about 2 miles to its end, then follow a jeep trail west, then south, to the entrance of Bell Canyon. You can then descend this shorter slot canyon until it meets with Little Wild Horse. It takes about four hours to do this loop, but the best photographic opportunities are in Little Wild Horse Canyon, so we'll concentrate on a round-trip inside this canyon.

Little Wild Horse Canyon starts revealing its strange splendor a few hundred feet further on. It begins with a series of very interesting holes and niches carved out by water action on the walls. At a height of about 200 feet, the latter are tightly constricted in some places, no more than a couple of feet wide at shoulder height. In some places, you'll need to place both hands on the rock wall and perform a series of push-up motions so you can move forward inside the highly slanted, shallow corridor. But, generally speaking, the walk is never difficult. However, be careful you don't get stuck and twist an ankle when the fault contracts down to a few inches under your feet.

Follow your exploration up-canyon for as long as your heart desires but go at least ½ mile to really take in the atmosphere of the place. After the first hundred yards or so,

*Little Wild Horse Canyon (photo by Steffen Synnatschke)*

the slot canyon widens, but a second section, even narrower than the first, and also much more interesting, awaits you a bit further on. Keep walking until you reach a sort of wide section, with some trees, about 50 minutes from the fork with Bell Canyon. The canyon continues on even higher, but by now you have done the most interesting part.

*Polished sandstone illusion*
*(Turn upside down to see the actual eroded niches)*

*Photo advice:* Little Wild Horse Canyon consists of a very brown type of Wingate and Kayenta sandstone near the ground with light colored Navajo sandstone on the very high walls. All this combines to make it quite dark, unless you visit the canyon around mid-day. There are, however, some wider spots where the sandstone takes on soft pinkish hues wherever the afternoon light is able to come through.

*Getting there:* Leaving Goblin Valley State Park *(see previous section)*, turn left soon after the park exit on a road marked by a sign saying Little Wild Horse Canyon. This road is generally well maintained and easily traveled in an ordinary passenger car or camper. It's a good idea to get the latest information from the Goblin Valley rangers since you'll be crossing a sandy wash about 2 miles from the intersection with the Goblin Valley road. In case of recent rains, the road may be washed out. You'll come to a parking area in about 5 miles. In case of flash flooding, your car will be protected here as it is above the riverbed. A sign tells about such a flash flood experienced by a visiting couple, with a photo showing their Landcruiser washed away by the high water. Take this very seriously, particularly on a summer's afternoon. Flash floods are generated by rain falling on the Reef far above the entrance of the canyon and you won't necessarily see it. If you are caught by a flash flood while you are in the canyon, you'll be in great danger. Never forget that it's storms such as these that are responsible for the creation of the beautiful walls of this slot canyon.

*Time required:* About 2½ hours round-trip from the parking area.

*Nearby locations:* Crack Canyon is another photogenic slot canyon in the vicinity. To reach it, take the Goblin Valley turnoff on UT 24. Instead of turning left to Goblin Valley SP, continue on Temple Mountain Road for about 2.3 miles; turn left on the Behind the Reef dirt road; continue for about 4 miles until you reach Crack canyon. Less photogenic Chute Canyon is about 2 miles further.

# Wild Horse Canyon

On the way to Goblin Valley and Little Wild Horse Canyon, you can look into nearby Wild Horse Canyon for a little known but interesting pictograph panel. Although quite small, the anthropomorphs depicted on the panel are finely drawn and very well preserved. As a bonus, you'll also be able to see Wild Horse Window, a spectacular alcove, lit by a hole in its roof.

After parking your car, look toward the reef to the northwest to spot Wild Horse Window; from here, it looks like some kind of cave. Try memorizing the topography around the window—which is not located in the main canyon, but farther north—as you'll lose sight of it once you descend into the canyon; this will help you locate it later on, after photographing the panel.

Descend into the wash and head west toward the reef for about ½ mile to the canyon's mouth, where you'll see Wilderness area markers. Enter the small light-colored narrows to the left and continue up-canyon. The walls become progressively taller and about 0.6 mile northwest past the markers, the canyon widens, assuming a wide circular shape. From here on, look up to the right to locate the previously-mentioned panel in its small alcove. To visit similar hard-to-find panels and to significantly increase your enjoyment and understanding of rock art, you might consider joining a field trip of the Utah Rock Art Research Association, aka URARA (see *Appendix*).

*Thou Shalt Follow*

Wild Horse Window is less than 0.2 mile north of the main canyon as the crow flies, in a side tributary. Reaching it requires finding your way over the slickrock without any obvious landmarks to guide you; some routefinding skills are therefore necessary for this detour. If you feel up for it after seeing the panel, retrace your steps toward your car; shortly before the canyon narrows you'll see a slickrock slope to the left, allowing you to easily climb on the plateau. Continue on the slickrock for a short while until you meet a little canyon leading northwest; walk up-canyon and you'll find the alcove within a few minutes. Shortly before the Window, there may be a couple of water holes in a wet year, which can be easily circumvented to the left.

*Photo advice:* A 28mm works best to capture the entire panel, which can later be cropped in panoramic format; you can also isolate some groups of anthropomorphs with a normal lens to fill the entire frame. While it's tempting to photograph the two roof openings from the back of Wild Horse Window with a super wide-angle (24mm or wider), the huge contrast between the inside of the alcove and the outside makes it very challenging; it is safer to frame the access canyon with only the entrance of the alcove.

*Getting there:* On UT 24, take the turnoff for Goblin Valley State Park; after 5 miles you arrive at Temple Mountain junction. Turn left, take Goblin Valley Road for about 0.3 mile and turn right on the third dirt road. Go another 0.3 mile from the paved road and park at the pullout to your left, just before the road descends into the wash.

*Time required:* Less than 1½ hour round-trip to photograph the panel. Add approximately 45 minutes for the Wild Horse Window extension.

*Nearby location:* Instead of turning left on Goblin Valley Road at Temple Mountain junction, continue straight on Temple Mountain Road for almost a mile and look to the right for an access to a wide parking area. Some paintings are located about 40 feet high up the cliff. Unfortunately, these beautiful pictographs have been "enhanced" with a chalk outline in recent years. A medium telephoto is necessary to photograph them.

If you follow Temple Mountain Road further north, you'll enter Sinbad Country, an attractive combination of vast desert expanse, small hills, buttes and grassland, with lots of interesting canyons and rock art waiting to be explored away from crowds. Temple Mountain Road is usually passable by passenger car, but may require a high-clearance vehicle at times. It goes all the way to I-70, offering an interesting alternative to reach Little Wild Horse Canyon or Goblin Valley SP from the Interstate (taking Exit 131 south).

## Along Interstate 70

As it crosses the San Rafael Swell between Green River and Fremont Junction, I-70 is without contest one of the most scenic interstates in the Southwest. This freeway was the last portion of the east-west interstate system to be finished, opening up an extremely remote part of rural Utah to visitor traffic. A series of rest areas line the freeway, allowing you to photograph spectacular views of the San Rafael area. All merit a stop, but with a bit more time you'll find a lot to explore and photograph on short road trips from the freeway.

Technically, the vast anticline called the San Rafael Swell doesn't begin before Fremont Junction on its western slope; however, the section of the freeway between Salina and Fremont Junction is just as spectacular.

Coming from Green River, the sudden presence of the swell is sharply felt as you penetrate the impressive barrier of the San Rafael Reef through Spotted Wolf Canyon. The first viewpoint is a rest stop located just before the Reef. There are great, unobstructed views to the north from a little hill above the rest stop.

The second rest stop on the eastern side, at milepost 142, has a fantastic view on the reef from above, looking down into Spotted Wolf Canyon and the Book

Cliffs on the horizon. It's a great wide-angle shot if you don't mind including the gently curving freeway in the foreground. For more intimate views of the reef you should visit Black Dragon Wash, which penetrates deep into the reef and offers an interesting rock art panel *(see section below)*.

Other rest stops along the freeway in the center of the swell are also worth

*The Reef through Spotted Wolf Canyon*

stopping. The north side of Exit 131 provides access to Buckhorn Draw and the Wedge Overlook via BLM road 332 *(see section below)* while the south side of this exit provides access to the Head of Sinbad via Temple Mountain Road *(see section below)*. Time permitting, the gravel road at Exit 116 brings you in about 18 miles to the town of Moore, which is 8 Miles from the Rochester Rock Art Panel *(see section below)*.

Exits 86 "SR-72" and 91 "SR-10" are the northern entry points for Cathedral Valley, as described in the Capitol Reef chapter. From Exit 86, UT 72 heading south to Loa is an enchanting highway with almost no traffic. It meanders through soft valleys before climbing to almost ten thousand feet to where you can find a few groves of early-turning aspen just past the Desert View rest stop. The rest stop has a distant but interesting view of Upper Cathedral Valley.

Continuing on I-70 toward I-15, the Fremont Indian State Park, located 21 miles southwest of Richfield at Exit 17, is a worthwhile stop to stretch your legs on the interstate. The museum has excellent exhibits of the Fremont culture, including a reproduction of a pit house. There is also a reconstructed pit house outside. Although there is a large quantity of pictographs, accessible from numerous interpretive trails, they are generally hard to locate. Be sure to ask for the various trail fliers to make your visit more instructive and enjoyable.

## Black Dragon Wash

The highlight of this popular rock art panel, located off I-70, is an interesting panel representing a strange bird-like figure resembling a pterodactyl.

To visit Black Dragon Wash, you must be coming from Green River, as there is no exit from the south side of the freeway. You could use one of the occasional median crossings, but these are normally for emergency use and the highway patrol frowns on it. Technically, there is no exit either on the north side, just an unmarked pull off area ¼ mile past milepost 147, which you'll find approximately ¾ mile beyond the bridge over the San Rafael river or about 13 miles west of Exit 157 on I-70, west of Green River. There is a marked BLM dirt road and a cattle gate, which you have to open and close behind you. Follow the road north for about a mile in open country, then turn left for another ¼ mile inside the reef; it is in decent shape and passable to a passenger car. With high clearance, you'll be able to drive the next 0.6 mile to a parking area located right below the panel. Passenger cars should stop before that, when things become rough.

The panel is on the north side of the canyon. It is at least 30 feet up on the cliff and appears rather small to the naked eye. Someone apparently decided one day that the red pigment had become too faint and drew a white outline with chalk around the dragon to make it easier to see. This exemplifies too well the risk of leaving prominent rock art unprotected. Outlining Indian rock art with chalk or drawing over it or around it is no different from painting over Michaelangelo's work in the Sistine chapel.

Once you have located the dragon, make your way up the rocky path that leads to the base of the ledge where it's drawn. Be extremely cautious as the path is slippery and the ledge is very narrow; one misstep could lead to a serious fall. About 60 feet to the left of the dragon, and a bit higher, is a small panel of human figures.

*Photo advice:* You'll need a 24mm to fit the dragon into your frame; it's about 7 feet wide from wing tip to wing tip. Bracket your exposure to obtain the best tonality.

*Time required:* 1 hour round-trip from I-70.

*Nearby location:* About halfway back from the Black Dragon parking area to I-70, you can turn west on a short ¼-mile spur road leading to the Petroglyph Canyon trailhead. Walk southwest along the reef for about ten minutes until you reach the mouth of Arch Canyon. Head inside the canyon and soon after its entrance take a short spur southwest and look for a small but undamaged panel on the north wall.

*The amazing Black Dragon*

## The Head of Sinbad

The Head of Sinbad is renowned for its two beautiful pictograph panels, which until now have been spared by vandals. This site is easy to visit while traveling on I-70. With the former access near milepost 124 now blocked by boulders, the only access as of this writing is from Exit 131 south on I-70.

*The Head of Sinbad pictograph*

Take the good frontage road west then head south. After 4 miles, go right for 1 mile then right again. Continue northwest for 3½ miles and turn right at the Dutchman's Arch sign, taking the narrow tunnel under I-70. After the tunnel, go right for ¼ mile, then right again at the next fork and continue straight ahead until you reach the car park and its wooden fence. This part of the road can be impassable for passenger cars.

The first panel is exquisite in its simplicity: A single shamanistic anthropomorph with an interesting hairdo, surrounded by two elegant and simply ornamented stick-like motifs and a curiously waving buck, revealing the artist's sense of humor. Do not miss the second panel, a bit to the left, where you can photograph an anthropomorph holding a snake; his neighbor is a dead ringer for E.T.

*Time required:* About an hour from I-70 including photography.

*Nearby location:* On the way back from the panel, cut right at the first fork and drive ½ mile west to see Dutchman's Arch, which is best photographed in the afternoon. Hardcore rock art aficionados may want to pay a visit to the somewhat faint Lone Warrior pictograph, protected behind his round shield. After returning under the I-70 tunnel, turn right immediately instead of going straight. After about 1½ mile, you'll see a sign for the Lonesome Warrior to the right. The pictograph is 0.4 mile from here, behind the second wooden fence.

## The Rochester Rock Art Panel

The Rochester is a large petroglyph panel consisting of a mix of animal figures, anthropomorphs and a kind of rainbow carved on smooth rock. It's easily accessible, via a good dirt road and an easy trail, and makes a good picture if you are looking for rock art. The location, on a rocky promontory overlooking the Muddy River 200 feet below, is also quite nice. If you are going toward the Wedge Overlook or Nine Mile Canyon from Fremont Junction on I-70, you should consider this short but interesting detour.

From Exit 91 on I-70, take UT 10 north and drive 12 miles to the town of Emery. About 3½ miles past Emery, near milepost 18, turn right in the direction of Moore for

*The Rochester panel*

½ mile, then south at the first gravel road to your right; this road has a small sign indicating the panel. Follow it for about 4 miles to the parking area. The easy ½-mile foot trail leads southward to several scattered groups of glyphs but the main panel, facing east, steals the show.

*Time required:* About 2 hours round-trip from I-70.

## The Wedge Overlook and Buckhorn Draw

To the north of Fremont Junction on I-70, UT 10 to Price offers the easiest access to these two popular sites located in the heart of the Swell, although it's possible to come from Exit 131 off I-70. Drive 38 miles to Castle Dale and a little over 1 mile north of town, take the marked and well-graded gravel road (CR 401), suitable to passenger cars in dry weather. Follow it east for 13 miles and, at the fork, turn south for about 6 miles on an equally good road leading to a breathtaking view of the San Rafael River at the Wedge Overlook. The viewpoint is 600 feet above the gorge—a great destination to photograph "Utah's Little Grand Canyon". There are trails following the canyon east and west leading to additional viewpoints.

Driving back 6 miles, turn right on BLM Road 401 for about 2.2 miles and right

*The Wedge*

again at the sign on BLM 332 to visit the Buckhorn Draw Area. About 2½ miles from the junction, you can park just past a cattle guard and follow a short trail heading east to a petroglyph panel. About 3½ miles further, park at the sign for the highlight of the road: The Buckhorn Wash Pictograph Panel, which has been repeatedly vandalized and restored. The panel, in the Barrier Canyon style, is right by the side of the road; it is fenced off but easily photographed with a normal lens to mild telephoto. These are, in my opinion, some of the finest pictographs in the Southwest. Road 332 continues for 23 miles toward I-70, which it meets at Exit 131. Along the way, it traverses the superb Buckhorn Canyon, followed by grassy open areas, allowing you to make a loop around the heart of the Swell. This is a remote area of magnificent scenery, although easily accessible, yet few people know about it. A great place for camping and relaxing.

## Nine Mile Canyon

Don't let the name fool you. Nine Mile Canyon is 40 miles long and takes at least half a day to thoroughly enjoy. The canyon got its name from a nine-mile triangulation done by one of J.W. Powell's topographers during the mapping of the area. Nevertheless, the 100-mile round-trip from Wellington to the gate which ends public access to the canyon provides an exquisite foray deep into the Book Cliffs wilderness. The road leaves from Wellington, southeast of Price, and takes you through one of the largest concentrations of rock art in North America. The road goes through a remote area offering an interesting variety of landscapes, from semi-alpine to fertile cultivated land to dry canyons. Due to the rarity of human presence, an abundance of wildlife can be seen on the road at dawn or dusk.

*The Hunting Scene in Nine Mile Canyon*

Although just driving this scenic backcountry byway is sheer pleasure if you have time on your hands, most photographers will want to visit the canyon to photograph rock art, and in particular the famous Hunting Scene panel, located near the end of the canyon.

*Photo advice:* Petroglyphs and pictographs, mostly of the Fremont era, can be found by the hundreds on the canyon cliffs, but unless you use a detailed booklet and drive very slowly, you will miss most of them. Stop at the Chevron gas station in Wellington and ask for the *Guide to Rock Art in Nine Mile Canyon (see Appendix)*. This useful booklet provides milepost information for many of the panels. If possible, bring binoculars to spot items high on the canyon walls. You will need a telephoto to photograph many of the rock art panels; others are at eye level or slightly above and call for a normal lens.

*Getting there:* The well-marked road leaves US 191 at the eastern end of the town of Wellington, about 8 miles southeast of Price. The road is called Soldier Creek Road after the Buffalo Soldiers, the famed troop of black cavalrymen who actually built it in 1882. A marker at the truck stop retraces the history of the road and points out the location of some of the more prominent panels. The road is paved for the first 12 miles, then becomes a well-graded dirt road suitable for passenger cars, even though it's not advisable in wet weather. Less than 9 miles after the end of the pavement, you reach the bridge over Minnie Maude Creek which marks the official entry into Nine Mile Canyon. The Hunting Scene Panel is located about 1.2 miles from the entrance of Cottonwood Canyon Road, which begins to your right about 24 miles from Minnie Maude Creek.

*Time required:* At least half a day from Wellington, but a full day will be more suitable for serious rock art hunters.

## The Crystal Geyser

Near Green River is a little-known but interesting natural phenomenon: A geyser—inadvertently "revealed" by someone drilling for oil! The trouble is: it isn't exactly Old Faithful! The geyser erupts only once or twice every 24 hours. So you'll need either luck, to be there at the right time, or patience. I was fortunate enough to see the geyser erupt on my very first trip here, so don't despair.

Even if you don't see the geyser erupt, you can still photograph the colorful travertine deposits cascading down to the river. They are created by the lime-saturated water flowing out of the pipe

*Photo advice:* Anytime in the day is fine to photograph the geyser if it's erupting. Be sure to protect your equipment if you're shooting at close range or some nasty whitish paste will blanket it and it will be hard to remove. The geyser is not hot so there doesn't seem to be a danger of getting

*The Crystal Geyser*

burns, but you should be cautious of where you step as there are a couple of hot bubbling mud holes next to it. Overexpose ½ stop to accurately convey the color of the column of water. The travertine deposits around the geyser make good subjects for abstracts.

*Getting there:* From Exit 164 on I-70 just east of Green River, follow the dirt road heading southeast for 2½ miles. At the junction, turn right and continue south, then west, for another 4 miles in a desolate landscape until you reach the geyser near the riverbank.

## Sego Canyon

Sego Canyon is as good as it gets for motorists who would like to see some prime rock art without sweating it out. If you are traveling on I-70 between Green

*Sego Canyon rock art*

River and Grand Junction, all you need to do is take Exit 187, about 25 miles east of Green River, drive north past Thompson Springs and continue for about 3½ miles on a paved road. Just follow the sign over the tracks and up canyon to an obvious parking area on the left side. It doesn't get any easier than that!

A short trail leads to a large and beautiful Barrier style panel. This panel is best photographed with a 50mm lens and a short telephoto. There are a couple of interpretive markers providing an overview of the various periods and styles of rock art.

If you walk a little bit along the road past the parking area, you'll see some large anthropomorphic figures painted on the sandstone just 60 feet from the fence. These impressive pictographs are badly faded and partially vandalized, but still worth the brief detour. ✿

*House on Fire*

Chapter 10

AROUND CEDAR MESA

*Kachina Bridge*

## AROUND CEDAR MESA

This chapter covers a vast territory stretching from the eastern and southern limits of the Cedar Mesa plateau to the Henry Mountains, with Natural Bridges National Monument at its epicenter.

On our journey, we will follow UT 95 from Blanding to Hanksville. UT 95 sees very little traffic except during the summer months. As of this writing, the area is experiencing a severe drought which has resulted in the temporary closure of the Hite Marina on Lake Powell, further reducing the usual traffic of motorhomes and trucks hauling boats on this spectacular road. Before visiting Natural Bridges NM, we'll do a foray to the south along UT 261 and in the vicinity of Mexican Hat. This is the *Trail of the Ancients*, at the heart of the Cedar Mesa Plateau, and it is known for its rich Ancient Puebloan heritage.

All along this chapter, we'll  explore a mix of interesting natural features and Puebloan ruins and rock art.


### Edge of the Cedars State Park

The little town of Blanding, located at the foot of the magnificent Abajo Mountains, would be unremarkable if not for the Edge of the Cedars State Park and its wonderful museum. The park definitely merits a stop for its exhibits of Ancestral Puebloan culture as well as modern Navajo and Ute artifacts. Behind the museum, there are some Pueblo-type ruins which were inhabited until about 1220 AD. They are only moderately interesting but pale in comparison with others—although you get a chance to descend into a reconstructed kiva.

*Getting there:* The park is in the town of Blanding on US 191 and to get there is a bit like following the yellow brick road as you are guided to the museum by a series of Puebloan icons painted on the surface of the paved road.

*Time required:* About 1 hour.

## Butler Wash & the Comb Ridge

About 11 miles from the start of UT 95, leaving US 191 south of Blanding, you'll find the Butler Wash car park on the right hand side of the road. An easy 1-mile round-trip trail takes you to an overlook with a good view of a nice balcony-shaped dwelling perched inside a grotto in the canyon below. Butler Wash looks its best in mid-morning. The dwelling is then evenly illuminated and the light is not yet too harsh. Earlier than that, you'll need to warm up the scene and later in the afternoon you'll be shooting against the light.

About 2½ miles further west on UT 95, you'll cross an enormous man-made cut in the ridge before the road opens up into the valley. You are passing through the great retreating cliff face of the Comb Ridge, stretching almost a hundred miles from north to south. Along with the Cockscomb and the Waterpocket Fold, the Comb Ridge is one of the big three anticlines traversing the Colorado plateau. From here, the views of the Abajo Mountains to the north and the Henry Mountains to the north-west are spectacular. As the road makes a blind curve through the cut, stopping is prohibited and you should park in the valley to observe and photograph the anticline or walk back up if you want to photograph from above. If you are coming from Natural Bridges, don't miss the small pullout just before the fence as you come into Comb Wash valley. It is a great vantage point with a fantastic view over miles of the ridge toward the south.

The west-facing cliff consists mostly of Wingate sandstone, with a bit of Navajo sandstone on top. It glows a rich red in the late afternoon sun and that's the best time to photograph it.

*Crossing the Comb Ridge*

## Mule Canyon

Mule Canyon is an outstanding location both for leisurely hiking and photography of small Puebloan dwellings and granaries.

The Mule Canyon system consists of two different arms, separated by about ½ mile at their entrance. Both the north and south forks extend for roughly 5 to 6 miles. They are both easy level walks, with few obstructions, a shallow stream, often dry or reduced to a trickle. They offer pleasant walks in solitude, inside sunny canyons with shallow walls. Both harbor nice ruins almost every mile or so, easy to spot and get to and fun to photograph.

The south fork of Mule Canyon is by far the most popular with photographers as it contains the striking 'flaming ceiling' ruin which has become an icon of the Colorado Plateau *(see my "House on Fire" image anchoring this chapter's front page)*. From the trailhead, head west up-canyon, following the mostly dry stream. After about 1 mile, you'll skirt a bend and find *House on fire* to the right. It is located under a cliff overhang, part of a small set of ruins and granaries just 20 feet above the canyon floor (37°32'38" 109°44'41"). After photographing the ruins, walk inside the small passageway to the left and look above for some handprints.

*Photo advice:* The best time to photograph *House on fire* is in late morning, to take advantage of the light bouncing from the slickrock slope below the ruins. This side of the canyon remains in the shade until late morning with no reflected light on the ruins; later in the day direct sunlight washes out the "flames".

*Getting there:* The two canyon trailheads are located on an unmarked county road (SJC 263) on the north side of UT 95 (at mile marker 102.3), ½ mile east of the marked Mule Canyon Ruin exhibit. The latter is a reconstructed kiva and is not particularly interesting. I have always perceived it as a decoy, built to steer people away from the canyons, while at the same time satisfying the curiosity of passersby who are in a rush. A small fee is required to visit all the noteworthy canyons on the Cedar Mesa plateau; you'll find a self-registration station near the entrance of the county road to that effect. Park about 0.3 mile after leaving UT 95 for *House on fire* in the south fork.

*Time required:* About 2 hours to photograph *House on fire* in the south fork of Mule Canyon; 5 to 6 hours to visit the entire length of the each arm.

## Grand Gulch

Grand Gulch has become the Mecca of Indian ruins and rock art on the Cedar Mesa plateau. During springtime and autumn, it attracts many visitors, particularly small groups, eager to explore easily accessible ancient Puebloan ruins while enjoying a laid-back backpacking experience in a pleasant canyon. The combination of moderately difficult terrain and a high concentration of well-preserved dwellings, granaries and rock art makes it a very rewarding trip.

Walking the entire length of the canyon from the main entry at Kane Gulch to the San Juan River is 53 miles and few people tackle such a daunting trip. Most people concentrate on the upper part of the canyon, which offers several exit points making it flexible to plan two to five-day trips. For those who would like to enjoy the wilderness experience without roughing it too much, there are accredited outfitters offering increasingly popular llama trips. I recommend these llama trips strongly to photographers, for they remove the burden of carrying camera equipment on top of your backpacking gear. If you are a large format photographer, this may well be your only option. If you want to see Grand Gulch without backpacking, it can be done with moderate effort on consecutive day-hikes.

From Kane Gulch, a 10-mile round-trip hike from the ranger station brings you to the confluence with Grand Gulch and good ruins at Junction Ruin and Turkey Pen Ruin. Bullet Canyon is a very rewarding entry point for short incursions into the Gulch. From the Bullet Canyon trailhead, Perfect Kiva and Jailhouse Ruin (37°26'18" 110°00'41") make a moderate, under 10-mile round-trip. An easier 10.6-mile day-hike in the central section of Grand Gulch is to the Big Man pictograph

*Big Man pictograph panel*

panel (37°27'16" 110°06'24"), reached by the well-maintained Government Trail and an easy up-canyon hike.

Arguably the best ruin complex in Grand Gulch, Split Level House is named for two connected dwellings located at different levels under an alcove, also sheltering a small kiva, granaries and pictographs; it is located 10 miles from the Kane Gulch trailhead and 13 miles from the Bullet Canyon trailhead, requiring an overnighter. A couple of hundred yards inside Sheiks Canyon, the Green Mask site has excellent pictograph panels; it is located 1.4 miles upstream from Bullet inside Grand Gulch.

*Getting there:* The Kane Gulch Ranger Station is on the east side of UT 261, about 4 miles south of its junction with UT 95. This is where you'll get your backcountry permit if you stay overnight; during the high season, permits should be reserved in advanced from the BLM Office in Monticello. Day hikers just pay the entry fee common to all hikes on the Cedar Mesa plateau. The Kane Gulch trailhead is just across the road from the Ranger Station. The Todie Canyon trailhead is located further south on UT 261 near milepost 25, at the end of a good unmarked 1½-mile dirt road; there is no sign. The Bullet Canyon trailhead is just past mile marker 22, followed by 1½ miles on CR 251. Both trailheads are easily reached by passenger car. CR 245 to the Government Trail is just opposite marked Cigarette Spring Road, 13 Miles south of UT 95. It is 8.6 miles to the trailhead, with the last 0.7 mile requiring high-clearance. All these roads are impassable during and after a rain.

*Nearby location:* Owl Creek Canyon and Fish Creek Canyon are a popular backpacking destination, usually done as a 2-day loop; you may want to plan a quick jaunt into Owl Canyon to photograph a well-preserved kiva just below the rim, only 0.8 mile round-trip from the trailhead. The well-signed road to the trailhead is located 1.1 miles south of the Kane Gulch Ranger Station.

## Road Canyon

Road Canyon is a very pleasant canyon, quite verdant and open, and it contains some of the most remarkable Ancient Puebloan dwellings, granaries and kivas on the Cedar Mesa plateau. You won't have to go far either, arguably the most photogenic dwelling which I like to call *Fallen Roof Ruin* is located less than 45 minutes from the trailhead. In recent years, it too has become an icon of the Colorado Plateau.

To get to the ruins from the trailhead, follow the well-trod 0.3-mile footpath taking you northeast to an easy entry point into a side canyon. Descend the steep route to the side canyon. If you don't see a cairn when you reach it, mark this point on your GPS or build a visual cue so you can find this turnoff when you get back. Getting out could otherwise be a problem, especially late in the day after several hours of exploration. Continue east-northeast for a while until the side canyon meets Road Canyon. Take your bearings at this junction too and turn right, proceeding eastward into Road Canyon on a now fairly obvious trail. A few hundred yards from the last turnoff, a tall hoodoo will come into view on the left side. Start looking up from this point on. The first ruin—the highly photogenic *Fallen Roof Ruin*—is not hard to find, but it does not jump at you either as it is perched more than a hundred feet above the canyon floor (37°23'46" 109°52'21"). Access to this ruin is easy, requiring only a bit of climbing on slanted slickrock, leaving the trail about 150 feet after passing the tall hoodoo.

Note that you may find the initial side canyon badly obstructed after particularly heavy rains. If that's the case, use the bypass trail starting immediately at the entrance of the side canyon. Instead of going downcanyon, climb up on the north side on an easy to follow footpath. This route completely bypasses the side canyon from the top, dropping you down into Road Canyon ½ mile later. There is an easy descent on a steep 10-foot wall of slickrock but there are plenty of holds and no rope is needed.

After photographing *Fallen Roof Ruin*, stay high above the canyon and con-

*Opposite page: Fallen Roof Ruin in Road Canyon*

tinue northeast until the end of the same narrow ledge to reach the next group of particularly well-preserved ruins in just a few minutes. Tread lightly near the ruins. Do not get inside or touch the walls with your hands or remove any artifacts. It is a privilege to visit such a lovely canyon and you should leave no trace of your passage.

*Photo advice:* The best light is in mid-morning, when *Fallen Roof Ruin* is still in shadow. Part of the ruin is in full light from midday to mid-afternoon; you can nonetheless get acceptable results during that timeframe on an overcast day. A vertical composition with a 24 or 28mm works best to encompass the entire alcove, with its pterodactyl-like pattern revealed on the collapsed ceiling.

*Getting there:* On UT 261, about 13 miles south of UT 95—almost a mile past milepost 20—turn left on Cigarette Spring Road (CR 239) just opposite Government Trail Road. Pay your fee at the self-register station, located almost 1 mile from the turn off, then drive straight ahead until you reach an unmarked spur road 2.4 miles further on your left. Turn onto this road, going north for a couple hundred feet until you find an obvious pullout and a small trail marker (37°23'27" 109°53'16").

*Time required:* 2½ hours round-trip to photograph the first two sets of ruins. A half day to enjoy more of the canyon at a relaxed pace.

## Mokey Dugway and Muley Point

About 23 miles south of UT 95 and less than 10 miles from the Road Canyon turnoff on UT 261, you reach the edge of the plateau at a place called Mokey Dugway, where the paved road suddenly turns graded gravel. Here, at an altitude close to 6,000 feet, you have a spectacular view of the Valley of the Gods about 1000 feet below. Monument Valley is also visible in the distance.

For even better viewpoints, take the dirt road heading west to Muley Point immediately before starting the descent from the plateau. There are two viewpoints: The first one, at about 3.7 miles, yields wonderful views of the goosenecks of the San Juan River. The second one, at about 5 miles, marks the end of the road and affords a closer and more open view of Monument Valley, as well as an almost 360° panorama, including Navajo Mountain, the Henrys, the Abajos and Sleeping Ute Mountain.

Returning to Mokey Dugway on UT 261, you descend an amazing portion of road, carved into the flanks of the cliff during the 1950's for the use of local uranium mines. It's all gravel road with almost 3 miles of hairpin turns descending steeply to the bottom, but it's wide and doesn't present any problems for a passenger car as long as you drive slowly. The pavement resumes as you near the bottom and in about 7 miles you reach US 163, where you can continue your trip southwest toward Mexican Hat and Monument Valley or northeast toward Bluff and Moab.

*Photo advice:* The views from the viewpoints are so incredibly vast that it is easier and probably more interesting to simply admire them than to photograph them. If you want to photograph Monument Valley in the distance, you'll need a telephoto in the 200-300mm range. The view is often too hazy, but you could get a good shot after a rain, with some nice clouds or a dramatic sky.

## Valley of the Gods

Right after descending the Mokey Dugway, you'll encounter an interesting track heading east and forming a loop around the place known as the Valley of the Gods. After a moderately spectacular portion in the vicinity of the Bed & Breakfast, you'll encounter imposing monoliths and buttes strewn about the valley. Although reminiscent from those found at Monument Valley, they do have their own flair. Though quite beautiful, Valley of the Gods doesn't offer the same photographic variety as the latter. The main advantage of the Valley of the Gods is that it is much less visited and an impression of solitude reigns here. You'll truly have the impression that you are embarking on an adventure, which is not the case in the highly controlled world of the Monument Valley Tribal Park. I particularly like the northern side of the valley, where the road abruptly turns south behind one of the tallest monoliths. I call this particular spot the *Rincon* and I like to park there and explore on foot. This area, located about 8 miles from either entry of the track, has by far the best views in the entire valley.

*Photo advice:* These Gods, immense monoliths rising high into the sky, won't disappoint you. If you arrive past mid-afternoon, when the rocks take very warm colors, take the track from its western entrance in order not to have the sun against you. In the early morning, take it from the opposite direction, you'll get good light and even better views.

*Valley of the Gods*

*Getting there:* The west entrance is at the foot of the Mokey Dugway on UT 261, less than 7 miles from US 163. The southeast entrance is on US 163, 8 miles northeast of Mexican Hat and about 4 miles from where it branches off UT 261. It is about 16-mile long; with caution, it is generally passable for passenger cars except during or after inclement weather.

*Time required:* At least 1 hour just to drive the loop; 2 hours if you want to do it at a more leisurely pace and take photos.

## Goosenecks of the San Juan

At the southern end of UT 261, there is a small but interesting Utah State Park largely ignored by travelers, who are either in a great hurry to get to nearby Monument Valley or in a euphoric state from visiting it.

Here, the San Juan River has cut out four successive bends over 1,000 feet in depth in a shale core, twisting and turning for almost 7 miles in a space of less than 2 miles. This view is more remarkable for being odd than for sheer beauty. You are presented with a geological phenomenon that defies the imagination.

*Photo advice:* The goosenecks make for eye-catching pictures no matter what size of wide-angle lens you have. There's no way you can get them all into one single shot, unless you shoot from a small airplane.

*Gooseneck of the San Juan*

*Getting there:* On UT 261, about 6 miles from the foot of Mokey Dugway or 1 mile from US 163, take SR 316 heading southwest for about 3½ miles until you reach the viewpoint at the edge of the plateau.

*Time required:* A detour of less than 1 hour round-trip from US 163.

## From Mexican Hat to Bluff

Less than 2 miles north of the Mexican Hat township, a well-graded dirt road leaves US 163 to wind around the southern side of Mexican Hat Rock, allowing you to pick up the view you prefer. I'll be the first to admit that photographing Mexican Hat Rock is a bit cheesy, but it's really tempting to stop and gawk. Judging by the number of cars that pull off for a close-up view and a quick snapshot, the temptation is universal. The second half of the afternoon offers better light on the rock.

Nearby, as you follow US 163 northeast toward Bluff, do not miss the colorful "Indian Blanket" patchwork on the cliffs overlooking the San Juan river, on the east side of the road. Farther up, as you head toward the junction of US 163 and 191, you'll be passing by the spectacular Lime Ridge before once again crossing our old friend the Comb Ridge, previously discussed in this chapter.

About 1½ miles past the Comb Ridge and approximately 4½ miles before reaching Bluff, you'll find Butler Wash Road heading north for about 21 miles until it reaches UT 95. Many interesting dwellings and rock art can be found along this dirt road. Among the most intriguing examples are the Wolfman and

Procession panels. For the Wolfman Panel, drive about 1 mile from the south entrance of Butler Wash Road, turn left just before a cattle guard and park. A short walk leads you to the panel, near the edge of the cliff. The Procession Panel—a 15-foot conga line of tiny marching figures following large animals—is about 5 miles further up on Butler Wash Road, requiring a 1.2-mile easy ascent to the top of the Comb Ridge. Inquire at the Recapture Lodge in Bluff *(see Appendix)* for more information about this site.

*Procession panel*

Not quite a mile past the junction of US 163 and 191, the marked road to the Sand Island Recreational Area leads to some mildly interesting petroglyphs. Sand Island is also a launching pad for rafting trips on the San Juan River. Wild Rivers Expeditions *(see Appendix)* offer a 26-mile 1-day rafting trip to Mexican Hat. The rare rapids won't delight thrill seekers, but photographers can expect beautiful scenery—especially near Mexican Hat. The trip stops at the River House dwellings, as well as at the impressive Butler Wash Petroglyph Panel with its large and originally adorned anthropomorphic figures.

About 3 miles east of Sand Island, Bluff makes a good stop between Monument Valley and Moab. Surrounded by the red cliffs that gave it its name and the interesting Twin Rocks, you'll find some oddly atypical Victorian style stone houses. These houses were built at the end of the 19th century by the same Mormon pioneers who founded the town following their epic Hole-in-the-Rock odyssey *(see Escalante Canyons chapter)*.

## Natural Bridges Nat'l Monument

Although not as spectacular as Arches, this park has a personality all its own; however, it only reveals its beauty and interest to those with enough time and willing to do some hiking. Natural bridges are eroded by the action of water flowing from rivers, as opposed to arches, which are eroded by wind and sand.

The three gigantic natural bridges—Sipapu, Kachina and Owachomo—are spectacular. Because of their particular geological origin, they are set deeply inside canyons, instead of being in the open like arches. This makes the bridges difficult to photograph from the top of the canyon, but if you take the time to go to the bottom you'll be rewarded by superb views of these huge bridges.

*Sipapu Bridge makes for an interesting shot from below*

The three bridges are located on a 9-mile one-way loop road. Sipapu Bridge is the longest, with a span of 286 feet, and is arguably the most elegant of the three. Forget the viewpoint close to the road, however, because the bridge appears totally lost among its whitish Cedar Mesa surroundings. Instead, take the 1.2-mile round-trip hike down into the canyon and you'll reach the bridge in less than ½ hour, including a brief stop halfway down the trail on a ledge providing a nice view of the bridge below. It's a 500 feet elevation drop, so it's fairly steep in places and you'll be using ladders. Sipapu is a nice mid-morning view and there are some spectacular angles looking up to the bridge from the bottom of the canyon, with some nice reflected light from the different walls.

Kachina Bridge, being just a bit shorter than Sipapu, is most notable for the thickness of its span. Just under 100 feet thick, it resembles a gigantic rock muscle stretched 130 feet above your head. The trail leading to Kachina Bridge from its overlook is a tad longer than Sipapu's; however, elevation gain is only 400 feet and the hike feels markedly easier. An added benefit is the presence of a kiva and pictographs behind a small talus south of the bridge.

If you have at least 3 hours available, I strongly recommend hiking the 5.6-mile loop between Sipapu and Kachina. The section at the bottom of White Canyon is an easy level walk alternating between a sandy path and the dry bed of the beautiful canyon. It's a unique opportunity to day hike inside a wild Cedar Mesa sandstone canyon in a relatively safe environment. On the way to Kachina, a few hundred yards past the confluence with Deer Canyon, look for ruins up on a ledge on the right side of White Canyon. The Horse Collar Ruin granaries are somewhat hidden at the back of this ledge. When you arrive under Kachina Bridge, don't proceed straight into the canyon; instead, turn immediately to the left to locate the path leading to the Kachina Bridge trailhead. On

*Owachomo Bridge with frozen creek*

the other side of the road, a good path will bring you back to the Sipapu parking area in less than 2 miles, passing through a pinyon juniper forest.

From the road, Owachomo Bridge is easy to reach and photograph, which is a good reason for not missing it, though it is dwarfed in comparison with the other two. If you're not in great shape, but still want to see a nice bridge, Owachomo is for you!

*Photo advice:* White Canyon consists of a very ancient, light-colored Cedar Mesa sandstone, which is difficult to expose on a sunny day. You'll have to find a way to isolate the bridges, preferably against the sky, to convey the true measure of their size and the feeling of power, which they project when close. There is only one way to do this, and that's by descending into the canyon. If your time is limited, you're most likely to do so at Owachomo, where the bridge is located only a few minutes from the road. In that case, don't stop when you arrive at the bridge, but continue under it and to the left, descending towards the creek flowing below. The creek makes a nice foreground and the angle you'll get from below provides an easy exposure of the bridge throughout the day.

*Sipapu Bridge*

*Getting there:* From Mexican Hat and US 163 by way of UT 261, with the added bonus of the beautiful viewpoints of Mokey Dugway and Muley Point, or by the superb UT 95 leaving from either Blanding or Hanksville. About 2 miles west of the junction of these two roads, you'll find the short UT 265 leading to the park's entrance.

*Time required:* 2 to 5 hours in the park, depending on the hikes you choose.

## Crossing Lake Powell

From Natural Bridges NM, you can cross Lake Powell in two ways. The main, most frequented route is UT 95 going straight towards Hite and continuing to Hanksville. You can also take UT 276, bearing due west to catch the Hall's Crossing to Bullfrog Marina ferry and then choose between the northern section of UT 276 or the Notom-Bullfrog Road leading to Capitol Reef.

In the first scenario, UT 95 follows spectacular White Canyon, dominated by the monoliths of Cheese Box Butte and Jacob's Chair. It is possible to descend into the canyon using a road located on the right hand side, about 2 miles past the *Jacob's Chair* sign.

Arriving at Hite Crossing, you'll leave the marina to the west and cross in succession the Colorado and the Dirty Devil rivers in the middle of an amazing landscape of petrified dunes. At the time of this writing, Lake Powell's level had receded drastically due to several years of continuous draught, and the Marina was out of commission.

*Quiet morning at Hall's Crossing (photo by Gene Mezereny)*

After less than 4 miles on the north shore, you reach a viewpoint overlooking Lake Powell (assuming its level is high enough) and providing an exceptionally nice vista. Past the viewpoint, the road begins its climb to the north, crossing a superb canyon of Entrada sandstone in the vicinity of Hog Springs, where it changes to Navajo sandstone.

Hog Springs' picnic area provides access to a small waterfall flowing into a pool on a 1-hour round-trip walk; perhaps more interestingly, it gives you the rare opportunity of photographing a very nice specimen of Barrier style pictograph, with no effort at all. From the parking area, walk along the right side of the road toward the south for about 400 feet. At the third post, find the path descending from the road, cross the small stream and head toward the big alcove. To the left of the alcove, you'll find Cleopatra, a well-preserved anthropomorph looking like it was just plucked out of Horseshoe Canyon's Great Gallery *(see Canyonlands–The Maze chapter)*. If you are looking for more discoveries, the area east of UT 95 has a number of side canyons waiting to be explored such as the nice, but technical, Leprechaun Canyon about 5 miles north of Hog Springs.

In the second scenario, via UT 276 west of Natural Bridges NM, you catch the John Atlantic Burr Ferry, which leaves Hall's Crossing for Bullfrog every two hours at even hours (odd hours from Bullfrog). The crossing takes ½ hour. As the schedule is subject to change and operating hours depend on the season, always verify it beforehand by calling (435) 684-3087. The service is usually interrupted for 4 to 6 weeks each winter. Once in Bullfrog you can rejoin UT 95 via lovely UT 276 along the Little Rockies. If you'd rather continue toward the Waterpocket Fold to Capitol Reef, leave UT 276 about 5 miles north of Bullfrog and take the Notom-Bullfrog Road (aka Burr Trail) alternately paved and graded but generally passable for passenger cars in dry weather. Almost 5 miles after leaving UT 276, consider stopping at the Pedestal Alley trailhead, where a 3-mile round-trip cairned trail leads through a stark desert landscape to some interesting pedestal rocks.

# Little Egypt

If you've enjoyed Goblin Valley *(see San Rafael Reef chapter)*, consider a brief stop at the Little Egypt Geological Site. Little Egypt is a free access site offering its share of goblins and hoodoos whose eroded shapes apparently evoked Ancient Egyptian temples for those who named it. Despite being more colorful—deep red with white striations—than their Goblin Valley counterparts, the formations fall a bit short in terms of photographic potential; their shapes offer less variety and they are too densely grouped together. Do not hesitate to explore each end of the site, you'll discover interesting hoodoos that are not visible from the car park.

*Photo advice:* Mostly oriented to the east, Little Egypt's formations look their best in the early morning sun. A wide-angle lens works very well here.

*Getting there:* On UT 95, about 20 miles

*Egyptian Hoodoos*

south of Hanksville or 6 miles north of the junction with UT 276, look for the *North Wash/Eagle Creek* sign and take the good track leading west. After roughly 1½ miles, a spur track appears on the right, leading to a large car park overlooking the site at the foot of the cliff.

*Time required:* About 1 hour.

# Arsenic Arch

Little known Arsenic Arch is a gem of an arch, well-hidden inside a tributary of Poison Spring Canyon. Lying isolated in the midst of a slickrock hill perched above the canyon, the small but elegant arch will delight dedicated arch hunters and photographers alike.

From where you park, walk north for almost ½ mile toward the canyon. Follow the rim until you spot the arch (38°06'20" 110°32'21")

*Arsenic Arch*

about 60 feet below the rim. The safest spot to descend from the rim is about 0.3 mile southwest (left) of the arch at (38°06'09" 110°32'29"). You'll have to skirt around a deep canyon to the right before you can reach the slickrock hill where the arch is located.

*Photo advice:* A 28 to 35mm lens is perfect to capture the entire arch. The best time to photograph the arch is at sunset, although early morning will work too.

*Getting there:* On UT 95, near milepost 20, just opposite the Little Egypt access road, turn east onto a sandy track normally in good condition in dry weather. There is a rocky wash to traverse after 0.6 mile, but the track becomes good after that. If you look carefully, you can briefly spot the arch on the left hand side from a hill located at about Mile 4.6, just before the signpost for the Sahara Sands. There is an obvious pullout to the right at Mile 5.2.

*Time Required:* About 2 hours from UT 95.

## Dirty Devil Overlook

While traveling on UT 95 from Hanksville to Hite or vice versa, you may want to take a quick side trip across the Burr Desert to the Dirty Devil River Overlook,

also known as Burr Point. It offers a remarkably expansive panorama of the canyon area formed by the Dirty Devil River, which is fed by the waters of Muddy Creek and the Fremont River.

*Photo advice:* The view is spectacular and would lend itself well to photography with a panoramic camera. This is a great late afternoon location.

*Getting there:* Drive about 15 miles south of Hanksville on UT 95 or 10 miles north of

*The Dirty Devil River from Burr Point*

the UT 276 junction and turn east at the Burr Point sign. Using caution, the 10-mile dirt road is generally suitable for passenger cars, except during and after a rain. ✿

*Fisher Towers reflection*

## Chapter 11

# AROUND MOAB

*Wilson Arch*

## AROUND MOAB

If there's one town in the Southwest that has changed drastically in the last twenty years, it's Moab. I knew Moab in 1975 when it was still a small hamlet with a couple of stray motels, a few odd restaurants and certainly no liquor. Today, with dozens of motels, Moab has become a cosmopolitan Mecca for tourists where they can buy cool bumper stickers saying "New York, Paris, London... Moab" and relax after a long day of hiking, rafting, four-wheeling or mountain biking in one of several micro-breweries in town.

Moab is certainly the jumping-off spot par excellence for those two scenic giants of the Colorado Plateau, Arches and Canyonlands *(see next chapters)*. However, the area around Moab contains quite a few remarkable sites that would be a shame to miss. This chapter deals with those sites that don't quite have the stature of National Parks and Monuments, but can be just as fascinating and full of photographic opportunities. While in Moab, be sure to look up Tom Till's exquisite photography in his gallery on Main Street.

### Potash Road

Scenic Byway 279 (aka Potash Road) begins off US 191, about 1.3 miles past the Colorado River Bridge north of Moab.

This highly scenic road follows the right bank of the Colorado River below steep Entrada sandstone cliffs adorned with desert varnish. Indian petroglyphs cover the canyon walls at some signed points and rock climbers from all over the world show off their skills—and colorful equipment—on the slickrock. This road provides access to landmarks such as Poison Spider Mesa and Corona Arch *(see next sections)* as well as to the main put-off and staging area for Colorado River trips in Canyonlands Nat'l Park and Cataract Canyon. Farther away, it leads to Thelma & Louise Point (remember the last scene of the movie…), the Shafer Trail and the White Rim Road *(see Island in the Sky chapter)*.

The road gets its name from the vast potash extraction site it serves; the plant is located about 1 mile before the end of a 17-mile paved road; the basins are a few miles further on a rough dirt road, where high-clearance is recommended. At the Potash site, water from the Colorado River is pumped into underground galleries where it dissolves potash salts, which are then aspirated back to the surface and into large evaporation basins. On the paper, it doesn't sound really exciting for the landscape photographer. However, the colorful basins display a spectacular palette, ranging from turquoise to deep dark blue and offering a shocking contrast with the red Entrada of the surrounding cliffs. To photograph this surreal sight, drive at least 5 miles past the end of the paved road to the farthest basins and find a slickrock ridge or a knoll close to the road to climb on for a better view. The best light is in late afternoon when it is evenly distributed on the whole scene. The evaporation basins can also been seen, albeit more distantly, from Hurrah Pass, accessible by high-clearance vehicle from Kane Creek Road. Kane Creek Road starts from the McDonald corner in downtown Moab and follows the south bank of the Colorado River (opposite SB 279) before following Kane Spring canyon and ascending the nice vantage point of Hurrah Pass. Another distant view of the basins is from Dead Horse Point State Park *(see Canyonlands-Island in the Sky chapter)* and Anticline Overlook *(see Canyonlands-Needles chapter)*.

## Poison Spider Mesa

I highly recommend a short drive or hike up Poison Spider Mesa for the extraordinary view it provides over the jumble of rocks and fins known as "Behind the Rocks", spread on the other side of the Colorado River. Although this is one of the most challenging 4x4 and mountain bike trails in Moab, the initial section leading to spectacular views can be tackled in a high-clearance 4WD SUV by

*Behind the Rocks, seen from Poison Spider Mesa*

experienced 4-wheelers. Unless you are a hardcore 4-wheeler, leave your car at the end of the Tie Rod Flats near Mile 2½ to avoid the difficult section known as the "Waterfall". From there, it's a short 0.3-mile walk to a superb open view.

*Photo advice:* You can also get good shots of the Behind the Rocks fins and cone-heads by climbing up one of the steep slickrock hills near the end of the initial switchbacks. Exercise much caution in doing so. A 200mm to 500mm telephoto will yield spectacular results shortly before sunset, with the extraordinary rocks lit up by the sun and the Manti-La Sals as a backdrop.

*Getting there:* Follow Potash Road (SB 279) for about 6 miles from the beginning of the road and exit at the Dinosaur Tracks sign. Passenger cars should stop at the parking area, but high-clearance vehicles can drive the first ½ mile of the track and park at the pullout under the electrical line. The track is strictly 4WD territory after that, although things get better between the end of the switchbacks and the challenging "Waterfall".

## Corona Arch

This is an easy, uncrowded and very rewarding 3-mile round-trip hike to two spectacular arches: massive, but elegant, Corona Arch with lovely Bowtie Pothole Arch along the way.

Corona Arch is one of the prettiest arches in the Moab area, thanks to its graceful span and an unobstructed view from both sides. Some people like to call it "Little Rainbow Bridge" and its shape is indeed reminiscent of the well-known landmark near Lake Powell *(see Around Page chapter in Volume 2).*

*Photo advice:* Afternoon works best to photograph Corona Arch from the slickrock bench. You can also walk under it and photograph it from the other side if you come around mid-morning.

*Corona Arch sunrise*

*Getting there:* Drive 10 miles from US 191 on Potash Road (SB 279) until you reach the marked car park for Corona Arch. The well-maintained trail climbs gently at first and makes use of safety cables and small ladders toward the end to reach the slickrock bench where the arches are located.

You can also park near a small canyon located ½ mile before the Corona Arch car park and hike through a thickly forested canyon and up to a plateau for a nice, but distant, view directly facing Corona Arch.

*Time required:* 1½ to 2 hours for the hike under the arches.

## Tukuhnikivats Arch

Tukuhnikivats Arch is an outstanding little arch, located at the southern tip of the area called Behind the Rocks, southeast of Moab. It has a very unusual square shape on one side and a rather rough texture. It makes a great photo, framing

the Manti-La Sal Mountains in the background. On your way to the arch, you'll pass on the left side of the track some outstanding fins and beehives of Entrada sandstone, in the shape of conical skulls.

*Photo advice:* A 28mm is required to frame the arch completely, as there is very little room to walk around it. Don't go much lower than 28mm or the Manti-La Sal Mountains will appear very small in the background. This is an excellent late afternoon location.

*Lovely Tukuhnikivats Arch (photo by Denis Savouray)*

*Getting there:* Follow US 191 south for a little over 12 miles from the Kane Creek Blvd. crossing in downtown Moab, where the McDonald is located. You'll come across a dirt road leading off to the right. Watch out as this dirt road is not posted on US 191 and is easy to miss; however, there is a small sign on the road itself indicating Pritchett Arch and a large signpost with a topo map of the area can be found a bit further. The road soon branches at 0.4 mile, with the left fork going toward Pritchett Arch as well as the northern section of Behind the Rocks. Take the right fork and head north for about 1.2 miles. When the dirt road begins to bear left, look to your right for a spur track heading north. Unless you drive a rugged 4WD—a must for this very rough track—park here. Follow the track toward the north for about 1.1 miles until it ends. Looking northwest, spot the small opening of Tukuhnikivats Arch (38°27'17" 109°27'10") high on your left. It looks very small from the bottom, but don't let this discourage you; it's not that small once you're there. The trail becomes very steep in the last 300 yards and could be dangerous if you hike alone.

*Time required:* 2½ hours round-trip from US 191.

## Wilson Arch

See an arch without leaving your car? Easy enough. About 25 miles south from downtown Moab, you'll find Wilson Arch right next to US 191. But if you want to climb to the arch to admire the beautiful view of the Abajo Mountains, prepare yourself for a rough ascent (about 150 feet of elevation gain in just 600 feet of trail). The descent on the slippery slickrock is even more difficult. Be extremely cautious and wear shoes with good traction. Sunrise and early morning is the best time to photograph the arch and get a nice red glow under its span. Mid to late afternoon works too but the arch is going to be directly lit.

## The La Sal Mountains Loop

This magnificent 62-mile loop from Moab offers a remarkable variety of landscapes, from alpine mountains to canyons. Along the 36-mile section between US 191 and UT 128, a number of viewpoints let you photograph the summits, the pine forests, the canyons above Moab, and the Moab fault in the background. It's hard to beat that. The loop rejoins the Colorado Riverway just past the lovely little community of Castle Valley, at the foot of the towering monoliths of Castle Rock and the Priest and the Nuns.

*Photo advice:* The preferred route is from the south, as the descent into Castle Valley is spectacular. The view from Castle Valley Overlook is best in the afternoon, when the Priest & the Nuns are getting very good light. This trip can be combined with a late afternoon arrival at the Fisher Towers *(see that section).*

*The Priest & the Nuns, near Castle Valley*

*Getting there:* From the south, drive about 7 miles south of downtown Moab (Kane Creek Blvd) on US 191 to catch the clearly marked loop, on the left. From the north, take UT 128 just before the bridge over the Colorado River and drive almost 16 miles to the Castle Valley sign, where you turn right. The road is paved except a very short graded gravel section, which is suitable for passenger cars. The upper part of the loop is closed or impassable in winter.

*Time required:* At least 2½ hours for the complete loop.

## The Colorado Riverway (SB 128)

You'll drive this outstanding Scenic Byway (UT 128) if you come from Colorado on I-70, on your way to Moab. If you come from US 191 either north or south of Moab, you will miss it, so I strongly recommend that you take at least an afternoon to drive it. It's a 30-mile one-way drive from the turnoff with US 191 north of Moab to the historic Dewey Bridge, where you can turn around.

This road provides superlative views as it follows the twists and turns of the Colorado River through Professor Valley, winding its way at the foot of red canyon walls alternating with wide-open areas offering tantalizing glimpses of the La Sal Mountains. You can include side trips to Negro Bill Canyon (well-known for its 4½-mile round-trip hike leading to Morning Glory Natural Bridge), Castle Valley and its impressive mesas reminiscent of Monument Valley, pretty Onion Creek Canyon, and the magnificent Fisher Towers (*see next section*), all extremely photogenic locations. All the beautiful scenery along this stretch of road is better lit after the middle of the afternoon and through sunset.

In spring and summer you'll see commercial raft trips floating down the Colorado River. There are no real rapids there, just a quiet float suitable for families. These half-day trips are more rewarding for the beautiful scenery than for their thrills, but they do provide a taste of the better multiday trips down river from Potash Road to Cataract Canyon. If you're interested in a more challenging experience, consider joining a 1 or 2-day rafting trip on Westwater Canyon, which offers a rough 17-mile descent of the Colorado River with many rapids. Outfitters in Moab and Green River offer this trip. The put-in is at the Westwater Ranger Station, located northeast of UT 128 and the takeout is near Cisco (*see Sego Canyon section in Chapter 9*).

*Nearby locations:* If you're interested in a more challenging whitewater experience, consider joining a 1-day rafting trip in Westwater Canyon, located northeast of SB 128. Outfitters in Moab and Green River offer this rough 17-mile descent of the Colorado River with many rapids. The put-in is at the Westwater Ranger Station and the takeout is near the quasi-ghost town of Cisco. This microscopic hamlet offers a foretaste of the plains characteristic of northwest Colorado, in startling contrast with the red rock landscape of the Moab area. You're left to wonder what the minuscule post office is doing here, lost in the middle of the plain, while most of the other buildings are either painted in psychedelic colors or nailed shut with wooden planks. My wife likes to call it "a little junk treasure".

## The Fisher Towers

Driving from Moab on SB 128 through Professor Valley, you'll reach the amazing Fisher Towers, rising almost a thousand feet high on your right, at the far end of Richardson Amphitheater. These monoliths are extremely photogenic, especially at sunset, when the dark brown and purple walls become almost completely red for just a few minutes. In the entire Colorado plateau, you'd be hard put to find a spot more red than this one at sunset. Don't miss the interesting little group of goblins and chimneys to the right of SB 128, just after you pass the track leading to the Towers.

*The Fisher Towers at sunset*

From the trailhead close to their base, follow the 4½-mile round-trip cairned trail going up and down around the Towers. There are plenty of great views along the way. After about 1½ mile, you reach the base of the Titan, which is the tallest tower. You can backtrack at this point, but I recommend that you follow the trail to its very end, where you'll eventually reach a ridge with a fantastic 360° panoramic view. From there, you can see and photograph the Towers with the shiny ribbon of the Colorado winding in the background, the very colorful badlands of Onion Creek Canyon on the other side and Castle Rock in the distance. Use hiking boots and exercise caution near drop-offs if the trail is slippery after a rain. In summer, take lots of water as the entire trail is in full sun in the afternoon.

*Photo advice:* The Fisher Towers are definitely an afternoon location. If you hike the entire trail, you should start in mid-afternoon in summer or shortly after mid-day in the wintertime, so you can be back before sunset to shoot the red monoliths from one of the pullouts on SB 128.

It's also possible to get stunning vertical shots of the Towers from the edge of the river with a medium to long telephoto lens, using their reflection in the water as a foreground. A polarizing filter is a must to control the amount of reflection. To get this shot, continue north on SB 128 for about 3¾ miles after the turnoff to the Fisher Towers and park about 150 yards past a cattle guard, at the second pullout on the left. Near a big flat rock along the road, you'll notice a small pathway descending to the edge of the river through the undergrowth. The slope may be muddy after a rain, so exercise caution. The path leads to a flat rock miraculously placed in the river close to the bank; depending on the water level you may have to stretch your legs to get to it. From this precarious vantage point, you get an awesome view of the distant Towers. Be there about one hour before sunset to avoid the shade at the bottom of the Towers and on the Colorado River. The Towers glow an astonishing bright red just before sunset. This shot can be caught with a medium telephoto and is even better in winter and spring, when the La Sals are capped with snow *(see the photograph anchoring this chapter).*

Some local photographers have also produced beautiful shots of the Fisher Towers with a full moon in the background. If you shoot the Towers just before they are in shadow, you can keep the exposure within a one-stop range over the entire picture and get a perfectly exposed moon in the deep blue sky.

*Getting there:* At the north end of Moab, just before the bridge, take SB 128 and drive 21 miles northeast from US 191 (or 5½ miles past the Castle Valley turnoff) along the Colorado River. The 2.2-mile track leading towards the Fisher Towers trailhead is marked and generally in good condition for passenger cars.

*Time required:* About 1½ hour for a short hike; 4 hours including the described hike and pre-sunset shot by the river.

*Nearby location:* If you've got a high-clearance vehicle, try a 1-hour foray by car into beautiful Onion Creek Canyon, following a perennial stream just south of the Fisher Towers. This is an outstanding backway, extremely scenic and with a high fun factor as you'll be crossing and recrossing the creek about two dozen times in shallow waters. The canyon gets quite narrow after a couple of miles and you'll find yourself constantly looking up at the impossibly red sandstone walls and tall spires. Drive almost 7 miles to where the canyon opens up into a valley and come back. This dirt road is well signed on SB 128, about 20 miles from US 191 and less than 1 mile before the Fisher Towers turnoff. I suggest that you do this drive prior to visiting the Fisher Towers to avoid the narrow canyon being totally in shadow and to reserve the late afternoon light for the Towers.

## The Entrada Bluffs

At Dewey Bridge, about 30 miles from the beginning of SB 128 near Moab, a well-maintained dirt and gravel road leads to the Entrada Bluffs area, providing scenic views along the way. For those with time on their hands and adequate driving skills, two rough 4WD roads lead south to a couple of spectacular viewpoints over the Colorado River and surrounding canyons. A topo map is essential for these two drives.

From the south end of Dewey Bridge, drive southeast for 1.2 miles on the well-graded Entrada Bluffs Road

*Pole Rim view (photo by Denis Savouray)*

leading to the Kokopelli Bike Trail and angle right on the faint 4WD track leading toward the electricity poles. This road is known as the Pole Rim Trail; it leads in about 5 miles to a dead-end close to the rim above the Colorado River. The Pole Rim Trail is for high-clearance 4WD only. The main challenge is a steep ascent about ½ mile from the beginning, following by an even steeper drop-off on slickrock. This is actually more scary than it looks, because traction is very good in dry weather. If you can clear that, you'll have no problem the rest of the way. Follow the road as it appears on the topo map. At the point where the road angles sharply northwest, make sure you don't stray off the main track or you could find yourself in a cul-de-sac. You can actually drive another ¼-mile past the point where the road ends on the topo. From here, walk north off-trail for about 20 to 30 minutes to avoid the higher cliffs obscuring the view of the Fisher Towers and find a suitable foreground for a terrific shot of the Colorado River with the Richardson Amphitheater, the Fisher Towers and the Manti-LaSal Mountains in the background.

After returning to the Entrada Bluffs Road, turn right, continuing toward the Kokopelli Bike Trail. About 3.8 mile past the turnoff to Pole Rim Trail (or about 5 miles from Dewey Bridge), you'll find a dirt road to your right. This rough 4WD high-clearance road leads southward in 4 miles to the ledge of Top of the World Mesa. As its name suggests, this location offers a superb panoramic view above Professor Valley and the east side of the Fisher Towers. The view from the ledge is quite reminiscent of what you see from the end of the Fisher Towers trail, albeit somewhat behind the Titan and the Towers proper.

*Photo advice:* The second part of the afternoon works best to photograph the Colorado River from Pole Rim; you may need an ND Grad filter if the light is bright. Top of the World is best in the early morning; in late afternoon you'll be shooting against the light. ❧

*Pillars of the Earth*

Chapter 12
ARCHES

*Storm on Delicate Arch (photo by Kerry Thalmann)*

# ARCHES

Almost everything has been written about Arches National Park in traditional guidebooks. What more can be said? That it's only been forty years since it was an isolated and little visited spot? That there was only a simple dirt track when Edward Abbey was a ranger here and wrote his seminal work, Desert Solitaire? Today, you're practically assured of finding a crowd rivaling that of the Grand Canyon, especially during the summer and on weekends.

Located just 5 miles north of Moab, this relatively small National Park is incredibly spectacular and exercises a particular attraction for visitors from all over the world, not only for its extraordinary concentration of arches, but also for its fantastic monoliths and fins with the Manti-La Sal Mountains in the background. The park can be visited year-round, but spring and fall are the best seasons. Summer is very hot and the long hours of bright sunshine make it difficult to photograph the park. Winter can be magical after a fresh dusting of snow.

It's possible to see the main sights in one day, as the very scenic paved road is only a 45-mile round-trip, including short side attractions. However, you should spend at least two days in the park if you want to do most of the rewarding hikes and photograph the highlights at the best time of day. The park is open 24 hours a day, so you'll have no problem being in the field before sunrise or for a moonlight walk, even if you stay in Moab instead of the park's campground.

## Park Avenue & the Courthouse Towers

After driving 2 miles up the high cliff past the Visitor Center and taking in the spectacular view of the Moab Fault, the Park Avenue viewpoint will be your first contact with the unique landscape of Arches Nat'l Park. The best light is in mid-morning or from mid-afternoon on. It is fun to shoot Nefertiti's Head and its beacon-like neighbor on top of the west cliff with a 200 to 300mm telephoto. Where the 1-mile trail pleasantly descending between the high walls of Park Avenue meets the main Park road at the Courthouse Towers viewpoint, you'll find the very photogenic Three Gossips. Nearby, the Courthouse Towers have some shadow from early spring to early summer. However, that's also the season when wildflowers appear in front of the butte called "The Organ" for a glorious photo made famous by Tom Till and many times imitated.

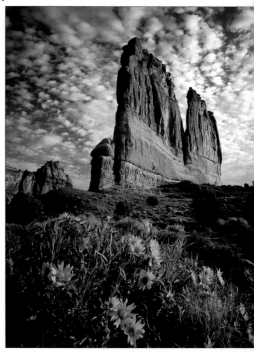

*Nearby location:* The Petrified Dunes are interesting Navajo sandstone formations, located close to the road and offering photogenic compositions, provided you're there at the right time.

Before sunrise, park at the Petrified Dunes pullout—2.3 miles past the Courthouse Towers viewpoint—and walk in the direction of the dunes. Once there, walk a little bit more into the heart of the dunes or until you come to a spot that seems picturesque and where you can't see your car. The sun rises behind the Manti-La Sal Mountains and directly lights the Great Wall, a series of rock faces several miles long that glow bright red with the appearance of the first sun rays. You can photograph these red walls with the petri-fied dunes in the foreground. A graduated

*The Courthouse Towers (photo by Tom Till)*

neutral density filter is a must to preserve the detail of the dunes and still cor-rectly expose the walls.

## Balanced Rock

Often photographed, always beautiful, Balanced Rock is a geological rebel, defying the unstoppable forces of erosion. Unfortunately, it is bound to lose its fight at some point and be toppled over like the rest. This will undoubtedly hap-pen very soon in geological time and could even happen soon in our own narrow human scale of time. So, don't wait; record its beauty for the sake of your children,

*Balanced Rock at sunset*

before it disappears forever. You can see it close up by doing the ¼-mile loop, but it also can be viewed from numerous vantage points farther away.

*Photo advice:* You can photograph it from close-up with a wide-angle lens or from the other side of the road with a 135 to 200 mm lens, to isolate it against the backdrop of the Manti-La Sal Mountains and get rid of the cars and tourists. The end of the afternoon is best to do this. Night photos under a full moon give great results and are fun to shoot. From this spot, I also like to shoot the tall pillars located near the Windows, using a 500 mm telephoto *(see front cover photo)*. There is also a good shot of Balanced Rock at sunset from the intersection of the Windows and Garden of Eden roads, also with a powerful telephoto.

## The Windows Section

This section of the park has a series of impressive arches that are easy to reach. From the parking area at the end of a 2½-mile side road, start your walk in the direction of Turret Arch and the North and South Windows. Near the South Windows, a spur trail lets you make a loop around the backside of the Windows; very few people use it and it's a real place for photography. Continuing past Turret Arch and South Windows, you'll come to a group of very interesting monoliths.

*Double Arch*

Exercising caution, you can climb to a rock behind North Window to shoot the classic photo of Turret Arch framed within the arch's opening. This is an excellent early- to mid-morning shot depending on the season. The NPS is considering making access to this shot permanently off limits due to the presence of cryptobiotic soil. Please check with a Ranger.

Back at the parking area, walk or drive to the Double Arch car park, from where you can walk right under the twin spans of this monumental arch.

If you are lucky enough to be at Arches in summer during the full moon, a midnight walk around this section of the park can be very rewarding. The heat radiating from the ground and currents of cool air mix in a delicious swirl around you and the rock formations of the Windows take on a fantastic quality.

*Turret Arch seen through the North Window*

*Time required:* About 1-½ hour.

*Nearby location:* On a short side road off the main road, Panorama Point provides a bird's-eye view of a good deal of the park, very lovely at the end of day, but too vast to be photographed with much success. You can, however, get a good morning view of Balanced Rock and also of the Devil's Garden with a 200 to 300 mm telephoto.

## Wolfe Ranch Petroglyphs

Most visitors stopping at the Wolfe Ranch parking area are anxious to be on their way to Utah's most prominent of icons: Delicate Arch. Few visitors go out of their way to look at these almost modern petroglyphs. This is sad, because it is such an interesting panel.

The small but well-preserved panel illustrates the way of life of local Ute tribes. Bighorn sheep, horses and riders are featured prominently on the panel. It is easy to assume that tribal artists endeavored to represent scenes of hunting.

*Photo advice:* The panel is well lit and surrounded by

*Ute petroglyphs at Wolfe Ranch*

vegetation. I find it beautiful, because of its simplicity, and a perfect subject for imaginative photography. The immediate area surrounding the mural is cordoned off, but the panel is close enough for standard lens or short telephoto photography. As with most rock art, well-exposed panels have a tendency to absorb more light and thus to turn gray on film on heavily overcast days. Be sure to have a warming filter handy for such occasions.

*Getting there:* At the Delicate Arch parking area, about 1.2 miles east of the main park road, follow the main trail past Wolfe Ranch. After a hundred yards or so, you'll come to a small wooden bridge. Immediately after the bridge, you'll find a small trail to the left. Follow it for another 200 yards until the panel comes to view. You can continue on this trail to meet the Delicate Arch trail.

## Delicate Arch

Arches National Park, and the State of Utah, wouldn't be the same without the extraordinary symbol of Delicate Arch. What sets this arch apart is not its size, but its incredibly graceful shape and stunning location above a curving slickrock basin with the Manti-La Sal Mountains in the background.

Delicate Arch is not so easy to get to and that's just as well because it some-what limits foot traffic, which is already very high. You can reach it by taking a trail that's about a 3 mile round-trip, half of which is marked by the footprints of previous visitors on the slickrock as well as by strategically-placed cairns. Though it may be easy to climb to Delicate Arch during the day—count on about 45 minutes one way—exercise extreme caution when descending after sundown and take a flashlight. It's easy to take a bad fall if you tend to shuffle along and not lift your feet sufficiently.

Visiting Delicate Arch in the middle of the day is not recommended. This is partly because the climb is quite hard and can be strenuous if the temperature is high, but also because the arch doesn't reveal all its splendor until late afternoon. In any case, Delicate Arch is the perfect hike to end your day in the park.

*Delicate Arch at sunset (photo by Nolan Thomas Jones)*

*Photo advice:* The best season for photographing Delicate Arch is winter, when the arch is entirely basked in sunset. In late spring, a small amount of shadow becomes visible at the bottom and by July, half of the arch is in shadow at sunset. Keep this in mind and don't arrive too late so you can avoid that nasty black shadow, even if you have to settle for less red on the arch. In summer, you'll be better off leaving the trailhead at least 1½ hour before sunset. You can get information at the Visitor Center or in town as to when the sun will set and figure the best time to climb to it. There aren't many angles to use at sunset. Backlit shots taken from the extreme left of the arch aren't very satisfactory and the view directly down the axis of the arch is only suitable for family photos. The best vantage point is from the edge of the rock ledge encircling the arch, where the trail comes out. Try to position yourself so that the highest peaks of the La Sal Mountains are profiled on the horizon between the base and the summit of the arch, a height of about forty feet. The

peaks are frequently adorned with a rosy veil during the last moments of sunset when the arch is lit up in red. If you can, stay a while after sunset to capture the residual lighting in the clouds and just to appreciate this sublime spectacle while the rest of the crowd hurries toward the parking area.

*Delicate Arch seen from the Viewpoint*

*Nearby location:* Past the Delicate Arch trailhead at Wolfe Ranch, the road continues for one mile to a distant viewpoint of Delicate Arch. It's quite interesting to go there to see how precariously the arch rests on the plateau. You reach the upper viewpoint at the end of a moderately difficult 1.3-mile round-trip trail. This hike should preferably be made before mid-afternoon, otherwise the arch will be in shadow. The view of the arch and the cirque from the ridge, with a 200-foot drop-off below you, is startling. From here, a 200mm telephoto lens will isolate the arch perfectly, but anything above 100mm will do. A 24mm lens is necessary for a panoramic view of the cirque and to include the butte to the right.

## The Fiery Furnace

On the east side of the main park road, the huge sandstone fins of the Fiery Furnace form a maze of confusing narrow canyons and dead-ending passage-ways. Ironically, the Fiery Furnace is the coolest place to be in Arches when it's hot, because you're almost constantly walking in the shade and there is always a light draft running through it. As many people have gotten lost in this labyrinth, you are encouraged to visit the Furnace with a ranger-led group. Nevertheless, it is possible to venture alone into this area off-season, after following a 20-minute video orientation and paying an extra fee.

For a first time visit, I strongly recommend that you join the guided walk, as it's so easy to lose your way—even with a compass or a GPS—and you'll miss several interesting highlights. A Park Ranger will show you hidden arches, such as Surprise Arch and Skull Arch, and explain basic facts concerning the geology and ecology of the park, such as the difference between an arch and a bridge, Entrada and Navajo sandstone, and the usefulness of cryptobiotic crust. The guided tour is given twice daily during the high season. It lasts about 3 hours, at a relaxed pace, and you'll cover a distance of approximately 2 miles. You can reserve at the Visitor Center up to seven days in advance by paying an extra fee. Be careful, this tour fills up quickly. As your group may have as many as 25 bodies who must move together, it is not an ideal situation for photography. However, nothing prevents you from returning on your own the next day and retracing your steps, perhaps an hour before a scheduled guided tour. If everything goes according to plan, you'll have plenty of time for photography before the group catches up with you; if you get lost or something happens to you, stay put or retrace your steps and wait for the guided tour to arrive.

*Photo advice:* During the hike inside the Fiery Furnace, don't bother with anything else than a wide-angle! Follow the advice given in the Introduction chapter about photographing in slot canyons—even though there is often quite a bit more light inside the Furnace. If you don't have time to do the guided walk, you can descend for a short distance towards the fins to photograph them with a medium or long telephoto lens and compress the perspective. This works better from late afternoon till sunset. From the parking area, the fins can also form a good foreground with the La Sal Mountains behind them.

## Sand Dune Arch & Broken Arch

About 1½ mile before the northern end of the park road, don't miss the very short walk to Sand Dune Arch. It's a peculiar sight, hidden as it is between the walls of huge fins. It is difficult to photograph, but you'll be rewarded along the way by a great shot of a group of symmetrical fins, especially in late afternoon. Broken Arch is also nice and it's an easy flat walk. Consider continuing on the 2-mile loop trail, going through the campground and passing through narrow joints between the fins before returning to the Sand Dune Arch parking area.

*Fins near Sand Dune Arch*

# The Devil's Garden

Located at the end of the scenic road, about 18 miles from the entrance of the park, the Devil's Garden loop is a real pleasure, arguably one of the most rewarding half-day hikes of the Colorado Plateau. It's a moderately difficult, but spectacular, walk. On your way to superb Double-O Arch, you'll be passing by Pine Tree Arch, Landscape Arch (the longest in the park), Partition Arch and Navajo Arch. Past the spur trail to Navajo Arch, you'll climb high on a narrow ridge providing excellent views of the fins below.

From Double-O Arch, you can do the extension to Dark Angel—a solitary monolith overlooking Salt Valley. Nearby, you can see a little-known but inter-esting site of Indian petroglyphs. It is only a short detour so it would be a shame to miss it. With Dark Angel behind you, walk cross-country toward the southwest for about 250 yards to reach the edge of a low cliff. Exercising caution, find your way to the foot of the cliff and follow it to your left, bearing southeast. Look for the petroglyphs that are spread over several hundred yards. Return the way you came.

*Wall Arch... before the fall*

Back at Double-O Arch, you can retrace your steps to the trailhead or return by the more difficult Primitive Trail, which is beau-tiful and less crowded. The Primitive Trail is a cairned route passing through canyons formed by fins and slabs of sandstone, with some sections on steeply slanted ground (slippery when wet). The whole loop, includ-ing all the side trails (except the Indian petro-glyphs) and returning via the Primitive Trail, is 7.2 miles round-trip. You can shorten your hike by one mile by returning the way you came instead of taking the Primitive Trail. Take hiking shoes, a hat and lot of water on this trail. If you want to capture the best light on Landscape Arch and avoid the extreme heat of the day—especially in summer when it's cooking—you should begin the hike early in the morning. If you do it in mid- to late-after-noon, however, you'll have the advantage of good light on the most beautiful side of Double-O Arch and the nearby fins.

*Photo advice:* Wall Arch is no more. It collapsed sometime during the night of August 5 to 6, 2008. The best season to photograph Landscape Arch is in late spring and early summer, when there are no shadows on the arch in early morn-ing. The view in complete sunshine is only available in mid-morning during the rest of the year and a moderate warming filter will help restore the rich color

*Double-O Arch*

saturation of the sandstone. In 1991, a large block of rock fell from the 306-foot long span of Landscape Arch, causing the National Park Service to close the trail under the arch. The fence, which was put up to prevent people from venturing under the arch, severely limits your composition in framing Landscape Arch artistically. The best vantage point to photograph the arch against a background of sky is at the end of the short spur. Double-O Arch is one of the most spectacular arches in the Southwest. To photograph it, pass through the lower opening of the arch and climb the slickrock on the other side until you find a suitable location. A wide-angle lens is necessary to capture the entire arch. This side is in the shade in the morning and is best lit from mid-afternoon on, as most of the fins in the Devil's Garden area.

*Time required:* 4 to 5 hours for the complete loop. Add almost an hour for the detour to the Indian petroglyphs near Dark angel.

## The Klondike Bluffs

The Klondike Bluffs area offers a nice easy hiking experience coupled with some great sights and photography, away from the increasing stream of visitors. Outside of the season, it is entirely possible to spend a couple of hours in the Klondike Bluffs and never see a soul.

Although massive Tower Arch gets most of the attention, another striking landmark in the Klondike Bluffs area is the formation group known as the Marching Men, consisting of spires of various thickness and height aligned one behind another, very much like a soldier troop on the go. The pleasant loop from the trailhead near Salt Valley Road is 3.4 miles round-trip and takes at least two hours depending on the time you devote to photography.

*Photo advice:* Photography inside the Klondike Bluffs is generally best in late afternoon. To photograph the Marching Men in the best possible light, plan on returning from Tower Arch about 45 minutes before sunset and find a suitable location at the top of the sand dune where all the Marching Men appear in your line of sight from a slightly dominant position. This location requires a short telephoto. Alternately, you can walk down toward the middle of the last sand dune and photograph the group from below with a moderate wide-angle to standard lens.

*Getting there:* The easiest and most common way is to come via Salt Valley Road; its turnoff is on the main park road, 1 mile before the Devil's Garden area. This dirt road is usually in good condition, although it can be quite sandy in places or even impassable after a rain. After about 7½ miles, you see a first spur road to your left. This sandy 4WD road leads in about 3 miles to a parking area very close to Tower Arch; there is a nasty ramp that needs to be negotiated around mile one. Also, if you use this road, you'll miss the hike through the beautiful scenery of the Bluffs—including the Marching Men. Instead, take the next road to the left, leading in 1.3 miles to the main trailhead; it is passable by 2WD vehicles. If you came to Tower Arch using the first sandy 4WD road, you'll encounter the Willow Flats 4WD road, returning to the main park road opposite Balanced Rock. Note that this is a very sandy and difficult road; every year visitors get stuck on it and have to be pulled out.

Returning to Salt Valley Road, it's relatively easy to leave the park by continuing north on this road for 11 miles until the intersection with Thompson Road. Turning left, you'll then reach US 191 in about a mile and turning right you can reach Thompson in 7½ miles to visit the Sego Canyon rock art site 3½ miles further *(see San Rafael Swell chapter)*. I have driven the northern section of Salt Valley Road in a 4WD

*The Marching Men*

vehicle and feel it would present no difficulties for a high-clearance vehicle in dry weather. As always, get directions in town or at the Visitor Center to find out the exact condition of the road.

Another way to access the Klondike Bluffs area, if you feel adventurous and have a 4WD, is to take the BLM road leaving from US 191 just before reaching the airfield when coming from Moab, driving directly toward the bluffs. There is a BLM sign on the gate and a fairly large parking area. Close the gate behind you and proceed on the well-maintained dirt road. Things worsen at the sandy wash crossing and the road becomes very narrow and poorly maintained after that. Drive as far as you feel comfortable, then park and walk toward the bluffs.

*Nearby location:* If you leave the park from the north via Salt Valley and Thompson Road, consider stopping at the Copper Ridge Sauropod Track site. It has impressive fossil tracks of a brontosaur and carnivores from the Jurassic period, unfortunately difficult to photograph. To get there, leave US 191 at milepost 148.7, about 4 miles south of the Thompson Road turnoff (8½ south of Exit 182 on I-70 at Crescent Junction or 20 miles north of the Colorado Bridge near Moab). Cross the railroad tracks on the east side of US 191 and follow the dirt road—suitable for passenger cars in dry weather—for about 2 miles to a parking area. The tracks are about 100 yards up the hill to the east.

## Courthouse Wash Rock Art

If you still have some time available in Moab and are interested in rock art, consider a brief stop along US 191 just north of town to observe an interesting Barrier style panel. The 50-foot Courthouse Wash panel is located within the southern confines of the Arches Nat'l Park, displaying a juxtaposition (sometimes a superposition) of anthropomorphs and abstract figures. Unfortunately, the pictographs were seriously vandalized in 1980 and are quite faint, which makes them hard to photograph.

To find the panel, drive out of town past the Colorado River bridge and pull out at a large car park on the right side of US 191 (at milepost 129, immediately after crossing Courthouse Wash). Walk east, crossing the mouth of Courthouse Wash and, still walking along US 191, bear southeast uphill to the base of the cliff. You'll find the panel less than ½ mile from where you parked.

Time permitting, you can hike up Courthouse Wash as much as you like toward the inside of the park, following the pleasant perennial stream bed with its cottonwoods and willows.

*Time required:* 1 hour from Moab for the rock art panel. ✿

*Dawn of the Mineral Age*

Chapter 13

CANYONLANDS — ISLAND IN THE SKY

*Mesa Arch at sunrise*

# CANYONLANDS — ISLAND IN THE SKY

I heartily recommend Canyonlands Nat'l Park to those who love sweeping canyon panoramas, river goosenecks, outstanding rock formations and who wish to escape the Grand Canyon crowds. I have recommended and continue to recommend this park to innumerable visitors. They return unanimous in their opinion that some of the views are as vast and impressive as those of Grand Canyon.

Just twenty five years ago this park received only 10,000 visitors a year and had no paved roads. Today, though not as heavily visited as Arches, it's become a destination of choice for tourists, 4x4 enthusiasts, mountain bikers, hikers and certainly for photographers. Madison Avenue and Hollywood have also discovered it, and you can see it in more and more movies, TV ads and music videos. Let's hope it won't have a negative impact on the park in years to come.

Canyonlands Nat'l Park consists of three districts separated by the two rivers merging in its center: the Colorado River and the Green River. Each district has its own distinct flavor: To the north, Island In the Sky and Dead Horse Point form a vast peninsula overlooking the canyons and is easy to visit. To the southeast, the Needles district is particularly remarkable for the diversity of its geological features—pinnacles, arches, grabens and canyons—requiring a lot of hiking or 4-wheel driving. To the west, the Maze is wild and desolate and visiting its intricate network of canyons and mesas is only for the most adventurous with mountain bikes or rugged 4WD vehicles.

Lacking bridges on the rivers, these three districts are separated by hours of driving. Just to get a glimpse of the three districts, one needs several days; several trips are a more realistic approach to enjoy some of the many trails. To gain a true perspective of the vastness of the park and understand its geography, geology and diversity, you would need to fly over it. Given the extreme temperatures that affect this region, the best time to visit is undoubtedly spring and the first part of autumn.

Due to the specific character of each of the three districts, as well as the huge distances separating them, each is described under its own chapter. The present chapter concentrates on Island in the Sky which is the most accessible—as well as the most visited—of the three districts in the park. A scenic road provides easy access to expansive views from a high mesa top (reaching 6000 feet of elevation) overlooking dozens of miles of canyon country. This paved road is SR 313, heading southwest about 11 miles north of Moab on US 191. The Visitor Center is located about 21 miles past the junction and the road continues for another 12 miles until it dead-ends at Grand Viewpoint Overlook.

## Dead Horse Point State Park

Even if you do not have much time, don't miss Dead Horse Point State Park for an outstanding panorama of the area. This small park, located near the entrance to Canyonlands National Park (Island In The Sky), offers the prototypical view of the American West canyons, as pictured in many ads and movies.

*Photo advice:* The best location is at Dead Horse Point Overlook, at the very end of the road, a few hundred yards past the narrow neck; it offers two panoramic views: To the southwest, the bend of the Colorado River with its superb mesa at the center and, on the opposite side, a view of the canyons with the Manti-La Sal Mountains in the background. From the parking area, the choice of views is limited. Walk on the Rim Trail around the viewpoint and pick a foreground you like, which will best show the depth of the canyon and the immensity of the terrain. A 28 to 35mm lens is ideal for the river bend. For the panorama of the canyons and the La Sal Mountains, you can give free rein to your imagination if you

*Contemplating Canyonlands*

have a zoom. Any focal length will highlight something different. The bend is best photographed in the early morning, with the sun rising on the left, but sunset is equally beautiful. It's also nice to photograph the bend before sunrise or after sunset using a warming filter to avoid a bluish tint on the mesa. In fact, the subject is so awe-inspiring that even mid-day photos can be impressive with a polarizing or warming filter. On the other hand, for the panorama of the canyons, a morning or evening light is essential to best render depth and contrast. With a bit of luck and patience, the high clouds will be basking in the last gleams of sunset and the snowy peaks of the La Sal Mountains will be a vivid pink. For a slightly different view of the eastern canyons, you can also walk to Basin Overlook, about halfway between Dead Horse Point Overlook and the Visitor Center.

*Arch near Long Canyon*

*Getting there:* The turnoff to Dead Horse Point State Park is on UT 313, 14½ miles from US 191 and before the entrance to Canyonlands. From the turnoff, drive 8 miles to Dead Horse Point Overlook at the very end of the road.

*Time required:* About 1½ hour round-trip to get there from Moab and 1 hour on location. However, you will most likely want to visit this place at the same time as Island in the Sky. The complete circuit of the viewpoints—to Grandview Point, including the side roads—can be done in a long half day at a hurried pace, though that will mean sacrificing taking pictures at either sunrise and/or sunset and missing interesting sites such as Aztec Buttes and False Kiva.

*Nearby location:* If you have a high-clearance vehicle, you can return to Moab by way of Long Canyon Road and Potash Road (SB 279). You'll find Long Canyon Road 6.3 miles from Dead Horse Point Overlook (or 1.7 miles from SR 313). After a tad over 3 miles on a good gravel road, you reach Pucker Pass, offering a nice open view with the canyons below and the Manti-La Sal in the background. From here on, the road becomes rough for about 4 miles and somewhat steep in places, as you descend slowly through an impressive landscape of huge sandstone cliffs. At one point, you'll pass under a huge boulder that has fallen from the cliff, forming a sort of arch with just enough room for your SUV to get through. Look for a beautiful horse hoof-shaped arch to the left at the junction with Potash Road. Long Canyon Road is passable most of the time, except after heavy rains; be sure to inquire about its condition at the Visitor Center.

# Mesa Arch

Mesa Arch, located about 6 miles south of the Island in the Sky Visitor Center, just before the junction with Upheaval Dome Road, offers an outstanding photographic opportunity, which has become a "classic" of the Southwest. If you go during the day, you'll see the entire superb spectacle of these immense canyons framed through a magnificent arch perched on the edge of a precipitous drop... really pretty, you say. Yes, but there's better still if you're willing to pay the price: you'll have to get up well before dawn to catch it at its very best for a truly magical photograph.

Start by getting the precise time of sunrise for that day. You can get this information on your GPS or the day before at the Visitor Center or in town. Plan to be at the Mesa Arch parking area about ½ hour before sunrise. From Moab, plan on almost 1 hour travel time to get there. Park your car and take the short trail; it's a 15-minute walk. This will give you enough time to find a spot, prepare your equipment and try to visualize in your mind's eye the extraordinary spectacle that will soon be unveiled. Don't rush it, even if the sky is already very light. There will still be some time before the sun actually appears and nothing will happen without its presence.

When the sun makes its appearance, far beyond the canyons, the underside of the arch will glow a vivid red, offering an absolutely sublime spectacle. The sun rises on the left of the arch in summer and on the right in winter. In either case, it's possible to frame it inside one of the arch's pillars.

You'll get the best results by spot metering on the sky just above the arch. As a general rule, a clean northern sky is as neutral as a gray card and can be metered on accurately. Do not meter under the bridge where the light is too intense and would severely underexpose your picture. If your camera doesn't have spot measuring, just trust your metering system and add ½ stop overexposure—but not more—to be safe. You'll have a good 15-minute window of opportunity to photograph the underside of the arch basking in intense red light, gradually turning orange and yellow on the edges. Work briskly, the first five minutes are the most intense. You'll have a hard time containing your excitement in the face of such a magnificent spectacle. For the grand finale, position yourself so the sun appears masked just behind the edge of the arch and bracket a couple of stops on each side.

You'll get excellent results with lenses ranging from an extreme wide angle to 35mm.

*Another view of Mesa Arch*

A 35mm lens will allow you to get better detail of the canyons through the arch and of the Manti-La Sal Mountains in the distance.

If you back up about 70 feet, a hillock will also let you shoot partially through the arch with an 80 to 105mm lens, compressing the perspective of the canyons and the La Sal Mountains with the incandescent top of the arch.

A tripod is of course indispensable to maximize the depth of field. An artistic blur of the foreground or background would kill the impact of this classic landscape composition.

Mesa Arch can also be photographed at the end of the afternoon with the sun lighting the front of the arch and the canyons in the distance. The accent is then on the contrast between the strongly lit arch and the blue sky.

## Grandview Point & White Rim Overlook

At the very end of the main park road, Grand Viewpoint offers a breathtaking panorama and you won't regret the miles you've traveled to get to this spot. From the parking area's vista point, your eye encompasses hundreds of miles of

*Grandview Point sunset (photo by Lynn Radeka)*

canyon country, with the spectacular white-capped spires of Monument Basin in the foreground; you can even improve on this view by taking the easy 2-mile round-trip trail leading to the tip of the plateau. The view from the end of the trail includes even more territory to the northeast, as well as a closer view of Junction Butte, just ½ mile away. Due to the immensity of the landscape, it's not an easy task to capture this view, unless you have a truly spectacular sky or you crop a panoramic view without the sky. You can also zoom in on a specific spot, such as Monument Basin. This view is best just before sunset.

For an even better view, drive back less than a mile towards the Visitor Center, stop at the picnic area and hike the 1.8-mile round-trip trail leading, at the right fork, to the lesser-known White Rim Overlook. This easy trail is quite interesting in itself and the overlook is a great early morning location with an outstanding view of Gooseberry Canyon and Monument Basin.

## Green River Overlook & Murphy Point

If you're on the Island toward the end of the afternoon, go to the Green River Overlook or to Murphy Point, set up your tripod and get ready to capture another grandiose vista.

The popular view from the Green River Overlook is a no-brainer; on Upheaval Dome Road, soon after the turnoff on SR 313, take the good 1½-mile gravel road to the large parking area, then walk only a couple of hundred feet to a fantastic view of Soda Springs Basin. This is a great evening location, when no haze is present. You may want to walk northwest along the rim for a little while to look for locations that inspire you, but you can't go wrong just staying at the main viewpoint. There are some small bluffs slightly to the left of the overlook, with a great view and plenty of space for your tripod. Camping at nearby Willow Flats campground is very convenient to get an early morning start for other Island-in-the-Sky locations, such as nearby Mesa Arch.

Murphy Point also offers a great panoramic view of the western side of the White Rim with a closer view of Soda Springs Basin, the Murphy Hogback and the tip of the Island-in-the-Sky to the distant south. Like the Green River Overlook, it is a great place for sunset photography, but the 4-mile round-trip jaunt deters many and you're likely to have the place to yourself.

## Aztec Butte

Aztec Butte has a small but very photogenic concentration of Ancient Puebloan dwellings and granaries. Given that it's only a 2-mile round-trip hike from the road, you shouldn't miss it.

From the trailhead, follow the good trail until you reach the base of the butte, climb the steep slickrock face to the top and take the trail to the right, passing the rather mundane top ruin. The path then continues toward the back of the butte where you'll find a series of alcoves and granaries, but the best is yet to come. Continuing the loop around the butte, you'll arrive on its northwestern side at an unusual and highly photogenic granary built inside an eroded sandstone alcove supported on each side by pillars. Unfortunately, part of the wall of the granary has recently collapsed and it is not as photogenic as it used to be.

*Aztec Butte Ruin*

Continue around the butte to rejoin the trail descending on the slickrock. The second butte is worth a quick visit to see two more granaries.

*Photo advice:* The granary is facing northwest and the best time to photograph it is in mid-afternoon. Closer to sunset, the right pillar of the alcove causes the dwelling to be in the shade. A 28mm works perfectly to capture the ruin with the horizon showing through the left pillar.

*Getting there:* On the road leading to Upheaval Dome, park at the marked Aztec Ruin trailhead, less than a mile from the junction with SR 313.

*Time required:* 1 to 1½ hour.

## False Kiva

False Kiva is a hauntingly beautiful photographic location made popular by Tom Till. Hidden under a vast alcove at the edge of Island in the Sky, False Kiva has all the ingredients of a great Canyon Country shot. It consists of a low circular ruin forming an ideal foreground to a classic Canyonlands grand scenic, with the silhouette of Candlestick Butte balancing the shot beautifully. False Kiva is not featured in the park's literature and chances are there won't be any other soul during your visit, which will only reinforce the beauty and serenity of the place. Despite its circular shape, the ruin is not a kiva. Notes on the origin of the name are found in a metal box also containing a visitor's log book. Do not disturb the ruins in any way and leave no trace of your passage so other photographers can enjoy this very special place.

*Photo advice:* The best time to photograph False Kiva is in the second part of the afternoon, when the cliffs to the southwest and Candlestick Tower in the background take on a superb golden hue. You may get good results by waiting until sunset and shooting an ambiance picture where the ruins are not in full sun. The ruins themselves receive less light as they are tucked in under the alcove and in full shadow before sunset. At that time, you'll need a 3-stop ND Grad filter to maintain detail in the ruins while keeping the background correctly exposed, or you can try a polarizer if you have a fairly good blue sky in the background. If you're shooting digital, take several tripod-based shots using your remote control under- and overexposing by 2 stops. You can later combine the best exposed foreground and background shots in your digital darkroom. A 28 mm is perfect to frame the ruin and part of the alcove. Below 24mm, you'll start losing much of the background.

*Getting there:* On the road leading to Upheaval Dome, park at the pull-out for the Alcove Spring trailhead, less than 4 miles from the junction with SR 313. On the other side of the road, walk back about 250 yards in the direction of SR 313 and look to the right for a well-trod footpath leading west.

Follow the sandy footpath for about ten minutes to the edge of a small cliff. Bypass the cliff by descending on the slickrock to the left. There are a few cairns present during this brief off-trail section. The visible trail resumes at the bottom and you reach the edge of the rim about 5 minutes later. A steep trail to the right leads down some talus. This trail has been greatly improved in recent years. It is now cairned and easy to follow but still a bit treacherous due to the loose stones rolling under your feet; walk down cautiously, this is not the place to twist an ankle. The trail eventually levels out as you reach the foot of a massive alcove. As you continue on the ledge toward the northern end of the alcove, look to your right for a footpath angling back and ascending the slope diagonally toward the southern end of the alcove. The steep ascent on small loose stones is brief and yields no clue of the presence of the False Kiva, which you discover at the last second, upon reaching the hidden platform.

*Time required:* 1½ to 2 hours round-trip with time to appreciate and photograph the site.

*Nearby location:* On the east side of the pull-out, you'll find the trailhead for the Alcove Spring Trail, leading in a little bit over 5 miles to Upper Taylor Canyon and the 1.8-mile loop trail around the impressive Moses and Zeus spires. You can also reach the Moses and Zeus monoliths by 4WD from the White Rim Road via the 5-mile long Taylor Canyon Road *(see White Rim Road section)*.

## Upheaval Dome

Located at the end of the 5-mile side road from the SR 313, this geologic phenomenon, which looks more like a crater than a dome, is quite interesting

*Opposite page: Stormy afternoon on False Kiva (photo by Denis Savouray)*

to observe. In and around the crater, the various geologic layers of the park are particularly well displayed and easy to observe because of the angle of the walls. It's a perfect opportunity for a little refresher course on the geology of the plateau and to learn to distinguish between the colors and the strata of the various sandstone formations.

An easy 2-mile round-trip trail leads to two successive overlooks from the edge of the crater. The first overlook is the better one to take photographs, although it's difficult to photograph the crater successfully anyway.

*Nearby location:* Driving back a few hundred yards toward SR 313 from the Upheaval Dome parking area, you can also take the easy 1-mile round-trip trail to the top of Whale Rock, from where you have good views of the dome in the earlier part of the day.

## The Shafer Trail

Branching off SR 313 about a mile from the Visitor Center, the 5-mile long Shafer Trail lets you descend, amongst superlative views, onto the White Rim plateau a thousand feet below. There, it joins with Potash Road to the left and the White Rim Road to the right. Originally an old cattle road used by ranchers since the late 1800's, it was enlarged in the fifties during the uranium boom. You can observe its spectacular switchbacks carved right into the flank of the steep canyon cliffs from the Shafer Trail viewpoint, located about ½-mile past the Visitor Center.

You'll need a 4WD or at least a high-clearance vehicle to descend the scary-looking—but not technically difficult—Shafer Trail and get a close-up view of the Colorado River and the famous White Rim Road. Needless to say, this trail must only be driven in dry weather, very slowly, using low gears and never in a passenger car.

The Shafer Trail can be easily integrated into a highly scenic loop drive, starting and ending up in Moab. In the course of one day, you can watch sunrise at Dead Horse Point or Mesa Arch, visit Island in the Sky including some of the short hikes described above, descend the Shafer Trail and spend some time on the beginning of the White Rim Road—at least as far as Musselman Arch—before returning to Moab by way of the Potash Road and SB 279, passing Thelma & Louise Point along the way. A memorable day by any standards, amply justifying the rental of a 4WD vehicle for the day in Moab if you don't have one.

## The White Rim Road

To visit the extraordinary White Rim and Monument Basin in greater depth, including spectacular features such as Monument Basin and Soda Springs Basin, you'll have to allow for a multi-day trip to cover the 100 miles of this popular loop. Although most of the road is suitable for high-clearance vehicles, there are some steep rocky spots where 4WD and low gear are necessary. This road is also a favorite of vehicle-assisted mountain biking groups. Most of the time, the road winds along the edge of the rim of the flat plateau halfway between the Island in the Sky mesa and the Colorado and Green rivers. It's an unforgettable trip and, all in all, not too difficult to accomplish, provided you reserve your permits well in advance.

In spring or early autumn, you can do this trip at a relaxed pace without suffering from summer's heat or icy winter nights. On this arid plateau, where wood fires are no longer allowed, nighttime temperatures drop well below freezing by November and remain so until early March.

*Photo advice:* There are countless opportunities for photography along the track, starting with the Shafer Trail switchbacks. About 1.2 miles past the junction with the White Rim Trail, you can follow the short Gooseneck Trail for a nice overlook on the Colorado River. About 2 miles further, you'll find the turnout to Musselman Arch, an interesting flat span above the basin below that some people like to cross. Look for the nearby Standing Rocks, which can be reached by walking up the rim from the arch. Almost 8 miles further, Lathrop Canyon provides the only access to the Colorado River via a rough and sandy road.

The most interesting section of the White Rim is without doubt Monument Basin, reached about 15 miles further and where photographic opportunities abound.

*The White Rim at close range*

Past the spur road to the White Crack campground, the western side of the trail offers outstanding views of the Green River and the great monoliths of the Maze: Ekker Butte, Cleopatra's Chair, Buttes of the Cross, and more. Beyond the Murphy Hogback and Soda Springs Basin, Turk's Head is an outstanding shot requiring a 21mm to frame the entire gooseneck of the Green River. As you progress further north past Candlestick Tower, you'll come level to the Green at Potato Bottom and, after a steep climb, reach the spectacular location of the Fort Ruin, smack in the middle of a great gooseneck. Take the 4.2-mile round-trip trail crossing the narrow mesa high above the river to the remnants of two Ancient Puebloan towers before descending to an old cabin on Fort Bottom.

In most instances, you'll be photographing along the road in the middle of the day and a skylight or polarizing filter will be useful.

*Getting there:* It is recommended to drive the White Rim Trail clockwise. From the top of the Shafer Trail on SR 313, you are looking at 75 miles of rough dirt road (without counting the side roads such as Lathrop Road, White Crack or Taylor Canyon) to rally Mineral Road, where you still have another 13 miles of good trail to finish the loop on SR 313, 8 miles north of your starting point. As you can see, it is quasi-impossible to do this loop in one day and you must therefore plan a camping trip. A quota system is in effect for all camping trips and it's necessary to make your reservation several months in advance. Only a few permits are issued every day, based on the very small number of primitive campsites located along the road. Some of these campsites are unique, like that of White Crack, at the southern tip of the trail, which has only a single car site. You will be alone on the edge of the canyon, with Junction Butte in front of you and the long ribbon of the Colorado River quietly flowing a thousand feet below. Island in the Sky is behind you, over a thousand feet higher, and a magnificent starry sky serves as your roof. The immensity and solitude of the surrounding canyons is impressive. The only other human beings for over 40 miles around are the few at the other campsites scattered along the trail. Candlestick, on the western side of the loop, is also a great single car campsite.

If you have no time for a multi-day trip or if you couldn't obtain a camping permit, day-driving is allowed on the White Rim Road as long as you are out by the end of the day. This opens up several possibilities: From the Shafer Trail (or Potash Road) you can drive to Gooseberry Canyon or even to Monument Basin in one extra-long summer day if you begin at sunrise; from Mineral Road, you can drive and visit Fort Bottom and even Taylor Canyon and the Moses & Zeus Spires.

*Time required:* 2 to 3 days for the entire loop with a motorized vehicle, depending on how much time you want to spend. ✿

*Druid Arch*

## Chapter 14

# CANYONLANDS — THE NEEDLES

*The fantastic Needles panorama at sunrise*

## CANYONLANDS — THE NEEDLES

The Needles district is much less visited than Island in the Sky. One reason is distance, as it is a cul-de-sac with only one way in and out, far away from the amenities of town. Another is that there is little to see from the scenic road proper—not even viewpoints like at Island in the Sky. The main attractions of this district can only be explored by day hiking, backpacking and 4-wheel driving. The Needles area has a wonderful network of trails, all well marked at the trailheads and made easier to follow thanks to many cairns along the way. Those with enough time and who are not discouraged by the effort will not regret their visit to the Needles. They'll discover a wide variety of geological features, including colorful spires rising hundreds of feet above the ground, many mushroom-like sandstone formations, massive arches, grabens and canyons, as well as much rock art and alcove dwellings left by the early inhabitants.

The most practical way to visit the Needles is to camp at Squaw Flat, which fills up quickly during the high season. This will let you photograph these extraordinary needles in the early morning, while the light is at its best, beginning a long and rewarding day of exploration in the area. If you can't camp, you can always resort to staying in a motel in Moab or Monticello, but it makes it considerably harder to be on location during the golden hour.

Moab offers all the advantages of modern civilization as well as a central location for exploring the surrounding parks, but it is 75 miles (about 1-½ hour) from the Visitor Center. Monticello can save you time as it is only 49 miles away. Also, this small town at the foot of the Abajo Mountains has a bit of an alpine flavor, which is quite pleasant. Regardless of your starting point, you turn off US 191, almost opposite an interesting monolith called Church Rock, for the last 35 miles leading to the Needles' Visitor Center on UT 211. The turnoff is about 40 miles south of downtown Moab and 14 miles north of Monticello.

From Monticello, you can also take the all-paved Harts Draw Road and get some nice but distant views of the park down the northern side of the Abajo Mountains before catching up with UT 211 about 2 miles before Newspaper rock. The winding Harts Draw Road shaves about 7 miles off the trip but almost no time. Past Newspaper Rock, UT 211 becomes particularly scenic as it follows the superb red cliffs of Indian Creek canyon. Under the right light and windless conditions, there is an interesting photo opportunity of their reflection in a little lake located on the right side of the road, 7½ miles past Newspaper Rock.

If you get to or from the Needles before sunrise or after sunset in winter, watch out for deer that often cross the road between Newspaper Rock and US 191.

## Newspaper Rock

After passing by the base of the Abajo Mountains, UT 211 enters the lovely, shallow canyon of Indian Creek, along which you'll stumble upon Newspaper Rock State Park, about 12 miles from US 191. Even if you aren't a fan of Puebloan

pictorial art, you really should stop to see these remarkable petroglyphs carved in the rock, very close to the road. A couple of them have been found to be 1,500 years old, but the majority were carved more recently over a period of several hundred years. This is one of the largest panels of petroglyphs you are likely to find on the Colorado plateau. These petroglyphs are very easy to photograph at any time of the day, but are better lit in the afternoon.

*A cornucopia of petroglyphs at Newspaper Rock*

## The Scenic Drive

The Scenic Drive winds for about 16 miles round-trip from the Visitor Center through red rock country with some distant views of the spires. The first stop along the road is Roadside Ruin, a nice Ancestral Puebloan granary only a few hundred yards from the road. Further up, after about a mile on a side gravel road leading to the Salt Creek area, you reach Cave Spring. This pleasant and easy trail, only 0.6 mile round-trip, leads to a grotto near a perennial creek where you'll find some rock art and a well-preserved cowboy camp with original items left by the last occupants. The trail passes two ladders and continues on slickrock with good views of the surrounding area.

At the intersection of the Scenic Drive and Elephant Hill Road, you'll find a lovely flat prairie. It makes an excellent foreground for the view of the Needles in the morning or to observe them from the road with your binoculars.

Almost 2 miles farther, the short Pothole Point loop contains a group of water-holes carved into the slickrock by erosion. These potholes are quite interesting when they are filled with water and you can see myriads of tiny organisms swimming in them. Nearby, you can see some nice examples of cryptobiotic soil along the trail. Be sure not to step on it, as it literally takes decades to regenerate.

Shortly before the end of the road, the 2.4-mile Slickrock Trail makes a loop along the mesa top overlooking the canyon. The best viewpoint is at the end of the trail, where Junction Butte and the Island in the Sky district are in full view. If you don't want to walk all the way, the first viewpoint on the Slickrock Trail—a short ½ mile from the start of the trail—offers a panoramic view of the cliffs with the Manti-La Sal Mountains in the background. At sunset, there are miles of cliffs that glow red while the snowy peaks are tinted pink. Big Spring Canyon Overlook, at the very end of the road, is not spectacular but offers an easy access to a lovely canyon, if you prefer not to do too much walking.

## Squaw Flat

For a fantastic view of the Needles at sunrise, take the Big Spring Canyon trail from the Squaw Flat parking area, close to the campground. In less than a mile, you'll come to a viewpoint overlooking the Needles. An 80 to 200mm zoom lens would be perfect here, allowing you to get different shots with the rising sun striking the walls. A polarizing filter will help accent the relief and darken the sky a bit so that the needles will stand out perfectly.

After having photographed the sunrise from this view-point, you might want to follow the very scenic trail descending into Big Spring. It's an easy walk in a wooded canyon bottom and the scenery is enchanting. A little under 3 miles down the trail, you'll come to a second viewpoint, even closer to the Needles. From there, you can best capture them using a 70 to 135mm lens.

*Sentinels of stone line up the Needles horizon*

## Elephant Hill

A mostly gravel road leads in 3 miles from the scenic road to the base of Elephant Hill. There, you'll find the famous 4x4 track of the same name, as well as the foot trail heading south to Chesler Park and Druid Arch. From the highest point on this road, you can get a beautiful panorama of the Needles district. A few hundred yards after the "blind curve" sign, you'll see a small slickrock hill to the right. You can easily climb on it for an excellent view of the entire area, including the Needles. The view is particularly majestic at sunset with a medium to long telephoto. Watch out for the cryptobiotic soil, however.

The challenging Elephant Hill 4x4 track is only for specially equipped vehicles and carries a substantial risk of vehicle damage. No behemoths there either, the Squeeze Play section is very narrow. This track requires excellent mastery of driving on slickrock and of your vehicle's reactions. Elephant Hill is not the only difficult spot on the track, sections such as the Silver Stairs have some rock steps that are at least as challenging. On the other hand, you can also do this route on foot for a short distance from the 2WD parking area, as there are good views of the Needles after you've crossed Elephant Hill. It's also very entertaining to see the 4x4s negotiate the slickrock grades. The Elephant Hill 4WD track leads to Devil's Kitchen and

*First light on Needles formations*

its very nice primitive campground surrounded by huge rocks. To return to the Elephant Hill parking area, take Devil's Lane and head north to New Bates Wilson Camp via the above-mentioned Silver Stairs section. There, instead of turning right to finish the loop, you can continue northwest to an overlook on the confluence of the Green and Colorado rivers. Arriving at Devil's Lane just after leaving Devil's Kitchen, you can also head south to the Grabens area, past the challenging 4WD section of SOB Hill, to reach the west side of Chesler Park and the Joint Trail *(see next section)*.

*Time required:* The minimum loop of almost 10 miles from the Elephant Hill 2WD parking area can be accomplished in half a day (assuming you were able to negotiate all the 4WD obstacles without inflicting damage to your vehicle). It is best to devote two days to this trip, camping at Devil's Kitchen along the way; you can then visit Chesler Park from its western access and take a side trip to the Confluence Overlook on your way back.

## Chesler Park

This extraordinary group of spires, with strongly colored horizontal striations, is located beyond the needles that are visible from the Scenic Drive and the Elephant Hill gravel road. The extremely ancient spires of Cedar Mesa sandstone

*Exquisite Chesler Park in its tallgrass setting*

are located in the center of a remarkably verdant basin surrounded by a circle of needles. The tall grasses in the park form a magnificent foreground and a singular contrast with the large spires.

Located on a saddle at the northern edge of the basin, the Chesler Park Viewpoint can be reached on a beautiful slickrock trail sometimes only materialized by cairns. It's a 6-mile round-trip from the Elephant Hill parking area, requiring about 3 hours. The last 200 yards, on a slope nicknamed Fat Man's Misery, are moderately challenging.

If you don't mind adding another 1-½ hour to your hike, walk back down Fat Man's Misery and take the nice trail to your left, leading to Devil's Kitchen and passing at the foot of several beautiful needles. This allows you to return to the parking area by way of the Elephant Hill 4x4 track. If you are considering driving it later, it's a good way to gauge the infamous rock steps and make sure you and your vehicle will able to make it.

However, if you really want to get the most out of Chesler Park and take photos in late afternoon light, you'll have to descend into the "park" from the Viewpoint. From there, walk the 5-mile loop around it in a clockwise direction, passing through the Joint Trail—a narrow crack in the rock about 60 feet deep and ¼-mile long located at the southern tip of the loop. The entire loop from the Elephant Hill trailhead is about 11 miles, using the shortest route. This may seem a bit long, but once in the "park", you'll progress rapidly over flat ground most of the time and the entire loop can be completed in a 6 to 7 hour hike, leaving enough time for pictures, rest and enjoying the scenery.

Another possibility is to walk into Chesler Park to campsite CP2 and turn left (east) to descend into Elephant Canyon. From there, you can return north to the parking area or hike south to Druid Arch *(see next section)*.

Watch out for the heat and possible dehydration if you do these hikes in summer. Even in late afternoon, the heat is still intense.

*Photo advice:* Best early in the morning for the view of the Needles from the beginning of the trail and from Chesler Park Viewpoint, but afternoon is preferred for photographing the spires from the south. You can get distant pictures of the spires from the viewpoint just before the east entrance of the Joint Trail; follow the cairns on the slickrock and climb on a small ridge overlooking the "park", with some red round rocks on white sandstone making a beautiful foreground. For the closest and best views of Chesler Park, follow the side trail toward backcountry campsites CP3, 4 and 5 until you find a suitable spot.

## Druid Arch

Druid Arch is one of the most striking arches of the Colorado Plateau, definitely worthy of the Top Five. It would certainly be yet another overused icon of the Southwest if it were more accessible. As it is, the shortest 11-mile round-trip hike discourages many visitors. For those who are ready to put in a reasonable effort, however, Druid Arch is a fantastic photo destination. From the Elephant Hill trailhead, the mostly level walk follows the Chesler Park Viewpoint trail for 2.1 miles before reaching a fork. At this junction, the sign indicates two ways to reach Druid Arch: The shorter one takes you southward directly to the arch via Elephant Canyon. The other one leads first to the Chesler Park Viewpoint, then into the "park" to remote campsite CP2 where you turn left to descend into Elephant Canyon and rejoin the direct trail to Druid Arch. If you don't mind doing an additional 1.8 miles, I highly recommend this second alternative, which allows you to combine a visit to Chesler Park and Druid Arch into one hike for a minimal additional effort. Walking in Elephant Canyon on sand or slickrock is rather easy and not much different from any other walks in the Needles area. The upper part of the canyon reveals awesome views as you penetrate deeper inside the needles. There is one easily negotiated dryfall and a fixed iron ladder to be climbed in your final

*Druid Arch from the upper viewpoint*

approach to the arch.

*Photo advice:* If you get to the arch in the morning, continue up the steep cairned trail until you reach a large platform on the northeast side of the arch. This is the best vantage point for morning photography of the arch. A moderate wide-angle lens will work best. In the afternoon, the arch is backlit from this point. Retrace your steps, descending to the wash between the ladder and the dryfall. Follow the wash to the southwest, skirting the arch until you end up on the opposite side. Climb cautiously on the slickrock to find some good vantage points.

*Time required:* 6 to 8 hours for the entire loop, depending on which way you decide to pick.

## Horse Canyon, Salt Creek and Angel Arch

Horse Canyon and Salt Creek used to be two popular destinations for 4WD enthusiasts looking for a more thorough exploration of the Needles District. At this time, the Horse Canyon track is still open to limited 4WD traffic, subject to obtaining a permit first at the Visitor Center. It is best to reserve your back-country permit well in advance; walk-in permits may also be available for the next day, but don't count on it. The track along Salt Creek has been closed to vehicular traffic since 1998. This imposes a 20-mile round-trip backpacking trip in order to see spectacular Angel Arch.

The access track to this area leaves south of the Cave Spring trailhead *(see Scenic Drive section above).* After 0.3 mile, you reach the locked gate (for which you receive the combination of the day with your permit) and at 2½ miles, you reach the junction of Salt Creek and Horse Canyon.

*Angel Arch at sunrise (photo by Kerry Thalmann)*

Take the left fork for Horse Canyon. The track goes on for 8 miles; it is not very challenging but there are some deep pockets of sand in places. You'll pass below Paul Bunyan's Potty, an interesting pothole arch with a suggestive streak of desert varnish flowing through and out of it. A short telephoto will capture it perfectly. About 2 miles from the junction, a 0.7-mile spur track leads to Tower Ruin, a nice ruin located under an alcove, high on the cliff. A short trail leads to the base of the ruin where you can catch a better glimpse, but do not climb into the ruin; use a medium telephoto to capture it. Continuing about 3½ miles on the main track, you'll find a small side canyon to your right; its entrance is soon blocked for vehicles. Walk about 20 minutes one-way and you'll see to your right the interesting Thirteen Faces panel.

Almost a mile further on the main track, look for the 1.6-mile round-trip spur trail leading to lovely Castle Arch. A bit farther, at the end of the track, dedicated arch hunters can also see Fortress Arch at the end of a 2-mile round-trip footpath.

Back at the junction with Salt Creek Road, you can drive south for 1 mile inside the wash until you reach Peek-a-Boo Camp. This is the trailhead for the Peek-a-Boo trail, leading west to Squaw Flat by way of Lost Canyon. From the trailhead, hike up to the window above the camp and look for the nearby panel of Fremont Indian petroglyphs representing shield-like figures.

From Peek-a-Boo Camp, the track is closed to all vehicular traffic and if you want to admire and photograph spectacular Angel Arch your only option is to backpack—after obtaining the necessary backcountry permit for at-large camping.

*Paul Bunyan's Potty*

The walk is level and easy, with patches of deep sand here and there. You'll be constantly following or crossing the mostly dry bed of Lower Salt Creek. During springtime, shallow water is present in the upper part of the creek. Watch out for the extremely aggressive deerflies that patrol the Salt Creek bed during spring and summer. The hike itself is not as beautiful as trails around Elephant Hill and Squaw Flat, but you can observe unmarked ruins, granaries and rock art panels along the way. After hiking 7½ miles from Peek-a-Boo Camp, take the left fork to Angel Arch and continue 1.8 miles to the arch. You can walk right below the spectacular span for close-up photography. A classic way to photograph Angel Arch is to include Molar Rock—a precariously top heavy rock in the shape of a tooth—in the foreground. Angel Arch is a sunrise and early morning photographic location, so it's preferable to camp not too far away, such as just north of the junction of Salt Creek and Angel Arch canyon.

*Time required:* Visiting Angel Arch on foot requires an overnighter and some at-large camping. This area rarely sees visitors nowadays outside of the season.

*Nearby location:* After visiting Angel Arch, continuing on Upper Salt Creek requires further backpacking and a car shuttle to the southern trailhead at Cathedral Butte, located 18 miles southwest from UT 211 on a good dirt road beginning about 1 mile north of the Dugout Ranch. From this trailhead, it's also possible to do an incursion into Upper Salt Creek until Upper Jump. This demanding 19-mile round-trip hike passes by several arches such as Wedding Ring Arch (about 6½ miles from the trailhead, on the east side) and numerous Puebloan ruins such as the Big Ruin, which is the largest in the park (about 6 miles from the trailhead, on the west side). Shortly before Upper Jump, you can see two famous Indian pictographs: The colorful All-American Man (about 8½ miles from the trailhead, on the east side) and the nice Four Faces (about 0.7 mile further, on the same side). Although strong hikers can tackle this round-trip incursion in one very long day, it is usually done as a one-way multi-day back-packing trip to Peek-a-Boo Camp or the Squaw Flat trailhead.

## Lavender and Davis Canyon

You may be wondering why Lavender Canyon Road makes such a long detour via Davis Canyon when your topo map indicates a more direct route? Some years ago, a prominent outdoor magazine published an article on the ten best places for car camping in America. One of them was Lavender Canyon! Lavender may be a great place for camping, but its remoteness and notorious quicksand make it a potential hazard for unsuspecting visitors. Hundreds of people flocked Lavender in the months following publication, seriously impacting the environment, creating incidents with the local ranchers and in a few instances requiring costly rescues. The NPS ended up closing the access route through private property, relocating it 3½ miles to the northwest, closer to South Six Shooter Peak, and instigating a permit/quota system.

Lavender Canyon is popular for its beautiful canyon walls, arches, lush vegetation and solitude. Although it is well within the limits of any high-clearance

4WD SUVs, Lavender should only be tackled by experienced and well-prepared visitors due to the occasional patches of treacherous quicksand one may encounter. Two cars, a tow strap and some shovels would just about eliminate any risks; however, the wash becomes very narrow for the last 2 miles of the track—about 1 mile after passing the park boundary—and your paint job may be given a rough treatment by the surrounding vegetation.

*Wonderfully riparian Lavender Canyon*

*Six-Shooter Peak*

After the initial 3 miles common to Davis and Lavender canyons, the signed Lavender Canyon Road follows a wide sandy wash passing through BLM and private land. After about 12 miles from UT 211, the wash enters a beautiful canyon of blond Cedar Mesa sandstone. 2 miles later, you reach the locked gate marking the park boundary. Although camping is no longer allowed inside the park, you can camp on BLM land just outside the boundary.

The backcountry desk of the Needles Visitor Center issues up to 10 day-use permits a day for Lavender Canyon. With your permit, you receive a combination for the lock—which is changed frequently—allowing you to open the gate and continue driving into the beautiful canyon. Close the gate behind you after you enter and exit.

Shortly after the locked gate, you'll encounter Natural Arch and Caterpillar Arch to your right, high on top of the canyon walls. Indian ruins are visible on the left side of the track. The area is remarkably pristine and riparian and Lavender Wash is usually a trickle once in the park. The wash becomes progressively narrower and the road ends shortly after passing Cleft Arch, a massive arch with beautiful streaks of desert varnish, located 3 miles from the park entrance.

Turning back toward UT 211, make a left at the turnoff to Davis Canyon, almost 3 miles before reaching the paved road. Davis is just as beautiful as Lavender, if not more so, and is a trove of Ancient Puebloan ruins.

The road inside the dry wash is quite easy with a 4WD vehicle and is not known to have quicksand. It ends at the park boundary about 5 miles from the turnoff. Park here, sign the register and hike into this pristine area to your heart's content. There are no arches in Davis Canyon, but many Puebloan dwellings, granaries and pictographs waiting to be spotted and explored. Look for the well preserved Five Faces pictograph panel which is less than 0.4 mile from the trail-head, somewhat hidden on the west side of the canyon. You can easily spend more than a day in Davis Canyon, following tracks and finding beauty in each and every side canyon. Camping is allowed only outside the park boundary.

*Getting there:* Approaching the striking silhouettes of North and South Six-Shooter Peaks as you drive on UT 211, make a turn on marked Davis Canyon Road, about 14 miles north of Newspaper Rock or 7½ miles east of the park's entrance station. For Lavender, bear left at the sign after almost 3 miles, leaving Davis Canyon to your right and eventually rejoining the old Lavender Canyon Road about 1½ mile ahead. Both roads are essentially tracks in the wash and directions are easy to follow.

## Canyon Rims

To reach the two Canyon Rims viewpoints—Needles Overlook and Anticline Overlook—take the well-marked road about 33 miles south of downtown Moab off US 191. Coming from the south the turnoff is 7 miles north of UT 211.

This good paved road reaches the Needles Overlook after 22 miles with little to see along the way. The view from the Overlook is spectacular because it is such an incredibly vast panorama; however, by this very nature it doesn't lend itself well to photography. The Colorado River is not visible and the Needles district is very distant, even with a telephoto.

Drive back about 7 miles and turn north on the well-graded dirt road leading in about 16 miles to the Anticline Overlook. Along the way, 13.7 miles from the beginning of the gravel road, look for a surprising arch shaped like a wine glass (38°25'46" 109°36'43"). The aptly named Wine Glass Arch is on the southern edge of a butte located on the left side of the road. The arch is fairly small and you'll need to get close to it to photograph it.

Less than 3 miles further, Anticline Overlook provides a panoramic view of Island in the Sky, the Colorado River, the Potash basins and Junction Butte. Even though this view is closer than the one from Needles Overlook, I do not rate it very high either for photography.

Still, both views are spectacular and worth the 2-½ hour detour from US 191 if time isn't an issue. ✿

*The Land of Standing Rocks*

Chapter 15

CANYONLANDS — THE MAZE

*The Fins and Ernie's Country*

## CANYONLANDS — THE MAZE

### Introduction to The Maze

As the name implies, the Maze is an intricate network of canyons. However, it also contains an amazing variety of fascinating rock formations spread out over a vast, wild and rugged area. As Canyonlands' most remote and difficult to access district, the Maze sees relatively few visitors; if you are adventurous, as well as looking for solitude and quiet, the Maze is for you. With the exception of the Horseshoe Canyon detached section, which can be visited in one day, you will need at least three days to explore the Maze by 4WD and a lot more if you're backpacking or mountain biking. Spring and autumn are the best seasons to explore the Maze. During wintertime, snow conditions often force access routes closures. In summer, the heat can become unbearable and there is no water along the trails. Regardless of the season, avoid rainy weather at all cost; it turns the clay roads into a quagmire and you could get stuck for days on end.

The Maze district of Canyonlands Nat'l Park is arguably one of the most remote areas in the continental United States and visiting it requires careful planning and preparation. First off, you'll need to have a 4WD high-clearance vehicle in tip-top mechanical condition. A short wheelbase with low-departure angle is recommended and so are rugged all-terrain tires with as many plies as possible. Large sport utility vehicles will not do well in the Maze, especially in some difficult sections like Teapot Canyon. They will most likely make it—although the stock tires may not—but you'll risk inflicting serious damage to the undercarriage, bumpers, mud flaps, running boards, etc. For additional security, you'll need a couple of extra tires, a high-lift jack, a compressor, a tow rope, a shovel, chains for all tires if there is a chance of snow, extra gas, lots of water, topographic maps and other necessities as you see fit for an extended 4WD road trip requiring total self-sufficiency. Needless to say, you also need good 4-wheel driving skills. A vehicle rescue from the Maze will cost you in the neighborhood of $2,500; not an outlandish figure when you consider that the Doll House is located 107 miles from the nearest town, mostly on a wretched trail. Oh, and don't you forget to bring your own port-a-potty, as required by the National Park Service.

If you plan to do any kind of hiking inside the Park, especially with photographic equipment, you'll benefit from being in good physical shape, as some of the hikes are long and strenuous. Most are on primitive trails, with exposure to cliff edges and steep routes requiring some scrambling and chimneying. Even if you are in good shape, you may experience a lot of discomfort if you are not used to hiking and carrying weight over long distances. A rope or a couple of 30-foot straps are necessary to lower packs in some difficult passages.

Any overnight trip to the Maze requires a backcountry permit, which has to be reserved well in advance if you go in spring or early autumn. During the off-season, you should have no difficulty getting a campsite by checking directly with the Hans Flat Ranger Station. Hans Flat is the official entry to the Maze; if you don't enter the Maze via Hans Flat Ranger Station, you must have a pre-reserved permit in your possession.

One final piece of advice: Bring a friend, preferably in a second vehicle. Do not venture into the Maze alone or without leaving specific details on your whereabouts. If you have neither the vehicle(s) nor the partner(s) for this trip, but have a few hundred dollars or

*The Wall, in the Land of Standing Rocks*

more to spare, you may consider hiring an outfitter to take you into the Maze. Let them wreck their vehicle and enjoy yourself free of concerns in one of the world's great wilderness.

*Getting there:* The following information is valid for all locations evoked in the next sections. There are three access routes to the various landmarks of the Maze. The most common way is to take US 24 to the Hans Flat turnoff, located about ½ mile south of the Goblin Valley Road turnoff *(see San Rafael Swell Chapter)*. This is about 20 miles north of Hanksville or 24 miles south of I-17 if coming from Green River. Follow the good graded dirt road for 25 miles. At the roofed signpost, follow the right fork for another 21 miles to the Hans Flat Ranger Station. The left fork leads in 7 miles to Horseshoe Canyon's trailhead. There are often pronghorns visible a short distance from the road in this area. Except during and after a rain, the road is passable by passenger car; however, 2½ miles southeast of Hans Flat Ranger Station (at the North Point Road Junction), a high-clearance 4WD becomes necessary, whether going west to Panorama Point or south toward the turnoff to the Flint Trail.

After descending the steep switchbacks of the Flint Trail, you can head northeast to the Maze Overlook or, if you want to visit the Land of Standing Rocks and The Doll House, go southwest, then northeast, traversing an extremely rough section around Teapot Rock. This section has some technically difficult spots and is extremely hard on tire walls and your vehicle's undercarriage.

An alternate way to visit the southern part of the Maze is to enter from the south on the usually well-maintained county road, leaving from US 95 near Hite. This road is located about halfway between the Colorado River bridge and the Dirty Devil River bridge and is easy to miss. It allows you to make good speed for the first thirty miles to Waterhole Flats and to avoid the switchbacks of the Flint Trail. However, this can lead to a false sense of security as it leads you smack into Teapot Canyon where things become suddenly hellish. Teapot Canyon is by far the most infamous portion of the road into the Maze. In my opinion, it would also be sad to miss the Flint Trail, which is a road of legend and part of the fun of visiting the Maze, much as the Shafer Trail is part of the White Rim Road experience. However, even if you enter the Maze from the north by Hans Flat, you can also exit via this southern route. Gas is available at the Hite Marina if your tank doesn't hold much.

A third way into the Maze is from Green River via a graded dirt road heading to Horseshoe Canyon (see section below).

## Horseshoe Canyon

Horseshoe Canyon is a detached section of Canyonlands National Park, located northwest of the Maze. It protects a series of outstanding early Fremont pictographs dating back from around 1000 BC and located inside a very scenic canyon. By a strange quirk of history, this canyon which was formerly known as Barrier Canyon, has lost its original name, but instead has lent it to a certain style of pictographs associated with the Fremont culture of the Late Archaic period—prior to the advent of agriculture. The crown jewel of Horseshoe Canyon is a large and well-preserved panel of intricately beautiful human and animal figures known as the Great Gallery, stretching over 120 feet of smooth slickrock wall. Most of the figures are life-size and some of them are over seven feet tall. They have large tapered torsos, no appendages and are quite ghostlike in appearance. A few figures are decorated with various patterns or surrounded by small birds and animals. The debate around the age of the mural has long been the subject of controversy, but most historians now endorse the above estimate, since a fragment was carbon-dated and determined to be approximately three thousand years old. Many have theorized that the figures are depictions of shamans in drug-induced spiritual states. Some even believe that they represent visiting space aliens. Regardless of your own interpretation, there is little doubt that the Great Gallery is the most spectacular panel of rock art in North America and an unforgettable experience.

The Great Gallery stretches out on a ledge located about 15 feet above ground. The area is cordoned off and, unless a park ranger is present, you'll need to admire and photograph the panel from a distance of about 30 feet, which makes it easy to capture either large portions of the panel or to focus on specific figures or groups of figures with a telephoto. To guarantee that you can observe and photograph the figures at close range—as well as listen to an interesting interpretation—you'll need to join a ranger-led hike; such hikes are usually organized from April through October on Saturday and Sunday morning (call the Hans Flat Ranger Station for more information).

*The Great Ghost... and Friends*

Upon close examination, you'll notice that some of the figures not only consist of pigment applied onto the rock, but that the rock itself is intricately pecked around the silhouette. One phenomenon you will easily notice without needing to get close, is the fact that some of the figures are pock-marked, leading some archaeologists to theorize that objects could have been thrown at them during rituals.

The hike from the trailhead at the top of the mesa to the Great Gallery is about 7 miles round-trip, but can feel longer than that when the weather is hot. It takes approximately 4 to 5 hours to accomplish, with enough time at the panels for observation, photography and rest. By hiking out early in the morning, you'll be able to take advantage of the best lighting conditions at the Great Gallery, as well as avoid the hottest part of the day as you climb back up to the plateau, which lies 750 feet above the canyon floor. It is a long climb—over a mile—and if you do it in mid-afternoon, it will be extremely hot. In late afternoon, however, the cliff will be partially in the shade.

At the bottom of the mesa, the canyon itself is absolutely gorgeous, with many cottonwoods providing welcome shade along the way. All through the hike, you'll be following a stream that usually seems to run with at least a small trickle of water, although it becomes frozen in winter.

*Wall of Spirits*

There are other pictograph panels along the way to the Great Gallery. The first one is easily spotted on your left, less than 20 minutes after the descent, and is called the High Gallery; you'll know why when you see it. The canyon is fairly wide and you'll need to cross the stream bed and walk on a trail to the right in order to visit the easily missed Horseshoe Shelter panel, a bit further up. About ½ mile further, you'll encounter a huge alcove on the right side; it makes for a nice resting spot, especially if you are hiking in the sun. Look for a few small pictographs toward the back of the alcove, unfortunately marred by some graffiti. If you look at the roof of the alcove, you will also note marks that seem to have been made by globs of wet mud thrown at the rock.

Continuing on 1¼ mile upstream, you'll eventually reach the main panel of the Great Gallery, to your right.

***Photo advice:*** As with all other large rock art panels of the Southwest, it's up to you to photograph what you want, from the wide scene encompassing the whole panel to the minutest detail.

Anything from a moderate wide-angle to a telephoto will work well at the Great Gallery. If no Ranger is present to unlock the fence, a long telephoto will be useful to isolate some particularly interesting anthropomorphs, such as the one with the tiny birds perched on its shoulder. Of course, you will want to photograph the Great Ghost, a large figure with a mysterious, ghostly appearance and intricate detail in the head. You'll find it to the left of the main panel, under a shallow alcove. Many of the other figures on the panel look like tapered mummy-like blobs of pigment with broad shoulders and two spots representing the eyes. On the whole, the "Gallery" gets its impact from the number of figures and size of the panel and moderate focal lengths will work best. Use different angles to impart some variety to your shots.

If you hike-in very early in the morning, you will have the ethereal experience of seeing the figures gradually illuminated by the soft morning light. On the other hand, if you end-up photographing the figures in bright sunlight, you may want to use a polarizing filter to eliminate glare. Also, keep in mind my general recommendation of using low-contrast film for rock art.

*Getting there:* From either Hanksville or I-17 west of Green River, take UT 24 to the Hans Flat turnoff (about ½ mile south of Goblin Valley road) and turn onto the graded dirt road. Follow it for 25 miles until your reach a fork with a roofed signpost; bear left and continue eastward for about 5 miles, then turn right and drive 2 miles to the car park and primitive campground near the top of the mesa. Alternately, there is a direct 45-mile graded dirt road from Green River to the above-described last junction; it leaves from Airport Road, south of town, and takes about the same time than using US 24. If you come all the way from Moab, count on approximately 2-½ hours of driving time.

*Shamans*

*Time required:* Allow a good part of a day for Horseshoe Canyon, including driving time both ways, especially if you come from Moab. If you're not going to explore other parts of the Maze, it's easy to visit Goblin Valley State Park in mid to late-afternoon of the same day (refer to the San Rafael Swell chapter).

## Panorama Point

Panorama Point affords a fantastic panoramic view of the northern Maze area and Island in the Sky, as well as close views of the Orange Cliffs. However, much like its Needles Overlook counterpart on the east side, the view is far too distant to make for interesting photography. Telephoto views rarely give any quality results because of the haze that usually blankets the area. If you are pressed for time, you can pass this viewpoint without too much regrets and head toward the Maze Overlook instead—although it's much farther. On the other hand, it is also the easiest way to catch a glimpse of the Maze, as it is only an hour's drive from Hans Flat Ranger Station by 4WD, without any technical sections, such as the Flint Trail or Teapot Canyon, along the way.

*Getting there:* 2½ miles south of Hans Flat Ranger Station, take the marked track leading east for 7½ miles, then follow the right fork for another 2 miles to the overlook. The left fork leads in 2½ miles to the base of Cleopatra's Chair, a huge monolith dominating the whole area.

## The Maze Overlook

This is without question the best vantage point over the Maze. You sit above the extraordinary labyrinths of Cedar Mesa sandstone and are relatively close. The impressive group known as the Chocolate Drops is right in front of you, only a mile or so away—a last remnant of organ-shale rock capping the sandstone and looking much like a row of nuclear submarine kiosks. The Land of Standing Rocks can be seen in the distance to the southeast, but close enough to yield good telephoto images with a 200mm if no haze is present. Elaterite and Ekker buttes are also fairly close and spectacular. This is a great spot to camp, relax and admire the Maze at its best. Late afternoon is the best time for photography. Approximately thirty minutes before sunset, you'll loose direct light over the Maze, but you'll get great colors in the sky if you have some clouds to the east. Early morning is very good for shooting in the direction of the Land of Standing Rocks. The side light brings out much detail to the maze of canyons at your feet. Don't wait too long: An hour after sunrise, the Maze will appear flat and the opportunity will be gone.

*The Chocolate Drops*

A very steep trail descends into the canyon bottom, leading to four different backpacking trails. One of these allows you to do a half-day trip to the Harvest Scene *(see following section)*.

*Getting there:* About 14 miles south of Hans Flat Ranger Station, go left and down the steep switchbacks of the Flint Trail for the 16-mile drive heading northeast to the overlook. It takes about 3 hours one way from Hans Flat Ranger Station.

## The Harvest Scene

The Harvest Scene is one of the largest and most intriguing group of pictographs on the Colorado Plateau. It is also one of the oldest. This Late Archaic panel derives its name from scenes of harvest depicting the life of the early hunter-gatherers who traveled through these canyons, at least that is the official explanation. Altogether, there are about a dozen or so figures, spread over roughly forty feet. They are smaller and less impressive than those of the Great Gallery. One striking difference is the lack of a foreboding ghostlike appearance in these

*The Harvest Scene*

figures. No wide torsos here, but some fairly elongated bodies. The horns on the heads on several figures suggest masks used in some shamanistic ritual. The fact that they have feet—but no arms—also contributes to make them a little bit more human-like.

*Photo advice:* Unfortunately, the panel is quite exposed to sun and wind erosion and the pigments have become very faint, making it difficult to see and photograph. If you are there in the middle of the day and the sun is shining directly on the panel, it will be difficult to bring out much detail, even with a polarizer. To photograph the Harvest Scene under optimum conditions, plan on being there preferably in the afternoon. The best light is late in the day, when the sun is just leaving the panel.

Photographing the panel is up to your imagination, however I would like to draw your attention to the large figure to the left, reminiscent of a telephone pole as well as to the interesting anthropomorph on the far right of the panel. Both isolate well vertically.

*Getting there:* There are two ways to get to the Harvest Scene, which is located in Pictograph Fork canyon. The most interesting way is via the shorter but much more exposed Maze Overlook trail *(see previous section for access to the trailhead)*, which winds its way 600 feet down a steep cliff and into the Maze. This trail is mildly technical and requires that you negotiate a series of moki steps and a short chimney. It is not overly difficult if you are normally agile and not afraid of heights. A rope or a couple of 30-foot straps will help greatly to lower your gear if you carry a camera backpack and a tripod. I suggest stashing a water bottle at the bottom of the cliff for later. Once in the Maze, follow the surprisingly verdant canyon to the south (left at the base of the cliff and around the eastern side of the Chocolate Drops) on a well-cairned path. Despite the cairns, do not venture inside the Maze without map, compass and a GPS. While walking, take regular bearings to be sure to find your way back. There are several small groups of pictographs visible along the way; some are very high up the canyon walls, so keep looking. The entire round-trip from the trailhead is almost 6 miles. Starting at daybreak, you can be at the Harvest Scene in 1-½ hour. My recommendation, however, is to start in mid-afternoon and come back shortly before sundown, catching good light at the panel and possibly a light breeze on the way back up. Incidentally, you'll find that climbing back up is much easier than coming down.

The other way to get to the Harvest Scene is the longer but more flat 9-mile loop starting from Chimney Rock in the Land of Standing Rocks.

## The Land of Standing Rocks

*The Land of Standing Rocks*

One great way to observe and photograph the vast area known as Ernie's Country is by walking down the Golden Stairs, an easy 2-mile hike down a sheer cliff composed of many different rock strata, hence the name Golden Stairs. If you're part of a group, you could arrange for your party to drop you at the Golden Stairs picnic area, located at the end of a short spur near the bottom of the Flint Trail. You could then take a leisurely walk down this spectacular path and then on to Land of Standing Rocks Road towards the Fins, where you can rendez-vous with your friends after they have negotiated the infamous road around Teapot Rock.

Walking down the Golden Stairs offers great opportunities to see a formation called the Mother and Child, best photographed from the beginning of the trail in early morning.

The Fins are beautiful and the backdrop of the Needles across the Colorado River make the scene very photogenic from the Land of Standing Rocks road, especially in mid-afternoon. Look for Cave Arch, easily located with the naked eye in front of the Fins.

After the jarring of Teapot Canyon or the sheer drop of the Golden Stairs, you'll be happy to enjoy a relatively smooth drive through the Land of Standing Rocks, with its spectacular and photogenic monoliths: the Wall, Lizard Rock, the Plug and Chimney Rock.

*Sunrise on the Maze*

*Getting there:* The Land of Standing Rocks is about 35 miles from Hans Flat, past the switchbacks of the Flint Trail and the infamous section around Teapot Canyon; count on 5 hours driving time.

## The Doll House

This is one of the most photogenic area in the Southwest, but also one of the most remote. The Doll House is 88 miles away from UT 24 on dirt and rocky roads and 65 miles by boat from Moab. But what a place; it's a bit like the Needles, with a whimsical flair thrown in; rocks on pot, you could say.

There are some very scenic camping spots dispersed throughout the Doll House, all pre-assigned at the Hans Flat Ranger Station when they issue your permit. One of these sites is located ½ mile to the southwest of the Doll House and has a good panoramic view. From the other campsites located very close to the Doll House, just wander amidst the formations and seek inspiration, you won't have difficulty finding it. I strongly recommend the 2-mile round-trip walk to the Granary. It goes through a couple of interesting joints, as on the Joint Trail in Chesler Park *(see Needles chapter),* before reaching the lovely and aptly-named Surprise Valley, a verdant graben that is a refreshing site in this universe of stone. There are also good views from the trail going north to Beehive Arch.

*Photo advice:* The Doll House is best photographed in late afternoon and at sunset. Take a general view from the vicinity of the southwest campsite with a medium telephoto, then wander on foot inside the Doll House proper, you'll be using a wide-angle most of the time. At sunrise, you may want to hike to Surprise Valley and down to the little granary or a short while down the Spanish Bottom trail to be on the sunrise side.

*Getting there:* The Doll House is located 5 miles past Chimney Rock at the very end of the Land of Standing Rocks Road *(see above section)*. It is 42 miles from Hans Flat Ranger Station and about 6 hours driving time.

The easiest way to reach the Doll House in summer is by boat from Moab. You can join one of the organized multiday trips bound for Cataract Canyon; many of them stop for the night at Spanish Bottom, which is at the foot of the mesa where the Doll House is located. If you arrive there in mid-afternoon, you can hike up and back the steep Spanish Bottom Trail in less than 3 hours for a quick peek at the Doll House. Alternately, you can arrange a private trip with a speed boat dropping you off at Spanish Bottom and picking you up the next day, but you'll have to carry all your water, camping and camera equipment up and down the trail, which gains 1,200 feet of elevation in only 1.2 miles on a rocky talus slope… not a fun experience.

*The whimsical Doll House*

Doing the trip in one day from Moab is feasible by jetboat. The boat will wait for you as you climb to the top of the mesa for a quick foray into the Doll House; however, you'll be there in the middle of the day and the light will be very crude. In any case, the view down the Spanish Bottom Trail is superb, but even more so is the view of the Doll House from the Colorado River as you come within a mile from Spanish Bottom on the jetboat.

## The Colorado River downstream from Moab

A boat trip down the Colorado River from Moab to Hite via Cataract Canyon is a fantastic experience including forays into side canyons along the way and world-class whitewater. The impressive rapids of Cataract Canyon begin soon after Spanish Bottom and are spread over 14 miles of the Colorado River before the latter turns into a quiet arm of Lake Powell. A multi-day rafting trip can be arranged either privately or with an organized tour *(see On the Go Resources in Appendix)*.

A shorter alternative is a one-day jet boat tour from Moab, without whitewater. In Summer, you can arrange for a jet boat to take you from Potash Road to Spanish Bottom and back, a fantastic 100-mile round-trip jour-

*The Colorado River near Lathrop Canyon*

ney on calm waters through the heart of Canyonlands Nat'l Park. This trip takes a whole day, passing through some of the most remote country in the Continental U.S. It is a wonderful alternative or complement to the White Rim drive (described in the Island in the Sky chapter). On your way to Spanish Bottom, you will marvel at the unbelievable scenery, as you travel through Shafer Basin, Pyramid Butte, the great gooseneck below Dead Horse Point State Park, Lathrop Canyon, Monument Basin, Junction Butte, the Loop, the Slide and the Confluence with the Green. The trip ends at Spanish Bottom, which provides access to the Doll House *(see above section)*. The return trip to Potash Road is even better in late afternoon, when the canyons turn golden. Such a private trip is better suited to a medium-size group as it is rather pricey. If you are willing to forsake some of the flexibility, you can also ride a jet boat delivering or picking up groups of kayakers or rafters at Spanish Bottom.

## Above Canyonlands

Although a scenic flight above Canyonlands Nat'l Park is not limited to the Maze district, I chose to include it in this chapter because for many people it is the only way to get an idea of this highly inaccessible section of the park. A flight can easily be arranged from Moab, Blanding, Monticello, or Telluride, CO. You can also arrange to be picked up and dropped off at the airstrip maintained by the wonderful folks of the Needles Outpost. Another possibility is to fly

*Aerial view of The Confluence*

back from Hite to Moab or to Needles Outpost at the end of a multi-day rafting trip, as offered by some outfitters. Most of the time, two or three people are necessary to book a scenic flight *(see On the Go Resources in Appendix)*.

Seen from a small aircraft, the landscape of Canyonlands Nat'l Park is extraordinary. A 1-hour flight is enough to view many parts of the three districts: The Needles, with its amazing Grabens, Chesler Park, Salt Creek, the confluence of the Green and the Colorado, Cataract Canyon, all of the fantastic formations of the Maze described in this chapter, the mesas of Island in the Sky and Dead Horse Point State Park, and more.

If you only take one small plane trip in the course of your journey through the Southwest, make it this one. You won't regret the money spent.

*Photo advice:* A 28 to 50mm lens is well suited to aerial photography of this area. Little or no depth-of-field is required, but you will of course need to keep the vibrations of the aircraft and your own movements in check. With low ISO, an aperture of f/4 or f/5.6 and a minimum shutter speed of 1/250 sec. represents the best compromise for sharpness and resolution. If you have a short gyro-stabilized zoom, it will work very well at the low end and give you an additional two stops to compensate for the movement of the plane. Check beforehand to see if the pilot will allow you to open your window. Some pilots charge an additional fee for this extra "service". If you're shooting with the window closed, place the lens as close as possible to the glass to avoid reflections; a polarizing filter can be helpful but may compromise your shutter speed with low ISO. In any case, disengage the autofocus and manually set the focus for infinity. If you shoot slides, use preferably a low-contrast film. Early morning or the end of the day is ideal for color and relief. Such a trip works very well in winter when the sun is mostly at a low angle, even close to midday. ✿

*Steamboat Rock*

Chapter 16

AROUND DINOSAUR

*Steamboat Rock aka Center of the Universe*

# DINOSAUR NATIONAL MONUMENT

Straddling the northeast corner of Utah and northwest corner of Colorado, Dinosaur National Monument is a bit out of the way of the classic "Grand Circle" tour for most people, but the rewards from a visit are many: Fantastic mountain and canyon scenery, two wonderful rivers offering great rafting, outstanding Fremont rock art, great camping, spectacular fall colors and few crowds. Oh, and I almost forgot... a remarkable Dinosaur Quarry exhibit!

Most people think of the Monument in terms of the Dinosaur Quarry, but the real star attraction is the 210,000 acres of rugged and beautiful country. Not that the Dinosaur Quarry isn't a wonderfully instructive attraction, but as a photographer the remarkable landscape of the park will be the main focus of your visit. Dinosaur is one huge park and very much an open book of geology with its tortured uplifts and exposed rock layers. It is also a rewarding place if you are looking for solitude and silence; Dinosaur sees less than 300,000 visitors per year—70% of which come in summer. This lack of heavy crowds, even at the height of summer, greatly contributes to a quality experience of the high desert. A scientific study conducted in the nineties has found the ambient noise in Dinosaur to be less than that of a recording studio. Take a hike on the Sound of Silence or Desert Voices trails early in the morning and you'll be able to experience this first-hand.

The solitude and silence are for a large part the result of the Monument's lack of through-access roads. Despite its enormous acreage, only four rather sinuous paved roads provide access close to the Monument's borders—and in one case a deeper foray inside its interior. Although these roads allow you to see some of the park's highlights, you'll need to take dirt roads, do a few day-hikes, or even consider a rafting trip, in order to see the park in-depth. Given the distances involved, count on spending three to five days to discover and photograph the park at an unhurried pace.

The Monument has two Visitor Centers: one is located 1½ miles east of the small town of Dinosaur, CO on US 40; the other is at the Dinosaur Quarry on UT 149, a few miles from Jensen, UT. All the comforts and trappings of civilization are available in nearby Vernal, west of the Monument on US 40.

## The Dinosaur Quarry

The remarkably well-designed Quarry structure houses fossilized dinosaur skeletons—with about 1500 bones purposely left exposed on the cliff face to be observed at close range by the public. The cliff containing the fossils can be viewed from two levels, but don't expect too much photographically. There are numerous exhibits explaining the evolution, reign and disappearance of dinosaurs, as well as how the bones ended up getting buried, then excavated, in this particular area. It is believed that some 150 million years ago, this area was part of a riverbed with a sand bank where dead dinos and other prehistoric creatures became deeply buried after eons of flooding. In later times, uplift and erosion caused the soft sedimentary layers to wash away, exposing the fossilized bones.

Despite the excellent exhibits, your curiosity about dinosaurs and paleontology will be better rewarded by attending one of the excellent short Ranger talks.

Needless to say, the place is a magnet for families with kids and school groups, but during springtime and autumn, you'll find the place very quiet, beautiful and enjoyable. From Memorial Day through Labor Day you must park at the lower Visitor Center and walk the short ¼-mile road to the upper Visitor Center and Quarry, or use the shuttle bus if you are rebuked by the slope.

*Getting there:* The quarry building is located ¼ mile from UT 149—the west entrance road to the Monument—about 7 miles north of Jensen on US 40.

*Time required:* 1 to 2 hours, depending on your interest in paleontology, preferably around midday when the light is too crude to photograph outdoors.

## Around Split Mountain

UT 149 continues for almost 11 miles past the Quarry turn-off, providing spectacular views of Split Mountain along the way. This road is known as Tour of the Tilted Rocks and a sign warns visitors that there are no fossils on display along the road. In fact there are no fossils to be seen anywhere else inside the Monument.

Darn, no more dino bones, only superlative mountain, river and canyon scenery! About 1 mile past the Quarry turnoff, you'll come to the Swelter Shelter on the north side of the road, a small cave used for thousands of years with a few Fremont

*Massive uplift near Split Mountain*

petroglyphs and pictographs. About a mile further, you'll encounter the 2.8-mile long Sound of Silence loop route, providing a glimpse at the arid desert environment and aiming to teach people how to find their way in the desert through a series of explanatory markers. The route follows Red Wash for about a mile before entering a narrow passage through a jumble of rocks. Bear right at all the junctions until you exit the narrow labyrinth and catch a glimpse of Split Mountain. The route continues on the bench forcing you to do some easy routefinding through gullies and ridges before rejoining the wash. It's a good idea to take the leaflet at the trailhead before embarking on this hike.

About 2½ miles from the quarry turnoff, take the paved road to your left leading north to the actual Split Mountain area, with its beautiful campground, picnic area and boat ramp. Stop at the scenic overlook to photograph the uplift and the massive bent dome in the background. This is a spectacular place and the closest you'll get to Split Mountain. Close to the campground entrance and boat ramp, you'll find the Desert Voices loop trail. The 1½-mile loop is one of the most educative and thought-provoking interpretive trails you'll find in any National Park or Monument. Although the signs were primarily designed to challenge young minds by raising their awareness of the desert and mankind's interaction with it, adults will do well to reflect on it too. A ½-mile connector trail links the Sound of Silence and Desert Voices trails together if you can arrange a short car shuttle. Both trails are best hiked in the morning, before the sun gets too high.

After coming back to the Split Mountain turnoff, the tour road follows the Green River to the east, affording highly photogenic views from the low plateau. It then traverses the beautiful private Chew Ranch after crossing the Green River, following Cub Creek before turning into a gravel road as it reenters the Monument. Shortly after the mildly interesting Elephant Toes Butte comes into view, you'll find two pullouts in succession with trails leading to the north to petroglyph sites. Both are a must for photographers, but the second one is particularly spectacular: A well-graded trail leads to the bottom of a sandstone cliff harboring pictographs of uncommonly large lizards.

The gravel road continues for another mile to reach the historic Josie Morris Cabin, set under a canopy of trees at the mouth of a 100-foot deep box canyon. Time permitting, explore the coolness of nearby Hog Canyon on a 1-mile walk.

*Photo advice:* The Tour of the Tilted Rocks road is excellent mornings and evenings. Although I tend to prefer late afternoon, there are outstanding morning views of the back of Split Mountain in the early morning from near Josie Morris' cabin. The best vantage point in the area is the Scenic Overlook above the Split Mountain campground. It offers a bird's eye view of the campground and the Green River with the red monocline directly ahead. Gazing at this vista, you'll have to admit that Split Mountain's name is well deserved. From here, it does look like it's been pried open and torqued by colossal tectonic forces, exposing remarkably colorful rock strata.

*Time required:* 1½ hour up to half a day if you choose to hike.

## Island Park Road & McKee Spring

The 18-mile long Island Park gravel road provides access to this remote section of the park that sees little visitation outside summer. Yet it provides access to some exquisite petroglyphs as well as spectacular views of the Green River. Although it is quite a long drive from the Quarry and Split Mountain, this road is actually located just to the north and behind Split Mountain as the crow flies.

Almost 11 miles from the beginning of the Island Park Road is one of the most outstanding Fremont petroglyph panels in Utah: the McKee Spring site. Although the site is not marked, you'll have no trouble locating it. About 0.6 mile after passing the interpretive booth marking the Monument's entrance on the right side of the road, you'll notice a couple of pullouts and a well-worn trail on the left side of the road, leading north toward a low cliff. A

*The beautiful McKee Spring petroglyphs*

short loop takes you through a few panels consisting of anthropomorphs and geometric designs, superbly chiseled and preserved in the beautiful ocher-color sandstone cliff and providing outstanding photographic opportunities under the right lighting conditions.

About 1½ miles further, and time permitting, you may want to take the ¾-mile spur road to Rainbow Park, which is essentially a boat ramp and a couple of primitive campsites with a mildly interesting view of the Green River as it enters Split Mountain. Instead, I recommend that you proceed directly to the Island Park Overlook for its superlative panoramic view of the large open valley formed by the Green River. From the Rainbow Park turnoff, continue for another ½ mile and turn right another 0.3 mile to the top. This is an amazing sight in the fall when the cottonwoods have turned. From the last turnoff, another 5 miles brings you to Island Park, which has a nice primitive campground, well shaded by large tracts of cottonwoods.

*Photo advice:* The McKee Spring petroglyphs can be photographed at close range and a normal lens works well here. The cliff is facing south and the glyphs can be photographed all day. The panoramic view from the Island Park Overlook requires at least a 24mm or shorter lens to take it all in. The view is toward the east so it's better to be here in mid to late afternoon.

*Getting there:* About halfway between Jensen and the Dinosaur Quarry on UT 149, turn northwest on Brush Creek Road for about 5 miles then turn right on a dirt road and drive 4 miles until you reach the marked Island Park Road. If you're coming from downtown Vernal, leave US 191 for 500N Street heading east for about 3 miles. Leaving Brush Creek Road to your right, turn left on Jones Hole Road (aka Diamond Mountain Road) for about 5 miles until you reach an unmarked road veering to the right; after a little less than a mile on this road, turn right at the T and another mile brings you to the marked Island Park Road to your left. From there, it is about 10 miles to the Monument's entrance on a graded gravel road. This road is open year-round and is usually suitable for passenger cars, but becomes impassable when wet.

*Time required:* at least 3 hours from Jensen or Vernal.

## Jones Hole

During the week you will encounter few cars along the narrow but very good paved road to Jones Hole and the Fish Hatchery, even at the height of summer. There are apparently few people willing to tackle the 80-mile round-trip drive from Vernal to this remote location and hike the 8-mile round-trip Jones Creek Trail to the Green River. It's a pity because this is one of the easiest and most beautiful trails in the entire Southwest, on a par with the Lower Calf Creek Falls *(see Around Scenic Byway 12 chapter)* as one of the top hikes for families with children; there is plenty to see and enjoy even a short distance from the trailhead. Although the elevation loss to the Green River is about 500 feet over 4 miles, the trail feels essentially flat. What makes this hike so beautiful is exquisite Jones Creek, constantly bubbling and scintillating at your side. This is one spectacular creek and a favorite of local fishermen on week-ends. The Fish Hatchery taps directly into the natural spring of Jones Creek and releases some of the purest waters you can find (it must nonetheless be filtered).

The trail begins at the bottom of the fish ponds and immediately enters a lush riparian environment. After about 1½ miles, just past a wooden footbridge, you'll reach the interesting Deluge Shelter pictograph panel on the right side. Another short trail just a bit further leads to more good pictographs. Shortly after that is the junction with the Ely Creek Trail, leading to a nice waterfall in about 0.3 mile and, 1½ miles further, to a box canyon area known as the Labyrinth.

At the junction, there is also a tiny but extremely pleasant backcountry campground (permit required). From this point on the canyon widens, revealing beautiful tall cliffs made of very ancient sandstone and limestone layers. During the remaining 2.2 miles from the Ely Creek Trail to the Green River, you're bound to encounter rafters on a short day hike to the petroglyphs and the waterfall; you may also encounter deer. The trail ends at the Green River in Whirlpool Canyon, which is wide and beautiful at this

*Rafting the Green River*

spot. Upstream, to your left, was the planned location for the dam that would have flooded Echo Park and surrounding canyons without the active opposition of environmental groups.

*Getting there:* From downtown Vernal, leave US 191 for 500N Street heading east for about 3 miles. There, bear left on Jones Hole Road (aka Diamond Mountain Road) and follow the signs until the end of the road at the National Fish Hatchery

*Time required:* 4 to 5 hours for the hike, with enough time to photograph and relax by the river, plus almost 2 hours for the round-trip drive from Vernal to the Fish Hatchery trailhead.

## Harpers Corner & the Journey Through Time Road

The 31-mile "Journey Through Time" road leading to Harpers Corner traverses a high plateau providing wide-ranging views of an immense wilderness with pristine habitat and virtually no human presence. The main vista points are located close to 8000 feet in elevation, allowing you to look down on a vast landscape of canyons, mesas, so-called "parks" and colorful geologic features. The journey begins at the Monument's Headquarters and Visitor Center on US 40, 1½ mile east of Dinosaur, CO.

The first overlook on the Harpers Corner Road is Plug Hat Butte, reached after about 4 miles and a short climb from the valley floor. The ½-mile nature trail offers panoramic views toward the south. There is good color from a fault down below, but the panorama is too vast for photography and lacks drama.

The road continues its ascent of the plateau toward Escalante Overlook, about 4 miles further, offering a similarly distant panoramic view to the west.

Having reached the high plateau, the road meanders through several miles of rather arid sagebrush steppe, eventually reaching the short Canyon Overlook road to your right, about 12 miles from the Escalante Overlook. Canyon Overlook provides great views of the Yampa Bench and the rugged canyons carved by the Yampa River. One can easily imagine the abundance of wildlife in such a huge wilderness.

A little over a mile past the sign marking the Colorado-Utah border, you'll see a road to the left with a sign announcing the hang-gliding take-off place. Reset your odometer here and about 1 mile beyond this road, look to the left for a large slab of flat slickrock covered by desert varnish close to the

*Anthropomorph on Harpers Corner Road*

road. Pull off the road and find a suitable location to park your car away from traffic. The best spot is actually on the left side of the road, so you might consider stopping here on the return trip from Harpers Corner. A barbed wire fence needs to be crossed in order to get to the slickrock slab, but don't be alarmed, you won't be trespassing on private property: The reason for the fence is that the park road is an NPS easement in the midst of BLM-administered lands; its purpose is to prevent range animals from wandering on the park road. The fence is low and stones have been strategically arranged to let you scale it easily. Once on the slickrock, you'll immediately spot some very photogenic petroglyphs carved on the ground into the desert varnish. This kind of horizontal carving is rare in the Southwest. If you enjoy rock art, you can easily spend an hour here scouting and photographing. Some of the most prominent petroglyphs include figures of cute little humanoids sporting antennas, footprints and bighorn sheep.

At about Mile 25, you'll pass the Echo Park Road to your right; we'll leave it for the next section. For now, continue for less than a mile to Island Park Overlook to catch a distant glimpse of the canyon formed by the Green River.

Shortly thereafter comes Iron Springs Bench Overlook with a superb view to the east toward the Yampa Bench canyons. I rate this overlook second only to the Harpers Corner Overlook.

A little over 3 miles further, the Echo Park Overlook has a picnic area and allows you to see Steamboat Rock in Echo Park, but the view is still too distant for interesting photography.

At last, you reach the Harpers Corner trailhead at the end of the road. The 2-mile round-trip trail straddles a narrow ridge ; it is relatively easy, with spectacular openings on both sides particularly to the west as you near the end. Nothing prepares you, however, for the breathtaking bird's eye view from Harpers Corner itself.

It is difficult to describe Harpers Corner without resorting to superlatives. I'll say only that it is one of the top panoramic views in the Southwest. The view is extremely open on all sides. Whirlpool Canyon appears right below to your left; the amazing upturned layers of the giant monocline caused by the Uinta uplift rise at an impossible angle 2400 feet below, with Lodore Canyon in the back; to your right, you can see the Mitten Park fault and the long slender silhouette of Steamboat Rock's ridge with the Green River in front, and the Yampa River nearing the confluence in the back. If you're going to spend any time in the Monument, you could return one last time to Harpers Corner so you can contemplate all the places you've been to!

*Photo advice:* Harpers Corner isn't a place for great sunrise or sunset. It is best photographed in mid-morning or afternoon light under a soft or dramatic stormy sky. Don't come too early in the morning or most of the views will be backlit, with the exception of Whirlpool Canyon to the west. Likewise, don't arrive too late in the afternoon or the jutting promontory at the end of the trail will cast a giant shadow on the Mitten Park fault in front of you. Don't get there in the middle of the day either or everything will appear washed out. If the light isn't right, forget photography and simply enjoy this truly unique view.

*Getting there:* The road leaves from the main Dinosaur National Monument Visitor Center, which also serves as Park headquarters. It is located 2 miles east of the junction of US 40 and CO 64 in Dinosaur, CO. Coming from the Quarry/Split Mountain area, you can also use County Road 16s as a shortcut; it leaves about 12 miles east of Jensen and joins the Harpers Corner Road 12 miles north of the Visitor Center. This road crosses BLM land and can provide alternate camping in case the Echo Park campground is full or closed. During wintertime, Harpers Corner Road closes at Plug Hat when snow drifts become too deep.

*Nearby location:* The little community of Dinosaur! Where else can you live on a street named Tyrannosaurus Rex? Be sure to stop for refreshments at the BedRock Depot and admire the photography of Bill Mitchem, a long-time local resident. His collection of photographs of the Monument is very extensive. The excellent Colorado Welcome Center has up-to-date information on the area and the entire State.

*Time required:* about 4 hours round-trip from Dinosaur.

## Echo Park

Echo Park ranks as one of my favorite places in the Southwest. It is a place of great power, beauty and spirituality; a temple of nature radiating a quiet energy pervading our consciousness in a positive, soothing way; a place where one feels humbled by nature but also very safe in her hands. Some people like to call Echo Park the Center of the Universe. Although the two places are very different, I can't resist a comparison with Upper Cathedral Valley in Capitol Reef. If you've experienced this special connection with nature in Cathedral Valley, you'll know what I mean and I believe you'll be affected in the same way at Echo Park. Go preferably after the rafting season is over (the rafting season lasts from mid-May to mid-September) or you may miss the feeling of remoteness, which is an important part of the experience. The perfect time to visit Echo Park is in the autumn when cottonwoods turn bright yellow against the deep blue sky and most visitors have left.

Let's begin where we left off at the previous section. Returning from Harpers Corner toward the Visitor Center, turn left after about 6 miles onto well-marked Echo Park Road. This is a fairly well-graded dirt/gravel road and although high-clearance vehicles are recommended, passenger cars can use it with caution, unless it has been damaged by recent rains. It is best to inquire on its current condition at the Visitor Center before you go.

The road descends steadily through the Iron Springs Bench before re-entering the Monument (as well as the State of Colorado) after almost 3½ miles, then follows Sand Canyon and its exquisite cream-colored sandstone cliffs. After about 7½ miles from the top, you come to the junction with the Yampa Bench Road. Bear left on marked Moffat County Road 156 to meet in less than 1½ miles lovely Pool Creek Canyon near the historic Chew Ranch. From there, the road follows the creek down to Echo Park for another 3 miles.

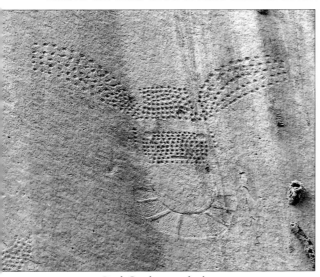

Almost 2 miles past the first Pool Creek crossing you'll come to the Pool Creek Petroglyphs, located to the left on the cliff above the stream. These Fremont petroglyphs are particularly interesting due to their intricate pointillist technique, consisting of closely spaced holes pecked into the sandstone. Although there are several petroglyphs, you'll be hard-pressed to observe the smaller ones without binoculars. The main one is located 35 feet above ground, requiring a 200mm telephoto.

*Pool Creek petroglyph*

About ½ mile further, you'll come to Whispering Cave—a long, shallow crack in the sandstone approximately 100 feet wide and situated at the base of a huge cliff. You can walk about 50 feet or more inside a narrow passage right behind the sandstone wall. The difference in temperature with the outside is striking. This is a good place to photograph from the inside, because you'll get a wonderful red glow.

*Whispering Cave*

Another ½ mile brings you to Echo Park—marvelous riparian oasis at the meeting point of the two awesome rivers: the Green and the Yampa. Echo Park is a superlative place for camping and you shouldn't miss the opportunity. You'll enjoy great photography and exceptional silence and solitude... as well as the constant company of deer.

Steamboat Rock is the obvious photographic subject here, with its odd bent shape. John Wesley Powell, who named Echo Park, climbed Steamboat Rock—not a small feat considering the lack of use of his partially-severed arm. During his climb of Steamboat Rock, he almost lost his life after having extended himself past his climbing ability. Powell found himself trapped on a tiny ledge and unable to move. It is said that one of his companions rescued Powell from his predicament by stripping off his long-johns and using them as a rope to pull Powell up to safety.

There are three interesting walks you can take from Echo Park; information on these three hikes is posted on the campground's bulletin board by the restrooms. The Sand Canyon trail starts along the east side of Steamboat Rock, passing the confluence of the Green and Yampa rivers and continuing along the Yampa where it meets with Sand Canyon to the right. Most people stop here but it is possible to enter Sand Canyon and hike up southward to the Yampa Bench Road or along the rim and back down into Pool Creek Canyon; more on the last part of this hike below. The Yampa River is the last major free-flowing tributary of the Colorado River system, although it narrowly escaped being dammed in the early 1950s, which would have put Echo Park and Steamboat Rock under water. A large public outcry helped defeat the Echo Park Dam project—a powerful reminder of how vital it is to let your voice be heard whenever we must fight back to preserve wilderness areas.

Another popular trail is Pat's Draw, located halfway between the campground and Whispering Cave on the west side of Echo Park Road. This canyon is located directly below Harpers Corner Road, discussed in the previous section.

The most popular trail is the Mitten Park Trail which follows the sandstone wall at the back of the campground, then ascends on a ledge above the Green River before dropping down into Mitten Park, where you find yourself right below the great Harpers Corner uplift.

There is one more "unlisted" hike that I strongly recommend to photographers; this hike leads to the top of the bench, just above Steamboat Rock and continues above the Green, providing an extraordinary view of the *Center of the Universe*. Although relatively short mileage-wise, this hike is mostly off-trail and requires some moderate routefinding skills and a bit of preparation. A topo map, as well as a compass or GPS is highly recommended. If you've never hiked off-trail but have "successfully" completed the Sound of Silence trail earlier *(see Around Split Mountain section)*, now is a good time to apply your newly-acquired experience in a real world situation. To find the trail, drive back into Pool Creek Canyon and locate the one-car pullout on the left side of the road, less than 0.2 mile past the petroglyphs. Look straight toward the cliff just ahead of you to the left and you'll see the Picasso Face—a striking disfigured human face sculpted into

*Picasso Face*

the sandstone by the whims of erosion. A mid-size telephoto in the 200mm range will capture the Picasso Face perfectly. About 50 yards to the right of the Face, you'll find a well-worn trail going up. It's a bit of a scramble at first, but it quickly turns into a good trail as you slowly gain elevation onto the sagebrush-covered bench. You should be able to follow the trail along Pool Canyon's rim for a while, but it becomes less obvious as you reach two successive gullies to the left, which you have to cross before resuming the climb toward the bench top through dense Junipers. One good way to avoid getting lost if you lose the trail is to mark the top of the mesa directly south of Steamboat Rock on your topo map and aim for this point. The entire walk is approximately 0.8 mile. Once you reach the top, you'll have a fantastic bird's eye view of Steamboat Rock, surrounded by cliffs. This view is best captured with a moderate wide-angle lens.

Time permitting, continue along the rim in the direction of the Yampa. There is a trail, but don't worry if you occasionally lose it. As long as you keep following the rim, even from a short distance, you won't become disoriented. Another mile or so brings you close to the confluence of the Green and the Yampa, with the surprisingly long east face of Steamboat Rock in front of you. This is a fantastic shot with a panoramic camera. From here, you can bear southeast until you find a safe way to descend into previously-mentioned Sand Canyon or you can return the way you came. A GPS will come in handy to find your way back to your car.

*Photo advice:* Mid-morning and late afternoon offer wonderful views of Echo Park and Steamboat Rock from a variety of vantage points on the high talus close to the Ranger's residence, or from the rim accessed via the above-described hike. My preference goes to late afternoon as the sun rays strike the left face of Steamboat Rock until very late due to the perfect orientation of Pool Creek Canyon. There are also very nice views along the Mitten Park Trail.

*Getting there:* Coming from Harpers Corner, you'll find the marked Echo Park Road to your left about 6 miles from the parking area. From the Visitor Center on US 40, drive 25 miles on Harpers Corner Road. Water is usually shut off at the Echo Park campground in late September or mid-October, however the pit toilets remain open.

*Time required:* From Vernal or Dinosaur, it is possible to visit Harpers Corner Road and Echo Park in a long day, but my advice is to camp at Echo Park and enjoy this beautiful place at a leisurely pace. Doing so, you can exit the Monument the next day via the interesting Yampa Bench Road *(see next section).*

*Steamboat Rock (photo by Bill Mitchem)*

## Yampa Bench Road

The Yampa Bench road follows the Yampa River for much of 40 miles from the Echo Park Road to US 40 at Elk Springs, with some spectacular overlooks of its canyon along the way. It is a graded dirt road with relatively few rough spots; although a high-clearance vehicle is recommended, it is passable with caution by passenger cars when dry and recently graded. As usual, it is essential to inquire at the Visitor Center about the state of the road before embarking. This is one long road and you wouldn't want to get stuck on it, although you're likely to meet a few other vehicles from time to time.

6½ miles from the junction with Echo Park Road, after crossing the bench for a while far from the river, the road reaches the first overlook at a huge meander. This is Castle Park Overlook. A short walk from the car park brings you to the rim and the incredible view below. Exercise extreme caution here, especially while photographing. You can wander a bit along the rim to look for an inspiring location. Framing the entire meander and some of the rim in the foreground requires a super wide-angle lens or a panoramic shot, but there are excellent views of the eastern meander by itself alongside Castle Park.

One mile further, as you near Hell's Canyon, you'll see the private Mantle Ranch Road to your left. Mantle Ranch used to be a working cattle operation within the borders of Dinosaur National Monument. The previous owners used to welcome visitors wanting to rough it for a week in a ranch still operating on "pioneer time", i.e. it had no electricity, no running water, no phone, and no mail. The ranch has now been sold and there is a dangling question mark on the future of the property, raising fears of private property development within the Monument. As of this writing, the ranch is still operating as usual.

Continuing for 1½ mile your next stop is the Harding Hole Overlook with a sweeping panorama of several smaller meanders, making another interesting photograph. The last direct view of the river is a little bit over a mile further at the Wagon Wheel Overlook, which has a slightly longer footpath to the overlook but provides similar views.

After that, the road moves inland passing the historic Baker Cabin before approaching the river one last time at the Haystack Overlook, reached via a side road almost 12 miles from Wagon Wheel Overlook. From here, you can walk to the edge of the cliff and look down over the Yampa. The Haystack itself is an impressive formation jutting out of the landscape and vaguely reminiscent of Gunsight Butte on Lake Powell *(see Photographing the Southwest - Vol.2)*. The road to the overlook is closed to visitation from April to mid-July to allow for an undisturbed nesting season of the Peregrine Falcons, whose eggs are seeded to other conservation areas around the country. A vast wooded area near the Monument's border was ravaged by wildfires in 2002 leaving a scarred landscape behind it, but if nature has its usual way new growth may be well underway by the time you read this.

Finally, you'll leave the Yampa Bench by climbing the east flank of Blue

Mountain and rejoining US 40 at Elk Springs by way of County Roads 14N and 14.

*Getting there:* From Harpers Corner Road, take the above-mentioned Echo Park Road, continuing straight on at the Yampa Bench turnoff almost 8 miles from the beginning of the road. Coming from Echo Park, drive up-canyon for about 4 miles and turn left on the Yampa Bench Road. From US 40, take County Road 14 at Elk Springs and continue for 13½ miles to the junction with 14N leading in 2 miles to the Monument's entrance. A useful NPS pamphlet entitled *Echo Park, Yampa Bench, and other unimproved Roads* is available. Although you won't have any difficulty finding your way without it, it's a nice thing to have.

*Time required:* 4 to 5 hours including stops at the viewpoints.

*Nearby location:* if you're coming to Dinosaur Nat'l Monument from the east and you're looking for a place to camp, consider the side trip to Deerlodge Park along the Yampa River. A small paved road

*Along the Yampa Bench*

leaves US 40 about 7 miles northeast of Elk Springs, leading to the campground in less than 14 miles. From May to July, you 're likely to meet rafting parties as it is the put-in for Yampa River trips. Outside this period, it's pleasant and quiet. The next morning, follow the footpath to where the Yampa enters a slickrock canyon, yielding a nice image.

## The Gates of Lodore

The stunningly beautiful Gates of Lodore are located in the far north section of the National Monument, a long ways from anywhere. It is the beginning of famed Lodore Canyon, which rises out of a completely flat area. The sudden emergence of the canyon is what makes Lodore so impressive. Most people who make it here are rafters intent on descending the rapids, but this spectacular location is for everybody, even non-photographers. So don't be rebuked by the mileage and motor to the Gates, you won't regret it.

Having said that, I must admit that I didn't visit Lodore on my first trip to Dinosaur Nat'l Monument many years ago and I was still hesitant on my subsequent visits. I'm glad I eventually did and I have since returned to enjoy this unique vista. One thing that proved an irresistible magnet was the Tolkienesque sounding name evoking an otherworldly setting of monumental proportions fit for heroic battle feats of great Kings of yore. And the reality… well with a little imagination and positive thinking, it is really not that far from this description.

Lodore is, quite literally, a one shot deal: A single entrance road, leading to a

*The Gates of Lodore*

single trail and a single viewpoint. That's it! If you come to Lodore for hiking and photography, you'll be tantalized by what lies ahead beyond the end of the trail. Unfortunately, you can't penetrate deeper into the canyon unless you take a raft trip. But, what a view from this vantage point located at the end of a 1½-mile round-trip trail. You'll be able to admire and photograph the abundant waters of the Green River entering the deep canyon with its dramatic dark red walls. The place has a definite ominous feel not unlike the Black Canyon of the Gunnison *(see Photographing the Southwest - Vol. 3)*, except that the river is wider and you are closer to the water. For a more intimate look into this remote section of the park, a raft trip on the Green River is necessary. For the photographer, it is not a simple matter because of several rapids made infamous by Major Powell in his memoirs under the name of Hell's Half-Mile, Disaster Falls and Triplet Falls. Still, with adequate protection for your equipment, a 4-day/3-night raft trip from Lodore to Split Mountain will be a memorable experience.

*Photo advice:* The best light is in mid-morning, using a normal lens.

*Getting there:* Coming from the southern part of the Monument, heading northeast on US 40 toward the town of Maybell, turn northwest on CO 318 and drive 40 miles to a marked well-graded dirt road to the left. Continue westward another 10 miles to the Gates of Lodore Ranger Station and campground. The trailhead is another 0.3 mile past the river put-in.

Alternately, you can come directly from Flaming Gorge via Dutch John and a good all-weather graded road leading to Brown's Park or from Jones Hole Road on a very scenic 4WD road through Crouse Canyon (which requires crossing a narrow suspension bridge with a 3-ton limit as you reach the Green River in Brown's Park).

*Nearby location:* Brown's Park Wildlife Refuge borders the northern boundary of Dinosaur Nat'l Monument. The Refuge serves as a nesting area for migratory waterfowl, and approximately 200 species of birds can be found here. It offers outstanding opportunities for bird watching and solitude and includes two campgrounds alongside the Green River. Brown's Park didn't attract only birds: it used to be a hideout for outlaws such as Butch Cassidy and the Wild Bunch, due to its remoteness and proximity to the Utah and Wyoming state lines.

# AROUND DINOSAUR

## Flaming Gorge

If you've come all the way to the far corner of Utah and Colorado to visit Dinosaur National Monument, it would be a pity not to go the extra distance and see the southern portion of Flaming Gorge National Recreation Area—only a short 50 miles from the Monument's entrance to the Quarry at Jensen. Flaming Gorge also makes a perfect stop if you're traveling between Moab and Jackson Hole—to visit Grand Teton and Yellowstone parks—especially Red Canyon where a lodge and several good campgrounds welcome the weary traveler.

Flaming Gorge National Recreational Area surrounds a 90-mile long reservoir created by the damming of the Green River in 1964. Although the largest portion of the reservoir lies in southern Wyoming, the most spectacular scenery is found in its southern section, at the foot of the Uinta Mountains of northern Utah. It is interesting to note that the Uintas are the only major east-west range in the United States. Here, the lake lies beneath steep cliffs that turn red at sunset, hence the Flaming Gorge name coined by John W. Powell during his exploration of the area. The southern section of Flaming Gorge is particularly appreciated by fishermen, so don't be surprised if the place fills up to capacity on week-ends during summer. During the week, you'll most likely have the place to yourself.

The main approach to Flaming Gorge NRA is from Vernal and US 191 on the Drive through the Ages Scenic Byway. This is a spectacular highway and it does a great job of explaining the various sedimentary layers you pass though a series of markers. Once you reach the vicinity of Flaming

*Red Canyon*

Gorge, the high-alpine landscape takes on a decidedly Wyoming flair. Immediately after entering Flaming Gorge NRA, follow UT 44 west toward Manila, leaving the dam several miles to the northeast on UT 260. The most spectacular spot in Flaming Gorge is Red Canyon, reached at the end of a 3-mile side road heading north, almost 4 miles west of the junction of US 191 and UT 44. This is also the site of the Red Canyon Visitor Center. There is a great view from inside the Visitor Center, perched at the edge of the canyon, although the glass window precludes any kind of photography. While at the Visitor Center, decide how

*Sheep Mountain*

you want to see and enjoy the park. If you want to linger, picnic, camp or hike the trails you must pay a small use fee. This fee doesn't apply to visitors just passing through and stopping only briefly at the viewpoints.

There are three outstanding viewpoints located on a paved loop trail just outside the Visitor Center; of the three, the main one (in the center) arguably offers the most spectacular view. The 2-mile round-trip walk from the Visitor Center to the Canyon Rim campground also has several outstanding viewpoints.

Returning to UT 44 on the Red Canyon Road, make a left on a side road marked "Scenic Overlook-Canyon Rim". It leads to a nice overlook near the Canyon Rim campground, although it doesn't offer as dynamic a composition as the three viewpoints near the Visitor Center. Less than a mile further you'll find the entrance to the Red Canyon Lodge, located on a lovely lake nestled between intensely green Ponderosa pines and Douglas firs.

Back on UT 44, aka Flaming Gorge Scenic Byway, the road meanders westward through a forested area of pine trees and the reservoir doesn't come again into view until Sheep Creek Bay, a shallow fjord following the Uinta Crest fault. During the descent, a couple of overlooks on the side of the road offer bird's eye views of the white and red cliffs plunging toward the deep blue waters. From these overlooks, the bay is a bit too far for effective photography. Dowd Mountain Overlook is another viewpoint in the Sheep Creek area; it is reached on a 4-mile dirt road, 10½ miles from the Red Canyon turnoff and 8 miles before reaching the Sheep Creek bridge. None of these views compare with what you see from the rim at Red Canyon.

*Photo advice:* At Red Canyon, the walls of the gorge are close together, plunging 1300 feet quasi-vertically into the lake. The contrast between the green vegetation, the red cliffs and the deep blue lake is especially photogenic in late afternoon as soon as the rock takes on the beautiful hues that gave its name to the gorge. Don't arrive too late, however, as the bottom of the lake is completely in shadow well before sunset. A standard wide-angle lens is sufficient to capture the depth of the canyon and its surrounding cliffs.

*Getting there:* From Vernal, follow US 191 north to the entrance of Flaming Gorge and take UT 44 immediately to the left.

*Time required:* 3 hours to a half-day to enjoy the different sites.

*Nearby location:* Just over 11 miles past the Red Canyon turnoff and shortly after the Dowd Mountain Road, turn left on a good gravel road, then right after 2¾ mile. This is the highly recommended 12-mile loop through the Sheep Creek Geological Scenic Backway, which rejoins UT 44 at the Sheep Creek bridge. The partly paved road soon meanders through a narrow canyon, providing outstanding views of colorful geological formations and great photo opportunities. Of particular photographic interest are the spectacular tilted red and white strata of the Uinta fault. At the heart of the fault, the road is eerily reminiscent of the Cockscomb, described in the *Along the Cockscomb* chapter. It is strange to find this heavily eroded and colorful area so far north, especially in this semi-alpine environment. There is an abundance of deer along the road and Bighorn sheep are also said to be present. It is more striking to start the loop from its south entrance; however, it can also be done in the opposite direction.

## Fantasy Canyon

Fantasy Canyon is a remarkable area of eroded siltstone and shale located roughly 40 miles south of Vernal. Fantasy Canyon is reminiscent of New Mexico's Bisti Badlands *(see Photographing the Southwest - Vol. 3)* albeit on a much smaller scale. It is lost in the midst of a foreboding landscape of oil and natural gas fields; "lost" is not an understatement, without the BLM signs guiding you through the maze of oil field roads, you'd be hard-pressed to locate this little gem. Despite the lack of interesting colors in the formations, this is a photographer's paradise and many have been trying to find this location ever since Michael Fatali published his striking photograph of Teapot Rock under the name "Back of Beyond".

The whitish siltstone material gets eroded at an extraordinary rate, probably quite noticeable in a lifetime—extraordinarily fast

*Isengaard (aka Teapot Rock)*

in geological terms—so be extremely careful of where you tread. It is easy to become over-excited in such a spectacular playground and to forget how fragile the formations are. Stay on the marked paths, relax and enjoy, there is always tomorrow. Come back to wonderful Dinosaur Nat'l Monument and you'll get a chance to revisit Fantasy Canyon in the process!

Many of the delicate formations have been given names by a local Boy Scouts troop; the names are stamped on tiny strategically located copper plates along the 0.6-mile loop. The most striking and photogenic of the many formations is without a doubt the famous Teapot Rock. It is a uniquely chiseled work of nature, defying both gravity and any kind of logic in erosion patterns.

*Photo advice:* Except for some formations on the fringe that can be photographed in early morning, most of the formations look best close to sunset. Don't be late as direct illumination of Teapot Rock is broken up by a small hill about 30 minutes before sunset. Don't expect the pale-colored limestone to produce the intense reds you may have seen on some photographs, even at sunset and using a saturated film and warming filter. You may need to apply some post-processing to the image to make it look its best!

*Fantasy Planet  (photo by Alain Briot)*

*Getting there:* The easiest, most practical way to reach Fantasy Canyon is from Vernal. Before you start, stop at the Vernal BLM Office *(see Appendix)* to get their park pamphlet, a map of the area (Vernal & Uintah County map) and a current road report. From the junction of US 191 and UT 40 in downtown, follow the latter southeast for 4 miles to Naples. There, take UT 45 (marked "Book Cliffs Access") going due south toward Bonanza and follow it for about 20 miles until it meets Glen Bench Road to your right, marked by a sign indicating "Mountain Fuel Bridge". Take this road and follow it southwest for about 13 miles to a dirt road marked "Fantasy Canyon" to your left. From this intersection, follow a series of short dirt roads eastward for 4½ miles through the Chapita Wells gas field. These clay roads are all well signed, graded and passable by passenger cars in good weather, unless damaged by heavy rains. They become impassable when wet, however, even to 4WD vehicles. Be sure to inquire at the BLM office in Vernal beforehand.

Alternately, if you are coming from the west on US 191/UT 40 and don't want to drive all the way to Vernal, take UT 88 for 17 miles toward Ouray and turn left immediately after the White River bridge. This road across the Ute Reservation is narrow but paved. After about 12 miles, you'll meet the afore-mentioned Glen Bench Road (at the point where you leave it when coming from Vernal). Cross it and follow the signs to Fantasy Canyon on various dirt roads for another 4½ miles.

It is also possible to come from the east via Bonanza but it requires some guess-ing in places and you'll be at risk of getting lost.

Whichever way you pick, be extremely careful driving on these roads. During the day, you'll encounter numerous large trucks barreling at full speed through the oil and gas fields. At dusk, you'll need to be constantly on the lookout for herds of deer and antelope roaming the area.

*Time required:* 4 hours round-trip from Vernal with plenty of time for exploring and photographing the formations.

*Nearby location:* At Mile 3 after you've left Glen Bench Road on the dirt road leading to Fantasy Canyon, you'll notice some very photogenic goblins on the left side of the road. These are worth a stop.

## Dry Fork Canyon/McConkie Ranch

The Dry Fork petroglyph panels represent one of the finest examples of Fremont rock art of the *Classic Vernal* variety.

Although located on privately-owned McConkie Ranch, northwest of Vernal, the friendly owners welcome visitors to the ranch, which has been designated a historic site; access is free but donations are accepted.

The numerous petroglyphs are disseminated on the north side of the canyon along a 200-foot high sandstone cliff. From the parking area you'll find two trails heading to the most interesting panels which are indicated by wooden signs. At the end of the ½-mile long lower trail, you'll find the famous and remarkably fine Three Kings panel. You'll need at least a 300mm telephoto to photograph the *Three Kings* panel, which is a good 120 feet above ground. Although truly outstanding, the petroglyphs are badly faded. There are a couple of other similar petroglyphs closer to the ground which—although they do not have the fine figures of the Three Kings—are also quite interesting to see and photograph.

*Three Kings*

One of the best example is the Big Foot panel located on the upper trail. Hardcore rock art aficionados can continue for several miles along the cliff to look for more panels, although the best ones are within ½ mile from the trailhead.

*Photo advice:* Early to mid morning or late-afternoon light is best to enhance the relief of most of the panels, as they tend to be washed out by direct sunlight.

*Getting there:* In downtown Vernal, turn on UT 121, continuing west for about 3 miles to Maeser, then turn right on 3500 South. Drive northward 6½ miles to McConkie Ranch's entrance to the right to reach the parking area, close to the cliff.

*Time required:* At least 1½ hour to enjoy the place and photograph the Three Kings and Big Foot panels. ✿

*Kiva Ladder*

APPENDIX

# APPENDIX

## A Glossary of not-so-obvious Terminology

Note: The terminology below pertains to the three volumes of
Photographing the Southwest.

*Alcove:* Shallow cave formed by the breakup of a sandstone layer weakened by
percolating water. Examples: Zion NP, Escalante river drainage.

*Anthropomorph:* Stylized figure with human-like attributes, as seen on rock
art all over the Southwest.

*Arch:* Natural opening eroded by wind or rain. Examples: Arches NP,
Canyonlands NP, all around Moab, Mystery Valley, Rattlesnake Canyon.

*Arroyo:* Spanish term used in place of "wash" throughout the Sonoran desert
region; see wash. Examples: Organ Pipe Cactus NM and Saguaro NP.

*Badlands:* Desert terrain forming strongly eroded shale or limestone
hills, frequently striped with spectacular colors. A translation of the French
"mauvaises terres", as named by French Canadian fur trappers. Examples: Old
Paria, Petrified Forest NM, Waterpocket Fold.

*Bajada:* Slope formed of multiple alluvial fans (fan-shaped deposits of sedi-
ments and debris found at the base of stream channels.) Examples: Organ Pipe
Cactus NM and Saguaro NP.

*Balanced rock:* Rock of hard material resting on top of a softer formation that
has been eroded away, leaving the former balanced on top of the latter. Examples:
Arches Nat'l Park, Chiricahua and Colorado Nat'l Monuments.

*Bedrock:* Solid rock of the earth's crust underlying sandstone layers.

*Butte:* Small, deeply cut mesa that has been protected from erosion by a hard
sedimentary layer on its summit. Examples: Factory Butte, Monument Valley,
Valley of the Gods, Lukachukai Mountains.

*Cairn:* Human-made conical pile of stones marking a footpath.

*Canyon:* Deep gorge formed by the course of a river. Found throughout the
Southwest. Examples: Grand Canyon, Canyonlands, Escalante river area.

*Cave:* Hole in a thick wall of sandstone formed by a spring-seep breaking up
the sandstone. Examples: Double Arch alcove (lower cave), Zion's subway.

*Confluence:* Points where two rivers or canyons meet. Examples: Green and
Colorado rivers in Canyonlands' Needles District, Buckskin and Paria in Paria
Canyon.

*Cross-bedding:* Intricately overlapped layers of sandstone. Examples: Zion
Plateau, Escalante, The Wave.

*Cryptobiotic soil:* aka cryptogamic soil or simply "crypto", Greek term for
"hidden life", a blackish crust inhabited by micro-organisms whose activity creates a network of fibers holding soil particles together. Unfortunately, crypto
is easily crushed by footsteps and car tires and takes decades to regenerate.
Examples: the Needles.

*Desert varnish:* Dark stripy patina on sandstone, formed by iron or manganese oxide processed by micro-organisms. Examples: Canyon de Chelly, Burr Trail, around Moab.

*Diatreme:* Gaseous eruption during which the shattered rock falls back into the pipe. Magma often flows upward through the weakened crust to create a dike around the diatreme. Also known as volcanic plug or neck. Examples: Shiprock, Agathla Peak, Church Rock.

*Dike:* Intrusive magma rise created when a crack occurred in the earth's crust. Examples: Shiprock, Agathla Peak.

*Fins:* Group of individually eroded rocks similar in shape to the fin of a shark and following vertical fracture lines. Examples: Arches Nat'l Park, Canyonlands' Maze District, Behind the Rocks.

*Flash flood:* Torrent of water suddenly formed by a violent rainstorm falling on non-porous soil. On the Colorado plateau, these torrents naturally gravitate towards fissures in the rock, forming narrows and slot canyons.

*Fold:* Rise formed by the irregular uplift of sedimentary layers of rock. See also Monocline. In the Waterpocket Fold, a layer located 6,000 feet deep inside the earth at its eastern end may be exposed as a surface layer in the west. Examples: Waterpocket Fold, the Cockscomb, Comb Ridge.

*Hogan:* Traditional Navajo dwelling, built of wooden logs.

*Goblin:* Variation of the Hoodoo; exclusively in soft sandstone. Evokes images of mythological creatures of a grotesque shape. Example: Goblin Valley.

*Gooseneck:* Bend in a river in the form of a loop. Examples: Goosenecks of the San Juan, Dead Horse Point, Horseshoe Bend, Capitol Reef.

*Graben:* Valley formed by a sinking of the ground between two parallel fault lines. Examples: the Needles, west of Elephant Hill.

*Hoodoo:* Pillar of eroded rock or sandstone, capped at the top by a more highly resistant layer. Examples: Bryce Canyon, Cedar Breaks, The Rimrocks, the White Rocks, Coal Mine Canyon, Tent Rocks.

*Kiva:* Underground ceremonial chamber built by Ancestral Puebloans and other native cultures of the Southwest.

*Kokopelli:* Ubiquitous anthropomorph, with its hunch back and flute. Common on rock art all over the Southwest.

*Laccolith:* Mountain formed by magma uprisings pushing horizontally and vertically through the thick layers of sandstone. Examples: all the most prominent mountains of the Colorado Plateau.

*Mesa:* Flat-top remnant of a plateau rising above the surrounding plain. Its name means "table" in Spanish. Examples: Monument Valley, Mesa Verde.

*Monocline:* Spectacular fracture in the ground, resulting in layers of sedimental rock exposed at a steep angle. Also known generically as "fold" and "hogback" when it's shorter in length. Examples: Waterpocket Fold, the Cockscomb, Comb Ridge.

*Natural Bridge:* Natural opening formed by water action piercing through thin rock at the bend of a river. Examples: Rainbow Bridge, Natural Bridges NM, El Malpais NM.

*Narrows:* Extremely narrow canyon formed by a watercourse that is often dry. Examples: Virgin Narrows, Paria Narrows, Buckskin Gulch.

*Needles:* Form of spire of Cedar Mesa sandstone eroded in the form of jagged points along fracture lines, also called minarets. Examples: the Needles and Maze districts of Canyonlands.

*Petrified dunes:* Ancient sand dunes turned to rock after being buried, then rounded and polished by erosion. Examples: Arches NP, Boulder, Hite, Round Rock.

*Petrified wood:* Remnant tree trunks from ancient forests submerged by volcanic ash, then exposed by soil erosion. Examples: Petrified Forest NP, Escalante SP, Wolverine area on Burr trail.

*Petroglyph:* Rock art done by pecking, scratching or carving.

*Pictograph:* Rock art painted on the surface of the stone.

*Playa:* Spanish for "beach", a dry lakebed formed by evaporation and consisting of dissolved minerals. Examples: White Sands NM.

*Pothole:* aka *Tinaja* in Spanish. A shallow pool formed in slickrock or limestone, sometimes even bedrock, by water dissolving the sand or rock particles, which are then washed away during storms. Examples: Canyonlands' Needles District, Hueco Tanks.

*Rincon:* Short abandoned loop in a river gorge or any short tributary in a canyon or valley. Examples: Escalante river drainage.

*Reef:* Natural rock barrier in the form of a ridge, formed by an almost vertical uplift of sedimentary layers. Examples: San Rafael Reef, Capitol Reef.

*Sand pipes:* Columns of light-colored rock of a phallic shape emerging in a haphazard manner from the earth. Examples: Kodachrome Basin.

*Slickrock:* Generic term used to describe exposed masses of hard sandstone polished by the elements, such as the Slickrock Trail of Moab, a favorite of mountain bikers. This sandstone becomes extremely slippery under rain, ice and snow. Examples: around Moab, Canyonlands.

*Slot canyon:* Narrow passage with smooth walls, formed not by constantly flowing water, but by the repeated action of flash floods. Examples: Antelope Canyon, Peek-a-Boo, Little Wild Horse, Wire Pass, Round Valley Draw.

*Spires:* Rock capped by a hard uppermost slab and eroded by rain into vertical towers. Examples: Fisher Towers, Monument Valley, Chimney Rock in Capitol Reef, Kodachrome Basin.

*Tank:* Large pothole. Examples: Capitol Gorge, Waterpocket Fold.

*Travertine:* Layered calcium carbonate formed by deposition from spring waters or hot springs. Examples: Havasu Canyon, Zion's Subway, Crystal Geyser.

*Volcanic plug:* See diatreme. Examples: Shiprock, Agathla Peak.

*Wash:* Dry watercourse channeling runoff water after thunderstorms.

*Window:* Hole trough a wall of rock, with edges not quite as defined as an arch. Examples: Arches NP.

# Maps

The maps are classified by scale, beginning with the largest and most general.

*Large scale road maps:* The best general road map is without doubt the Indian Country Guide published by the American Automobile Association (AAA). This remarkable guide/map is a sheer pleasure to read and use. It contains a surprising amount of dirt and gravel roads, with very accurate mileage and it does an excellent job of referencing little-known locations. Unless you intend to do some heavy-duty hiking or four-wheeling, this map is quite sufficient for an ordinary car-based tour of the "Grand Circle". The only sites in the present guide that are not covered by AAA's Indian Country Guide are a small part of San Rafael Swell Chapter (Wedge Overlook and Buckhorn Draw, Nine Mile canyon) and all the Around Dinosaur Chapter. They are adequately covered by the AAA Utah–Colorado map and Dinosaur National Park mini-guide. You can obtain these maps from any AAA office and many of the bookstores in the National Parks and Monuments as well as some gas stations.

*Detailed road maps:* Southeastern Utah and Southwestern Utah maps are published by the Utah Travel Council. Roads and tracks are indicated in a very precise fashion. These maps can prove very useful when used in conjunction with the Indian Country map, especially to find less important 4WD trails.

*National Park and Monument miniguides:* These wonderfully concise mini-guides are packed with all the essential information about the parks, their history, geology and fauna. You can get them at the park entrances or at Visitor Centers. Each has a detailed map of the highlights of the park to help you find your way around on roads and trails. For Grand Staircase-Escalante Nat'l Monument, you'll need the Visitor Information brochure; it includes a map introducing a very convenient numbering system that greatly helps in identifying and navigating the numerous backcountry roads in the area (including the southern part near US 89).

*National Park topographic maps:* If you plan on adventuring along the trails and roads in distant parts of the national parks, the topographic maps of the Illustrated Trails series, printed on waterproof paper, are extremely well made and highly recommended. I always use them for hiking in the parks.

*Topo! maps on CD-ROM:* A fantastic resource to plan your trip beforehand. The maps print spectacularly well and you can mark your intended route. Great to enter way points in your GPS. Delorme, Maptech and National Geographic make topo mapping software on CD-Rom. National Geographic's Topo! State Series is particularly good. On the web, topozone.com allows you to display at no charge small portions of topographic maps using GPS coordinates and to print them on your own equipment. This site and others, such as backpacker.com, offer a paying service allowing you to download and print personalized maps.

*4x4 topographic maps:* Fran Barnes' maps in the Canyon Country series are excellent. They are U.S. Geological Survey topo maps on which are superimposed the numerous and little frequented 4x4 trails. They are extremely practical if your primary purpose if to do some four-wheeling in the Moab area.

## Selected Bibliography - Guidebooks

You have a wide selection of materials from which to choose among the traditional guidebooks. Here are some of my favorites:

*National Geographic's Guide to the National Parks of the USA*, published by the National Geographic Society, (888) 225-5647; an excellent general reference work, very well illustrated with many photographs.

*Journey to the High Southwest* by Robert Casey, published by Globe Pequot Press, ISBN 0-7627-0499-3; a remarkably endearing and thoroughly documented travel guide to the Four Corners.

*Scenic Driving Utah* by Joe Bensen, published by Falcon Press, ISBN 1-56044-486-X; excellent resource for driving around Utah.

*Utah Byways* by Tony Huegel, published by Wilderness Press, ISBN 0-89997-263-2; nice to have in the glove box for good description of the Scenic Backways.

*Utah's National Parks* by Ron Adkinson, published by Wilderness Press, ISBN 0-89997-126-1: a great resource, very thoroughly researched.

*Hiking the Southwest's Canyon Country* by Sandra Hinchman, published by The Mountaineers Press, ISBN 0-89886-492-5; an excellent hiking guide to the Southwest, very complete, with great maps.

*Canyon Hiking Guide to the Colorado Plateau* by Michael Kelsey, published by Michael R. Kelsey Publishing, ISBN 0-944510-16-7; a remarkable resource for fit people wanting to explore canyons and remote places of the Colorado Plateau. To be used responsibly and according to the author's warnings and disclaimer. Hiking times are underestimated for almost everybody. Use maps with caution and not as your primary source of information.

*Utah's Favorite Hiking Trails* by David Day, published by Rincon Publishing, ISBN 0-9660858-1-7; great descriptions of a large number of Utah trails; highly recommended.

*Hiking Zion and Bryce Canyon NP* by Erik Molvar & Tamara Martin, published by Falcon Press, ISBN 1-56044-509-2; excellent hiking guide to these major parks.

*Hiking Grand Staircase-Escalante & the Glen Canyon Region* by Ron Adkinson, published by Falcon Guides, ISBN 1-56044-645-5; excellent hiking resource for the whole Escalante region.

*Trail Guide to Grand Staircase-Escalante* by David Urmann and Kevin Bowditch, published by Gibbs Smith Publisher, ISBN 0-879058-85-4; nice book, with good advice on the rarely-documented Kaiparowits Plateau.

*Hiking the Escalante* by Rudi Lambrechtse, published by Univ. of Utah Press, ISBN, 0874806313; the book to take if you'll be using the Hole-in-the-Rock road as a staging area for hikes.

*Hiking and Exploring the Paria River* by Michael Kelsey, published by Michael R. Kelsey Publishing, ISBN 0-944510-21-3; the comments for the Canyon Hiking Guide to the Colorado Plateau apply to this one too.

*Hiking Guide to Cedar Mesa* by Peter Francis Tassoni, published by University of Utah Press, ISBN 0-874806-80-1; excellent guide centering on the Cedar Mesa Plateau, with an abundance of GPS points.

*Canyonlands National Park Favorite Jeep Roads & Hiking Trail* by David Day, published by Rincon Publishing, ISBN 0966085825; the new standard for exploring Canyonlands Nat'l Park.

*Exploring Canyonlands and Arches* by Bill Schneider, published by Falcon Press, ISBN 1-56044-510-6; good hiking resource.

*Canyon Country Off-Road Vehicle Trails* (a collection) by Fran Barnes; a must for off-road driving in the Arches and Canyonlands area.

*Canyon Country Prehistoric Rock Art* by Fran Barnes, published by Arch Hunter Books, ISBN 0-915272-25-3; an excellent introduction to rock art.

*Guide to Rock Art of the Utah Region* by Dennis Slifer, published by Ancient City Press, ISBN 1-580960-09-X; very good resource for finding rock art sites.

*Guide to Rock Art of Nine Mile Canyon* by M. and J. Liddiard, no ISBN; a useful booklet for finding rock art panels in the canyon.

*Hiking Ruins Seldom Seen* by Dave Wilson, published by Falcon Press, ISBN 1-560448-34-2; excellent hiking guide covering the entire Southwest.

*Rock Art and Ruins for Beginners and Old Guys* by Albert Scholl Jr., published by Rainbow Publishing, ISBN 0-9704688-0-6; a fun guide to the major rock art sites.

*Canyon Country Geology for the Layman and Rockbound* by F.A. Barnes, published by Arch Hunter Books, ISBN 1-891858-18-1; one of many highly informative and easy-to-read guidebooks by Mr. Barnes. Highly recommended.

## Selected Bibliography - Other Recommended Reading

I cannot recommend too highly the following works, which I consider quintessential to a good understanding of various aspects of the Southwest. Reading these books during a trip in the American West reinforces the pleasure of discovery.

*The Southwest Inside Out* by Thomas Wiewandt and Maureen Wilks, published by Wild Horizons Publishing, ISBN 1-879728-04-4; a highly-innovative and approachable presentation of the natural features of the Southwest. Remarkably illustrated. Outstanding photography.

*Standing Up Country* by Gregory Crampton, published by Rio Nuevo Publishers, ISBN 1-887896-15-5; a wonderful resource on the human history of the Colorado Plateau, richly illustrated with outstanding photography.

*Mormon Country* by Wallace Stegner, published by the University of Nebraska Press, ISBN 0-803293-05-4; a fundamental work on the colonization of Utah by the Mormons; impartial, remarkably documented and an easy read. It would be a shame to cross Utah without knowing or understanding the remarkable saga of the Mormon pioneers.

*Architecture of the Ancient Ones* by A. Dudley Gardner and Val Brinkerhoff, published by Gibbs Smith, ISBN 0-87905-955-9; outstanding photography.

*The Exploration of the Colorado River and Its Canyons* by John Wesley Powell, published by Penguin Classics, ISBN 0-142437-52-2; Powell's extraordinary journals of his expedition, prefaced by Wallace Stegner.

*Centennial* by James Michener, published by Fawcett Books, ISBN 0449214192; a remarkable book, describing the conquest of the Western frontier through the fascinating saga of several characters and families over centuries.

*Desert Solitaire* by Edward Abbey, published by Ballantine Books, ISBN 0345326490; the classic among the numerous books by Abbey, the rebel ranger, at once liberal and redneck. Abbey depicts his love of the desert with a fine sensibility. It's the perfect accompaniment for a trip to Arches and Canyonlands.

*The Dark Wind* by Tony Hillerman, published by Harper, ISBN 0061000035; a novel with a cool Navajo cop as its reluctant hero. An excellent introduction to Navajo culture in the guise of a lively story. A must-read when crossing the Big Rez! Don't be ashamed of the "white guy" syndrome. If you get hooked on Navajo and Hopi culture, you'll naturally step up to serious works.

Needless to say, there are numerous coffee table books depicting the Southwest. These books by well-known photographers such as John Annerino, Jack Dykinga, Gary Ladd, Joseph Lange, David & Marc Muench, Eliot Porter, Lynn Radeka, Galen Rowell, Anselm Spring, Tom Till, Linde Waidhofer, Art Wolfe and many more are a pleasure to look at. They are also an excellent source of locations and a great way to improve your photographic skills through emulation.

## On the Go Resources

These resources are intended as a quick way of finding further information while you're on the road, by calling the appropriate agency. The phone numbers have been verified shortly before we went to press; however, prefixes and numbers can change and this information may be obsolete by the time you read it. I hope you'll find this list useful in your travels.

I have purposely avoided presenting a formal list of web sites, which would become rapidly be obsolete given the highly impermanent nature of web sites. A large number of links to interesting websites can be found at:
    http://www.phototripusa.com/e_resources.html

*National Parks & Monuments*
    Arches NP (435) 719-2319 or (435)719-2299
    Bryce Canyon NP (435) 834-5322
    Canyonlands NP/Island District (435) 259-4712 and (435) 719-2313
    Canyonlands NP/Needles District (435) 259-4711
    Canyonlands NP/Maze District (435) 259-2652
    Capitol Reef NP (435) 425-3791

Cedar Breaks NM (435) 586-9451
Dinosaur NM (970) 374-3000
Flaming Gorge NRA (435) 789-1181
Glen Canyon NRA (928) 608-6404
Grand Staircase-Escalante NM (435) 826-5499
Hovenweep NM (970) 562-4282
Natural Bridges NM (435) 692-1234
Pipe Spring NM (928) 643-7105
Zion NP (435) 772-3256

*State Parks*
Anasazi SP (435) 335-7308
Coral Pink Sand Dunes SP (435) 648-2800
Dead Horse Point SP (435) 259-2614
Edge of the Cedars SP (435) 678-2238
Escalante Petrified Forest SP (435) 826-4466
Fremont Indian SP (435) 527-4631
Goblin Valley SP (435) 564-3633
Goosenecks SP (435) 678-2238
Kodachrome Basin SP (435) 679-8562
Snow Canyon SP (435) 628-2255

*Other Parks & Organizations*
Archeology Vandalism Hotline (800) 722-3998
BLM of Hanksville (435) 542-3461
BLM of Kanab (435) 644-4600
BLM of Moab (435) 259-2100
BLM of Monticello (435) 587-1500
BLM of Price 435) 636-3600
BLM of St. George ((435) 688-3200
BLM of Vernal (435) 781-4400
Canyonlands-North Travel region (800) 635-6622
Canyonlands-South Travel region (800) 574-4386
Castle Country Travel Council (435) 637-3009
Color Country Travel region (800) 233-utah
Dinosaurland Travel Region (800) 477-5558
Hall's Crossing Ferry (800) 528-6154 and (435) 684-7400
Moab Information Center (800) 635-MOAB or (800) 635-6622
Navajo Nation Tourism Department (928) 871-6434
Paria Canyon-Vermilion Cliffs Wilderness (435) 688-3246
Utah Rock Art Research Association PO Box 511324, SLC, UT 84151
Utah Road Conditions (800) 492-2400
Utah State Parks and Recreation (800) 322-3770
Utah Travel Council (800) 200-1160

Note: All National Parks and Monuments and most travelers' bureaus will send you free documentation anywhere in the world to prepare your trip.

*Permission for Red Cave*
Dell Tait, 2410 South State, PO Box 12, Mt. Carmel, UT 84755
(435) 648-2522 delltait@color-country.net

*Equipment for the Virgin Narrows and the Subway*
Zion Adventure Company (435) 772-0990
Zion Rock & Mountain Guides (435) 772-3303

*Llamas, horses, hiking Concessionaires & Shuttle service*
Bryce Canyon Trail Rides (435) 679-8665
Bryce Scenic Rim Trail Rides (435) 679-8761
Red Rock n' Llamas (435) 335-7533 or (877) 955-2627
Escalante Canyon Outfitters (435) 335-7311 or (888) 326-4453
Paria Outpost & Outfitters (928) 691-1047
Needles Outpost (435) 979-4007
Recapture Lodge (435) 672-2281

*4x4 Rentals in Moab*
Arches Auto Rental (435) 259-4959
Canyonlands Jeep Adventures (435) 259-4413
Farabee's Jeep Rentals (435) 259-7494
Slickrock 4X4 Rentals (435) 259-5678
Thrifty Car Rental (435) 259-7317

*A few River Outfitters*
Utah Guides & Outfitters Associations (801) 495-2592
Adrift Adventures (800) 874-4483 or (435) 259-8594
Dinosaur Expeditions 800-345-RAFT
Navtec Expeditions (800) 833-1278 or (435) 259-7983
Splore (801) 484-4128
Tag-A-Long Expeditions (800) 453-3292 or (435) 259-8946
Western River Expeditions (800) 453-7450 or (435) 259-7019
Wild Rivers Expeditions (800) 422-7654 or (435) 672-2244
World Wide River Expeditions (800) 231-2768 or (435) 259-7515

*Flights Over Canyonlands*
Slickrock Air Guides (Moab) (866) 259-1626 or (435) 259-6216
Red Tail Aviation (Moab) (800) 842-9251 or (435) 259-7421
Mountain Flying Service (Moab & Monticello) (800) 954-8747
Needles Outpost (435) 979-4007

# RATINGS

Using a scale of 1 to 5, the following ratings attempt to provide the reader with an overall vision of each location, in order to facilitate comparisons and choices. Obviously, the ratings alone don't tell the whole stoty about a location and should be used only in cunjunction with the explanations of each section.

The ratings are assigned on the basis of four different criteria: overall interest of a location, based mostly on its scenic value (or its beauty and interest in the case of rock art and ancestral dwellings), photographic potential for those of you who happen to carry a camera :-) and level of difficulty to access each location with your vehicle and/or on foot.

The objectivity of ratings done by an author tend to be somewhat tainted by the individual's personal preferences. To minimize personal bias, I arrived at the ratings through a concensual process with a team of knowledgable friends and photographers. We based our assessments on the criteria below and I think we achieved even-handed results. I hope you'll find the ratings helpful in preparing your trip(s) to the Southwest.

| Rating | Scenic Value |
|---|---|
| – | Of no particular interest |
| ♥ | Mildly interesting, visit if nearby and/or time permitting |
| ♥♥ | Scenic location, worthy of a visit |
| ♥♥♥ | Very interesting, scenic or original location |
| ♥♥♥♥ | Outstandingly scenic or rewarding location - a highlight |
| ♥♥♥♥♥ | World-class location - absolutely tops |

| Rating | Photographic Interest |
|---|---|
| – | Of no particular photographic interest |
| ♦ | Worthy of a quick photo |
| ♦♦ | Good photo opportunity |
| ♦♦♦ | Good photographic potential and scenic subjects |
| ♦♦♦♦ | Outstanding photographic potential, highly original or scenic subjects |
| ♦♦♦♦♦ | World-class photographic location, "photographer's dream" |

| Rating | Road Difficulty |
|---|---|
| – | Paved road, accessible to all normal-size vehicles |
| ♠ | Dirt road accessible without difficulty by passenger car (under normal conditions) |
| ♠♠ | Minor obstacles; accessible by passenger car with caution (under good conditions) |
| ♠♠♠ | High-clearance required, but no major difficulty |
| ♠♠♠♠ | High-clearance 4WD required, some obstacles, no real danger |
| ♠♠♠♠♠ | High-clearance 4WD required, some risk to vehicle & passagers, experienced drivers only |

| Rating | Trail Difficulty |
|---|---|
| – | No or very little walking (close to parking area) |
| ♣ | Easy short walk (<= 1h r/t), for everybody |
| ♣♣ | Moderate hike (1 to 3h r/t) with no major difficulty or short hike with some minor difficulties |
| ♣♣♣ | Moderate to strenuous (3 to 6h r/t) and/or difficulties (elevation gain, difficult terrain, some risks) |
| ♣♣♣♣ | Strenuous (> 6h r/t) and/or globally difficult (elevation gain, difficult off-trail terrain, obstacles, risks) |
| ♣♣♣♣♣ | Backpacking required or for extremely fit dayhikers |

| Location | Page | Scenic Value | Photogr. Interest | Road Difficulty | Trail Difficulty |
|---|---|---|---|---|---|
| **3   Around Zion** | | | | | |
| Highway 9 on Zion Plateau | 63 | ♥♥♥ | ♦♦♦ | – | – |
| Checkerboard Mesa | 64 | ♥♥ | ♦♦ | – | – |
| Canyon Overlook Panorama | 64 | ♥♥ | ♦ | – | ♣ |
| Towers of the Virgin | 65 | ♥♥ | ♦♦♦ | – | – |
| Watchman (from the bridge) + Pa'rus Trail | 66 | ♥♥ | ♦♦♦ | – | ♣ |
| Court of the Patriarchs | 66 | ♥ | ♦♦ | – | ♣ |
| Emerald Pools (Lower + Upper) | 67 | ♥♥ | ♦♦ | – | ♣♣♣ |
| Angel's Landing | 68 | ♥♥♥♥ | ♦♦♦ | – | ♣♣♣♣ |
| Hidden Canyon | 69 | ♥♥ | ♦♦ | – | ♣♣♣ |
| Weeping Rock | 69 | ♥♥ | ♦ | – | ♣ |
| Observation Point | 70 | ♥♥♥ | ♦♦ | – | ♣♣♣♣ |
| Great White Throne | 70 | ♥ | ♦♦ | – | – |
| Temple of Sinawava + Riverside Walk | 71 | ♥♥♥ | ♦♦ | – | ♣ |
| Virgin Narrows (> Orderville Canyon) | 72 | ♥♥♥♥♥ | ♦♦♦♦ | – | ♣♣♣ |
| Kolob Canyon Road and Viewpoints | 75 | ♥♥♥ | ♦♦ | – | – |
| Middle Fork of Taylor Creek | 76 | ♥♥♥ | ♦♦♦ | – | ♣♣ |
| South Fork of Taylor Creek | 77 | ♥♥ | ♦♦ | – | ♣♣ |
| Kolob Terrace Road | 77 | ♥♥♥ | ♦♦ | ♠♠ | – |
| West Rim Trail | 78 | ♥♥♥ | ♦♦ | – | ♣♣♣♣ |
| The Subway (from the bottom) | 78 | ♥♥♥♥ | ♦♦♦♦♦ | – | ♣♣♣♣ |
| Right Fork of North Creek | 81 | ♥♥ | ♦♦ | – | ♣♣♣♣ |
| Smithonian Butte | 82 | ♥♥ | ♦♦ | ♠♠ | – |
| Grafton | 82 | ♥ | ♦ | ♠ | – |
| Water Canyon | 82 | ♥♥♥ | ♦♦♦ | ♠ | ♣♣ |
| Coal Pits Wash (autumn foliage) | 82 | ♥ | ♦♦ | – | – |
| Pipe Springs NM | 83 | ♥♥ | ♦ | – | – |
| Red Cliffs | 84 | ♥♥ | ♦♦ | – | ♣ |
| Snow Canyon - Hidden Pinion Trail | 84 | ♥♥ | ♦♦ | – | ♣ |
| Snow Canyon - West Canyon Overlook | 84 | ♥♥ | ♦♦ | – | ♣ |
| Snow Canyon - UT 18 Overlook | 84 | ♥♥ | ♦♦ | ♠ | – |
| Pine Valley | 85 | ♥♥ | ♦ | – | ♣ |
| Virgin River Gorge (I 15) | 85 | ♥♥ | ♦ | – | – |
| Coral Pink Sand Dunes | 86 | ♥♥♥ | ♦♦♦ | – | ♣ |
| Red Canyon Slot | 87 | ♥♥ | ♦♦♦ | ♠♠♠♠ | ♣ |
| Angel Canyon | 87 | ♥♥ | ♦ | – | – |
| Red Cave | 88 | ♥♥♥ | ♦♦♦ | ♠♠♠ | ♣♣ |
| **4   Around Bryce Canyon** | | | | | |
| Sunrise and Sunset Viewpoints | 91 | ♥♥♥♥♥ | ♦♦♦♦♦ | – | – |
| Inspiration Point & Bryce Point | 91 | ♥♥♥ | ♦♦♦♦ | – | – |
| Navajo and Queen's Garden Trails | 92 | ♥♥♥♥ | ♦♦♦ | – | ♣♣ |
| Peek-a-Boo Trail (from the rim) | 94 | ♥♥♥♥ | ♦♦♦ | – | ♣♣♣ |
| Fairyland Trail | 94 | ♥♥♥♥ | ♦♦♦ | – | ♣♣♣ |
| Mossy Cave Trail | 95 | ♥♥ | ♦♦♦ | – | ♣ |
| Yovimpai and Rainbow Points + access road | 95 | ♥♥♥ | ♦♦ | – | ♣ |
| Red Canyon - Pink Ledges trail | 96 | ♥♥♥ | ♦♦♦ | – | ♣ |
| Red Canyon - Arch Trail | 96 | ♥♥ | ♦♦ | ♠ | ♣ |
| Cedar Breaks NM Viewpoints | 97 | ♥♥♥ | ♦♦ | – | – |
| Cedar Breaks NM Wasatch Ramparts Trail | 97 | ♥♥♥ | ♦♦ | – | ♣♣ |
| **5   Around the Cockscomb** | | | | | |
| Cottonwood Canyon Road | 100 | ♥♥♥♥ | ♦♦♦ | ♠♠ | ♣ |
| Round Valley Draw | 101 | ♥♥ | ♦♦ | ♠♠♠ | ♣♣♣ |
| Grosvenor Arch | 102 | ♥♥ | ♦♦ | ♠♠ | – |
| Cottonwood Narrows | 103 | ♥♥ | ♦ | ♠♠ | ♣ |
| Lower Hackberry Narrows | 105 | ♥♥ | ♦♦ | ♠♠ | ♣♣ |
| Yellow Rock | 106 | ♥♥♥♥ | ♦♦♦♦ | ♠♠ | ♣♣♣ |
| Box of the Paria | 108 | ♥♥ | ♦ | ♠♠ | ♣ |

| Location | Page | Scenic Value | Photogr. Interest | Road Difficulty | Trail Difficulty |
|---|---|---|---|---|---|
| Wahweap Hoodoos (north access) | 108 | ♥♥♥♥ | ♦♦♦♦ | ♠♠♠ | ♣ |
| Wahweap Hoodoos (south access) | 108 | ♥♥♥♥ | ♦♦♦♦ | ♠♠ | ♣♣ |
| White Rocks (lower site) | 110 | ♥♥♥ | ♦♦♦ | ♠♠♠ | ♣ |
| White Rocks (upper site) | 110 | ♥♥♥ | ♦♦ | ♠♠♠♠ | ♣♣♣ |
| Rimrocks Hoodoos | 112 | ♥♥♥ | ♦♦♦ | – | ♣ |
| Old Paria | 114 | ♥♥♥ | ♦♦♦ | ♠ | – |
| Paria Canyon | 115 | ♥♥♥♥ | ♦♦♦ | ♠ | ♣♣♣♣ |
| Wire Pass - Buckskin Gulch | 116 | ♥♥♥♥ | ♦♦♦ | ♠♠ | ♣♣ |
| Cobra Arch | 119 | ♥♥♥ | ♦♦♦ | ♠♠♠ | ♣♣♣ |
| **6  Along Scenic Byway 12** | | | | | |
| Kodachrome Basin | 123 | ♥♥♥ | ♦♦♦ | – | ♣ |
| Skutumpah Road | 123 | ♥♥ | ♦♦ | ♠♠♠ | – |
| Willis Creek | 124 | ♥♥♥ | ♦♦♦ | ♠♠♠ | ♣♣ |
| Bull Valley Gorge | 125 | ♥♥ | ♦♦ | ♠♠♠ | ♣♣♣ |
| The Blues | 125 | ♥ | ♦ | – | – |
| Escalante Petrified Forest | 125 | ♥♥ | ♦ | – | ♣♣ |
| Circle of Friends | 126 | ♥ | ♦ | ♠ | – |
| Smoky Mountain Road | 126 | ♥♥ | ♦♦ | ♠♠♠♠ | – |
| Horizon Arch | 127 | ♥♥♥ | ♦♦♦ | ♠♠♠ | ♣♣♣ |
| Hell's Backbone Road | 128 | ♥♥ | ♦♦ | ♠♠ | – |
| Death Hollow (via Escalante Trailhead) | 128 | ♥♥♥♥ | ♦♦ | ♠ | ♣♣♣♣ |
| SB 12: Escalante > Boulder (via Hogback) | 130 | ♥♥♥♥ | ♦♦ | – | – |
| Escalante Natural Bridge (SB 12 > arch) | 130 | ♥♥♥ | ♦♦♦ | – | ♣♣ |
| Escalante River Trail (Escalante Trailhead) | 131 | ♥♥♥ | ♦♦♦ | ♠ | ♣♣♣♣ |
| Hundred Handprints | 132 | ♥♥ | ♦ | – | ♣♣ |
| Phipps Arch | 132 | ♥♥ | ♦♦ | – | ♣♣ |
| Lower Calf Creek Falls | 133 | ♥♥♥♥ | ♦♦♦ | – | ♣♣ |
| Upper Calf Creek Falls | 135 | ♥♥ | ♦♦ | ♠ | ♣♣ |
| SB 12: around Boulder Mountain | 135 | ♥♥♥ | ♦♦ | – | – |
| Anasazi SP | 135 | ♥♥ | ♦♦ | – | – |
| Burr Trail (> Long Canyon) | 136 | ♥♥♥♥ | ♦♦♦♦ | – | – |
| Burr Trail (Long Canyon > Notom Bullfrog Rd) | 136 | ♥♥ | ♦♦ | ♠♠ | – |
| Little Death Hollow | 137 | ♥♥♥ | ♦♦ | ♠♠♠♠ | ♣♣♣ |
| **7  Canyons of the Escalante** | | | | | |
| Hole In The Rock Road (except 5 last miles) | 140 | ♥♥ | ♦ | ♠♠ | – |
| Cedar Wash Arch | 141 | ♥♥ | ♦ | ♠♠ | ♣ |
| Zebra & Tunnel Slots | 143 | ♥♥♥ | ♦♦♦♦ | ♠ | ♣♣ |
| Devil's Garden | 144 | ♥♥♥♥ | ♦♦♦♦ | ♠ | ♣ |
| Chopock Canyon | 146 | ♥♥♥ | ♦♦♦ | ♠♠♠ | ♣♣♣♣ |
| Upper Harris Wash (> Escalante) | 146 | ♥♥♥ | ♦♦ | ♠♠ | ♣♣♣♣ |
| Neon Canyon / Golden Cathedral | 148 | ♥♥♥♥ | ♦♦♦♦ | ♠♠♠ | ♣♣♣ |
| Dry Fork + Peek-a-boo & Spooky Slots | 150 | ♥♥♥♥ | ♦♦♦ | ♠♠ | ♣♣♣ |
| Coyote Gulch (Crack in the Wall > Red Well) | 153 | ♥♥♥♥♥ | ♦♦♦♦ | ♠♠♠♠ | ♣♣♣♣♣ |
| Coyote Gulch (Crack in the Wall > Jacob Hamblin) | 153 | ♥♥♥♥♥ | ♦♦♦♦ | ♠♠♠♠ | ♣♣♣♣♣ |
| Chimney Rock | 157 | ♥ | ♦ | ♠♠♠♠ | – |
| Sunset Arch | 157 | ♥♥♥ | ♦♦♦♦ | ♠♠ | ♣♣♣ |
| Dance Hall Rock | 159 | ♥♥ | ♦ | ♠♠ | – |
| Broken Bow Arch | 159 | ♥♥♥ | ♦♦♦ | ♠♠♠ | ♣♣ |
| Hole In The Rock (at the end of the road) | 161 | ♥♥♥ | ♦♦ | ♠♠♠♠♠ | ♣♣ |
| Llewelyn Gulch | 162 | ♥♥ | ♦♦ | ♠♠ | ♣♣♣ |
| **8  Capitol Reef** | | | | | |
| Panorama Point & Sunset Point | 164 | ♥♥♥ | ♦♦♦ | ♠ | ♣ |
| Fruita Oasis (+ creek) | 166 | ♥♥ | ♦♦ | – | ♣ |
| Fremont Gorge Overlook | 166 | ♥♥ | ♦♦ | – | ♣♣ |
| Cohab Canyon + Fruita Overlooks | 168 | ♥♥♥ | ♦♦ | – | ♣♣ |
| Scenic Drive (including Capitol Gorge) | 168 | ♥♥♥♥ | ♦♦♦ | ♠ | – |
| Pionner Register + Waterpocket Tanks | 168 | ♥♥ | ♦ | ♠ | ♣ |

| Location | Page | Scenic Value | Photogr. Interest | Road Difficulty | Trail Difficulty |
|---|---|---|---|---|---|
| Golden Throne Trail | 168 | ♥♥ | ♦ | ♠ | ♣♣ |
| Hickman Bridge | 169 | ♥♥ | ♦ | – | ♣♣ |
| Rim Overlook + Navajo Knobs | 170 | ♥♥♥ | ♦♦ | – | ♣♣♣ |
| Cathedral Valley Loop | 170 | ♥♥♥♥ | ♦♦♦♦ | ♠♠♠ | ♣ |
| South Desert + Bentonite Hills | 172 | ♥♥♥ | ♦♦ | ♠♠♠ | ♣ |
| Upper Cathedral Valley | 173 | ♥♥♥♥ | ♦♦♦♦ | ♠♠♠ | ♣ |
| Lower Cathedral Valley | 175 | ♥♥♥ | ♦♦♦♦ | ♠♠ | – |
| Caineville Badlands | 176 | ♥♥ | ♦ | ♠♠ | – |
| Nottom Bullfrog Road (> foot of Burr trail) | 177 | ♥♥ | ♦♦ | ♠♠ | – |
| Strike Valley Overlook | 178 | ♥♥♥♥ | ♦♦ | ♠♠♠♠ | ♣ |
| Upper Muley Twist | 178 | ♥♥♥♥ | ♦♦ | ♠♠♠♠ | ♣♣♣ |
| Hall's Creek Overlook | 179 | ♥♥ | ♦♦ | ♠♠♠ | – |
| Brimhall Arch | 180 | ♥♥ | ♦♦ | ♠♠♠ | ♣♣♣♣ |
| Hamburger Rocks | 180 | ♥♥ | ♦♦ | ♠♠♠ | ♣♣♣ |
| Hall's Creek Narrows | 180 | ♥♥♥♥ | ♦♦♦ | ♠♠♠ | ♣♣♣♣♣ |

## 9   San Rafael Swell

| Location | Page | Scenic Value | Photogr. Interest | Road Difficulty | Trail Difficulty |
|---|---|---|---|---|---|
| Factory Butte | 183 | ♥♥ | ♦♦ | ♠ | – |
| Goblin Valley | 184 | ♥♥♥♥ | ♦♦♦ | – | ♣ |
| Mollie's Castle | 185 | ♥ | ♦ | – | – |
| Little Wild Horse Slot | 185 | ♥♥♥♥ | ♦♦♦ | ♠♠ | ♣♣ |
| Crack Canyon | 187 | ♥♥♥ | ♦♦♦ | ♠♠ | ♣♣ |
| Wild Horse Canyon (panel + window) | 188 | ♥♥♥ | ♦♦♦ | ♠ | ♣♣ |
| Temple Mountain Panel | 189 | ♥♥ | ♦ | – | – |
| Spotted Wolf Canyon (I 70) | 189 | ♥♥♥ | ♦♦♦ | – | – |
| Fremont Indian SP | 190 | ♥♥ | ♦ | – | ♣ |
| Black Dragon Wash | 190 | ♥♥ | ♦♦ | ♠♠ | ♣ |
| Petroglyph Canyon | 191 | ♥ | ♦ | ♠♠ | ♣ |
| Head of Sinbad Panel | 192 | ♥♥♥ | ♦♦♦ | ♠♠♠ | – |
| Lone Warrior Panel | 192 | ♥ | ♦ | ♠♠ | – |
| Rochester Rock Art Panel | 192 | ♥♥ | ♦♦ | ♠ | ♣ |
| Wedge Overlook | 193 | ♥♥♥ | ♦♦ | ♠♠ | – |
| Buckhorn Draw | 193 | ♥♥♥ | ♦♦♦ | ♠♠ | – |
| Nine Mile Canyon | 194 | ♥♥♥♥ | ♦♦ | ♠ | ♣ |
| Crystal Geyser | 195 | ♥♥ | ♦♦ | ♠♠ | – |
| Sego Canyon | 196 | ♥♥♥ | ♦♦♦ | ♠ | – |

## 10   Around Cedar Mesa

| Location | Page | Scenic Value | Photogr. Interest | Road Difficulty | Trail Difficulty |
|---|---|---|---|---|---|
| Edge of the Cedars SP | 198 | ♥♥ | ♦ | – | – |
| Butler Wash Ruin | 199 | ♥ | ♦ | – | ♣ |
| Comb Ridge | 199 | ♥♥ | ♦♦ | – | – |
| Mule Canyon South Fork (House on Fire) | 200 | ♥♥ | ♦♦♦♦ | ♠ | ♣♣ |
| Grand Gulch (Split Level House, Green Mask) | 200 | ♥♥♥♥ | ♦♦♦ | – | ♣♣♣♣♣ |
| Kane Gulch > Grand Gulch (Junction Ruins) | 200 | ♥♥♥ | ♦♦ | – | ♣♣♣ |
| Todie Canyon | 201 | ♥♥ | ♦ | ♠♠ | ♣♣♣ |
| Bullet Canyon > Jailhouse Ruin | 201 | ♥♥♥ | ♦♦♦ | ♠♠ | ♣♣♣ |
| Government Trail > Big Man Panel | 201 | ♥♥♥ | ♦♦♦ | ♠♠♠ | ♣♣♣ |
| Road Canyon (Fallen Roof Ruin) | 202 | ♥♥♥ | ♦♦♦♦ | ♠♠ | ♣♣ |
| Mokey Dugway & Muley Point | 204 | ♥♥ | ♦ | ♠ | – |
| Valley of the Gods | 205 | ♥♥♥ | ♦♦ | ♠♠ | – |
| Goosenecks of the San Juan | 206 | ♥♥♥ | ♦♦ | – | – |
| Mexican Hat & Indian Blanket | 206 | ♥ | ♦ | ♠ | – |
| Wolfman Panel | 207 | ♥♥ | ♦♦ | ♠ | ♣ |
| Procession Panel | 207 | ♥♥♥ | ♦♦ | ♠♠ | ♣♣ |
| Sand Island Panel | 207 | ♥ | ♦ | ♠ | – |
| Bluff & Twin Rocks | 207 | ♥♥ | ♦ | – | – |
| Rafting on the San Juan (Bluff > Mexican Hat) | 207 | ♥♥♥ | ♦♦♦ | – | ♣ |
| Sipapu Bridge | 208 | ♥♥♥ | ♦♦♦ | – | ♣♣ |
| Sipapu - Kachina Loop via White Canyon | 208 | ♥♥♥ | ♦♦ | – | ♣♣♣ |

| Location | Page | Scenic Value | Photogr. Interest | Road Difficulty | Trail Difficulty |
|---|---|---|---|---|---|
| Kachina Bridge | 208 | ♥♥ | ♦ | – | ♣♣ |
| Owachomo Bridge | 208 | ♥♥ | ♦♦ | – | ♣ |
| Hog Spring & Cleopatra | 210 | ♥♥ | ♦♦ | – | ♣ |
| Pedestal Alley Trail | 210 | ♥♥ | ♦ | ♠ | ♣♣ |
| Little Egypt | 211 | ♥♥ | ♦♦ | ♠ | ♣ |
| Arsenic Arch | 211 | ♥♥♥ | ♦♦ | ♠♠ | ♣♣ |
| Dirty Devil Overlook (Burr Point) | 212 | ♥♥♥ | ♦♦ | ♠♠ | – |
| **11   Around Moab** | | | | | |
| Potash Road (paved part) | 214 | ♥♥ | ♦♦ | – | – |
| Potash Road Basins | 215 | ♥♥ | ♦♦ | ♠♠♠ | – |
| Poison Spider Mesa ( > Waterfall) | 215 | ♥♥ | ♦♦♦ | ♠♠♠♠ | ♣ |
| Corona Arch & Bowtie Arch | 216 | ♥♥♥ | ♦♦♦ | – | ♣♣ |
| Tukuhnikivats Arch | 217 | ♥♥ | ♦♦♦ | ♠♠ | ♣♣♣ |
| Wilson Arch | 218 | ♥♥ | ♦♦ | – | ♣♣ |
| La Sal Mountains Loop & Castle Valley | 218 | ♥♥♥ | ♦♦ | ♠ | – |
| Colorado Riverway (SB 128) | 219 | ♥♥♥ | ♦♦ | – | – |
| Cisco | 219 | ♥ | ♦ | – | – |
| Fisher Towers | 219 | ♥♥♥♥ | ♦♦♦♦ | ♠♠ | ♣♣♣ |
| Onion Creek Canyon | 221 | ♥♥♥ | ♦♦ | ♠♠♠ | – |
| Pole Rim View | 222 | ♥♥♥ | ♦♦♦ | ♠♠♠♠ | ♣ |
| Top of the World | 222 | ♥♥♥ | ♦♦ | ♠♠♠♠ | – |
| **12   Arches NP** | | | | | |
| Park Avenue & Courthouse Towers | 225 | ♥♥♥ | ♦♦♦ | – | ♣ |
| Petrified Dunes | 225 | ♥ | ♦♦ | – | ♣ |
| Balanced Rock | 225 | ♥♥ | ♦♦♦ | – | – |
| Windows Section | 226 | ♥♥♥♥ | ♦♦♦♦ | – | ♣ |
| Panorama Point | 227 | ♥ | ♦ | – | – |
| Wolfe Ranch Petroglyphs | 227 | ♥♥ | ♦♦ | – | ♣ |
| Delicate Arch (top) | 228 | ♥♥♥♥♥ | ♦♦♦♦ | – | ♣♣ |
| Delicate Arch Viewpoint (below) | 229 | ♥♥♥ | ♦♦♦ | – | ♣ |
| Fiery Furnace | 229 | ♥♥♥ | ♦♦ | – | ♣♣♣ |
| Sand Dune Arch & Broken Arch | 230 | ♥♥ | ♦♦ | – | ♣ |
| Devil's Garden (> Double-O Arch) | 230 | ♥♥♥♥ | ♦♦♦ | – | ♣♣♣ |
| Klondike Bluffs | 232 | ♥♥♥ | ♦♦♦ | ♠♠♠ | ♣♣ |
| Copper Ridge Sauropod Track | 233 | ♥ | ♦ | ♠♠ | – |
| Courthouse Wash Panel | 234 | ♥♥ | ♦ | – | ♣ |
| **13   Canyonlands Island in the Sky** | | | | | |
| Dead Horse Point SP | 237 | ♥♥♥♥♥ | ♦♦♦♦♦ | – | ♣ |
| Long Canyon Road | 238 | ♥♥♥ | ♦♦ | ♠♠♠ | – |
| Mesa Arch | 239 | ♥♥♥ | ♦♦♦♦ | – | ♣ |
| Grandview Point | 240 | ♥♥♥ | ♦♦♦ | – | ♣ |
| White Rim Overlook | 240 | ♥♥♥ | ♦♦♦ | – | ♣ |
| Green River Overlook | 241 | ♥♥♥ | ♦♦♦ | ♠ | – |
| Murphy Point | 241 | ♥♥♥ | ♦♦♦ | ♠ | ♣♣ |
| Aztec Butte | 241 | ♥♥ | ♦♦♦ | – | ♣♣ |
| False Kiva | 242 | ♥♥♥ | ♦♦♦♦ | – | ♣♣ |
| Alcove Spring Trail | 243 | ♥♥ | ♦ | – | ♣♣ |
| Moses & Zeus (via Taylor Canyon) | 243 | ♥♥ | ♦♦ | ♠♠♠♠ | ♣♣ |
| Upheaval Dome | 243 | ♥♥ | ♦ | – | ♣ |
| Shafer Trail | 244 | ♥♥♥♥ | ♦♦ | ♠♠♠♠ | – |
| Potash Road (Shafer Trail > SB 279) | 244 | ♥♥♥ | ♦♦ | ♠♠♠ | – |
| White Rim Road (loop) | 244 | ♥♥♥♥♥ | ♦♦♦♦ | ♠♠♠♠ | ♣ |
| Fort Bottom Trail | 245 | ♥♥♥ | ♦♦ | ♠♠♠♠ | ♣♣ |
| **14   Canyonlands Needles** | | | | | |
| Newspaper Rock | 249 | ♥♥♥ | ♦♦ | – | – |
| Roadside Ruin | 250 | ♥ | ♦ | – | – |
| Cave Spring | 250 | ♥♥ | ♦ | ♠ | ♣ |

| Location | Page | Scenic Value | Photogr. Interest | Road Difficulty | Trail Difficulty |
|---|---|---|---|---|---|
| Pothole Point Loop | 250 | ♥ | ♦ | – | ♣ |
| Slickrock Trail | 250 | ♥♥ | ♦♦ | – | ♣♣ |
| Squaw Flat / Big Spring Trail | 250 | ♥♥♥ | ♦♦♦ | – | ♣♣ |
| Elephant Hill (2WD Road + uphill hike) | 251 | ♥♥ | ♦♦ | ▲ | ♣ |
| Elephant Hill 4WD Loop (+ Confluence) | 251 | ♥♥♥ | ♦♦ | ▲▲▲▲▲ | – |
| Chesler Park Overlook | 252 | ♥♥♥ | ♦♦ | ▲ | ♣♣ |
| Chesler Park Overlook + Loop inside the Park | 252 | ♥♥♥♥ | ♦♦♦♦ | ▲ | ♣♣♣ |
| Druid Arch | 253 | ♥♥♥ | ♦♦♦ | ▲ | ♣♣♣ |
| Horse Canyon | 254 | ♥♥♥ | ♦♦♦ | ▲▲▲▲ | ♣♣ |
| Salt Creek - Peek-a-Boo Camp | 255 | ♥♥ | ♦♦ | ▲▲▲ | – |
| Salt Creek - Angel Arch | 255 | ♥♥♥ | ♦♦♦ | ▲▲▲ | ♣♣♣♣ |
| Upper Salt Creek > Upper Jump | 255 | ♥♥♥ | ♦♦♦ | ▲▲ | ♣♣♣♣ |
| Lavender Canyon | 256 | ♥♥♥ | ♦♦ | ▲▲▲▲ | – |
| Davis Canyon | 257 | ♥♥♥ | ♦♦♦ | ▲▲▲ | ♣♣ |
| Needles Overlook | 258 | ♥♥ | ♦ | – | – |
| Anticline Overlook | 258 | ♥♥ | ♦ | ▲ | – |
| **15  Canyonlands The Maze** | | | | | |
| Horseshoe Canyon > Great Gallery | 262 | ♥♥♥♥♥ | ♦♦♦♦ | ▲▲ | ♣♣ |
| Panorama Point | 265 | ♥♥ | ♦ | ▲▲▲▲ | – |
| Maze Overlook | 265 | ♥♥♥ | ♦♦♦ | ▲▲▲▲ | – |
| Harvest Scene | 266 | ♥♥♥ | ♦♦ | ▲▲▲▲ | ♣♣♣ |
| Land of Standing Rocks | 268 | ♥♥♥ | ♦♦♦ | ▲▲▲▲▲ | ♣ |
| Doll House + Surprise Valley (via 4WD road) | 269 | ♥♥♥♥ | ♦♦♦♦ | ▲▲▲▲▲ | ♣♣ |
| Doll House + Spanish Bottom (via jet boat) | 269 | ♥♥♥♥ | ♦♦♦♦ | – | ♣♣ |
| **16  Around Dinosaur** | | | | | |
| Dinosaur Quarry | 275 | ♥♥ | ♦ | – | – |
| Split Mountain - Sound of Silence Loop Trail | 276 | ♥♥ | ♦ | – | ♣♣ |
| Split Mountain - Desert Voices Loop Trail | 276 | ♥♥ | ♦ | – | ♣ |
| Split Mountain - Scenic Overlook | 276 | ♥♥ | ♦♦ | – | – |
| Split Mountain - Cub Creek Panels | 276 | ♥♥ | ♦♦ | – | ♣ |
| McKee Spring Panels | 277 | ♥♥ | ♦♦♦ | ▲ | – |
| Island Park Road & Overlook | 277 | ♥♥ | ♦♦ | ▲ | – |
| Jones Creek Trail | 278 | ♥♥♥ | ♦♦ | – | ♣♣♣ |
| Harper's Corner Drive | 279 | ♥♥♥ | ♦♦ | – | ♣ |
| Harper's Corner Overlook (at trail's end) | 281 | ♥♥♥♥ | ♦♦ | – | ♣ |
| Echo Park | 282 | ♥♥♥♥ | ♦♦♦ | ▲▲ | – |
| Steamboat Rock Overlook + Rim | 284 | ♥♥♥ | ♦♦♦♦ | ▲▲ | ♣♣♣ |
| Yampa Bench Road | 286 | ♥♥♥ | ♦♦ | ▲▲ | ♣ |
| Deerlodge Park | 287 | ♥ | ♦ | – | ♣ |
| Gates of Lodore | 287 | ♥♥♥ | ♦♦ | ▲ | ♣ |
| Brown's Park Wildlife Refuge | 288 | ♥♥ | ♦ | ▲▲ | – |
| Flaming Gorge - Red Canyon | 289 | ♥♥♥ | ♦♦♦ | – | ♣ |
| Sheep Creek Scenic Backway | 291 | ♥♥ | ♦♦ | ▲ | – |
| Fantasy Canyon | 291 | ♥♥♥ | ♦♦♦♦ | ▲▲ | ♣ |
| Dry Fork / McConkie Ranch | 293 | ♥♥♥ | ♦♦ | ▲ | ♣♣ |

*Warning:* Road Difficulty ratings are for normal, dry conditions. Driving conditions can change dramatically during or after a rain, even more so on clay roads or roads that follow the course of a wash. As an example, the popular and well-used Cottonwood Canyon Road—rated 2 in difficulty—can become impassable after a rain and stay so for days on end, even with 4WD. Severe weather can dramatically alter conditions for extended periods of time. When the road was last maintained also has a huge impact on its condition and can alter the rating by 1 level in either direction. Always check current road conditions with local authorities before you leave.

# INDEX

## A not so brief blip about the Author

I was born in Paris, France. Thanks to an open-minded family, I attended school in Paris, London, Barcelona and several cities in Germany. I hold degrees in modern languages and international business.

A couple of years after college, I did the best thing a young person can do to widen his or her horizons and gain an understanding of our world and its wonderful diversity: I set out on a 20-month trip around the world, photographing extensively.

From 1976-1981, I lived in Tokyo, becoming a permanent resident of Japan and teaching at Sophia University. During this time, I also worked as a freelance photographer and pursued my research on the origins of Sumo and its ties with the Shinto religion, resulting in *Sumo – Le Sport & le Sacré* published in 1984. My years in Japan have had a profound influence on my life, my philosophy, and my photography.

I immigrated to the United States in 1982, settling in Southern California and creating Graphie Int'l, Inc, specializing in software, multimedia and, later on, internet technologies. Constant exploration and photography of the Southwest resulted in the publication of *Land of the Canyons* in 1998. In 1999, I permanently switched my focus from the software industry to a full-time career as a fine-art photographer, author and publisher, spending a good deal of my time in the Southwest.

I have been photographing since the age of 11, paying my dues to the B&W chemical lab for many years before becoming an early adopter of Cibachrome. I prefer shooting 2¼" medium format. Although I have shot Hasselblad and Mamiya, I now do the majority of my photography with two Fuji 645 rangefinder cameras, which I find well-suited to my style of photography. In the past, I have also used a 35mm Olympus OM-4 system extensively, especially for extreme wide-angle and long-telephoto shots. Nowadays, I use Canon and Olympus dSLR cameras regularly. When shooting film, I use Fujichrome Velvia almost exclusively. In my work, I seek to challenge the imagination with images characterized by bold colors, unique textures and a striking sense of depth, ranging from starkly minimalist compositions to complex abstracts. ❀